New Face of Terrorism
Ethnic, Domestic and Foreign

New Face of Terrorism
Ethnic, Domestic and Foreign

V T Patil

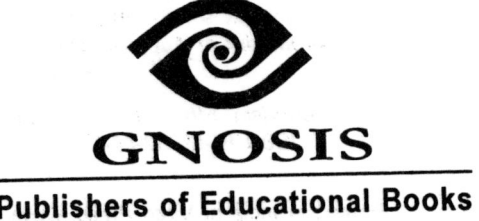

GNOSIS
Publishers of Educational Books

Worldwide Circulation through Authorspress Global Network
First Published 2008
by
GNOSIS
E-35/103, Jawahar Park
Laxmi Nagar, Delhi-110 092
e-mail: authorspress@yahoo.com

Copyright © 2008 Author
An Imprint of Authorspress

New Face of Terrorism, Ethnic, Domestic and Foreign
ISBN 81-89012-54-1

Printed in India at Virgo Press, Delhi.

Preface

Terrorism today is a ubiquitous phenomenon within the context of a globally unstable political climate, an issue of major importance at par with such problems as poverty and unemployment. Using sustained, clandestine violence—murder, kidnapping, bombings—to achieve a political or religious purpose, the spectre of terrorism as a meaningful and realistic threat has begin to pose unprecedented problems. The September 11, 2001 attacks on the Twin World Trade Centre Towers was a watershed moment in the history of terrorism widening the limits and boundaries which terrorists had not even dared to cross before. Today, as the range of terrorist acts continue to evolve and expand, the often-quoted, phrase, 'One phrase', 'One man's terrorist is another man's freedom fighter' reflects genuine doubts about what terrorism actually means, what it entails and how deep is this malaise.

One of the worst features of contemporary terrorism is the deliberate killing of civilians to intimidate the civilian population or government. As a result, in popular usage, influenced by politicians and the media terrorism has become synonymous with not just guerrilla warfare tactics on government institutions, but as a sort of anti-establishment enterprise adamant on imposing its will on the people. The quest for spectacular horror effects in order to attract media coverage, as well as its international dimension, has made terrorism a phenomenon which is deeply rooted in today's world and which perpetuates constant political instability in a vicious circle. In democracies, the need to protect civil liberties, the difficulty of proving conspiracy, and the devastating nature of terrorist outrages have also shifted the emphasis from deterrence to prevention. Currently, by general consensus the most effective means of frustrating terrorist activity is through detailed intelligence obtained primarily by prevention of terrorist networks.

This book, written as a political analysis of the issue of terrorism, explores and examines the new styles and range of terrorism by small groups, cults, individuals as well as international networks with access to weapons of mass destruction. Depending upon their scope, terrorist outfits are classically typified into three categories: ethnic, domestic and international or foreign. At all three levels, these organisations are responsible for creating a climate of terror which instils undesirable and reprehensible fear, and a milieu of constant, draining vigilance. To make matters worse, the scientific advancements of out times have only aided terrorists in maintaining a sustainable programme of horror and violence. The book makes an incisive, penetrating analysis of what makes up for terrorism in general, and its ever changing face. Charting its origins and development through the ages, the book engages in a deep and insightful discussion of the causes and tactics of terrorism, looking at contemporary violence through the lens of political ideologies, religious conflicts, socio-economic factors and ethnic tensions. The new face of terrorism, which is highly deadly in its penetrative power and consequences, is studied with the aim of making it clearer to readers the ramifications of a continuously evolving enterprise like terrorism, its sponsorship and logistics in the contemporary world, its motivations and goals, as well as the strategies to control and curb it. In addition, the text also presents forth the most up-to-date information on terrorism, understanding the ways in which terrorism affects culture, economics and politics all important hallmarks of a human society.

It is hoped that the erudition and insight of this book foster a better understanding of the issue of terrorism.

V T Patil

Contents

Preface   *v*

1. **New Face of Terrorism**   **1-16**
   1.1. Influencing Factors of New Terrorism
       1.1.1. Cultural Factors
       1.1.2. Political and Organisational Factors
       1.1.3. Technological Factors
   1.2. Future Challenges

2. **Types of Terrorism**   **17-30**
   2.1. Definitions of Terrorism
   2.2. History of Terrorism
   2.3. Types of Terrorism
       2.3.1. Civil Disorder
       2.3.2. Political Terrorism
       2.3.3. Non-political Terrorism
       2.3.4. Quasi-Terrorism
       2.3.5. Limited Political Terrorism
       2.3.6. Official or State Terrorism

3. **International Terrorism**   **31-68**
   3.1. International Terrorism During 1980s
   3.2. Terror and Resistance
   3.3. Concept of Retaliation
   3.4. International Terrorism in South Asia

3.4.1. Al Qaeda, the Taliban, and Pakistani Terrorist Groups
3.4.2. Pakistan-U.S. Anti-Terrorism Cooperation
3.4.3. Madrassas and Pakistan Islamists
3.4.4. Terrorism in Kashmir and India
3.5. Countering International Terrorism in Britain
   3.5.1. Characteristics
   3.5.2. Principles
   3.5.3. Protecting the Public
3.6. Changing International Terrorism

4. State Sponsored Terrorism 69-86

4.1. Cuba
4.2. Iran
4.3. Iraq
4.4. Libya
4.5. North Korea
4.6. International Economics and State Sponsored Terrorism
   4.6.1. International Trends
   4.6.2. Economic Performance of Country Groupings

5. Domestic Terrorism 87-122

5.1. Domestic Terrorism in the United States
   5.1.1. Organisations Associated with Domestic Terrorism
   5.1.2. Acts of Domestic Terrorism
5.2. Domestic Terrorism in India
   5.2.1. Causes
   5.2.2. Role of the Diaspora
   5.2.3. Funding
   5.2.4. Sanctuaries
   5.2.5. Al Qaeda in India

5.2.6. Role of Pakistani Mercenaries
5.2.7. Domestic Counter-terrorism Policies
5.2.8. External Counter-terrorism Policies
5.2.9. Counter Terrorism Strategy
5.2.10. Counter-terrorism Techniques
5.2.11. Intelligence-sharing on Terrorism
5.2.12. Regional cooperation in South Asia
5.3. Domestic Terrorism in Pakistan
5.4. Suicide Terrorism in Sri Lanka
    5.4.1. Suicide Terror Organisations
    5.4.2. Suicide Attacks
    5.4.3. Women Suicide Bombers
    5.4.4. Black Sea Tigers

6. **Religious Terrorism**   123-138
   6.1. Motivation
   6.2. Irish Terrorism
   6.3. Religious Terrorism in South Asia
   6.4. Religious Terrorism in Balkan Provinces
   6.5. Religious Terrorism in Eurasia
   6.6. Religious Terrorism in North Africa
   6.7. Religious Terrorism in Middle East
   6.8. Rise of Religious Fundamentalism

7. **Dynamics of Ethnic Terrorism**   139-148
   7.1. Ethno-nationalistic Terrorism
       7.1.1. Pogrom
       7.1.2. Combat 18
       7.1.3. Black Panther Party
       7.1.4. Ku Klux Klan

8. **Democracy and Terrorism**   149-164
   8.1. Political Culture and Legitimacy
   8.2. Democracy in the Muslim World

8.3. Terrorism and the Rule of Law
    8.3.1. Ignoring the Rule of Law

9. Psychology of Terrorists — 165-186
9.1. Theoretical Approach
    9.1.1. Instinct Theory
    9.1.2. Drive Theory (Frustration-Aggression)
    9.1.3. Social Learning Theory
    9.1.4. Cognitive Theory
9.2. Biological Approaches
9.3. Raw Empirical Approaches
9.4. First Generation of Psychological Research on Terrorism
    9.4.1. Psychoanalytic Theory
    9.4.2. Narcissism
    9.4.3. Early Typologies
9.5. Contemporary Psychological Research
    9.5.1. Motives and Vulnerabilities
9.6. Psychopathology and Preventing Terrorism
    9.6.1. Major Mental Illness
    9.6.2. Psychopathy/Antisocial Personality
    9.6.3. Psychological/Personality Abnormality
    9.6.4. Suicide Attacks
9.7. Understanding Terrorist Personality Traits
9.8. Understanding Individual's Life Experiences and Preventing Terrorism.
    9.8.2. Role of Ideology in Terrorist Behaviour
9.9. Influence of Culture on Terrorist Ideologies

10. Globalisation, Terrorism and Democracy — 187-202
10.1. Globalisation, September 11 and Terror War
10.2. Attacks on Democracy

Bibliography — 203-206
Index — 207-209

1
New Face of Terrorism

The attacks on the World Trade Centre and the Pentagon on September 11 confirmed that terrorism had acquired a new face. Terrorists were now engaged in a campaign of suicide and mass murder on a huge scale. After the thousands of deaths on September 11, it was evident that at least one group would stop at nothing. Terrorism was not always like this. Its history is as much European as Middle Eastern, and as much secular as religious. Far from being wilfully indiscriminate, it was often pointedly discriminate. Yet there are some common threads that can be traced through the history of terrorism. What happened on September 11 was a sinister new twist in an old story of fascination with political violence.

The word 'terrorism' entered into European languages in the wake of the French revolution of 1789. In the early revolutionary years, it was largely by violence that governments in Paris tried to impose their radical new order on a reluctant citizenry. As a result, the first meaning of the word 'terrorism', as recorded by the Académie Française in 1798, was 'system or rule of terror'. This serves as a healthy reminder that terror is often at its bloodiest when used by dictatorial governments against their own citizens.

During the 19th century terrorism underwent a fateful transformation, coming to be associated, as it still is today, with non-governmental groups. One such group—the small band of Russian revolutionaries of 'Narodnaya Volya' (the people's will) in 1878-81—used the word 'terrorist' proudly. They developed certain ideas that were to become the hallmark of subsequent terrorism in many countries. They believed in the targeted killing of the 'leaders of oppression'; they were convinced that the developing technologies of the age—symbolised by bombs and bullets—enabled them to strike directly and discriminately. Above all, they believed that the Tsarist system against which they were fighting was fundamentally rotten. They propagated what has remained the common terrorist delusion that violent acts would spark off revolution. Their efforts led to the assassination of Tsar Alexander II on 13 March 1881—but that event failed completely to have the revolutionary effects of which the terrorists had dreamed.

Terrorism continued for many decades to be associated primarily with the assassination of political leaders and heads of state. This was symbolised by the killing of the Austrian Archduke Ferdinand by a 19-year-old Bosnian Serb student, Gavril Princip, in Sarajevo on 28 June 1914. The huge consequences of this event were not the ones that Princip and his fellow members of 'Young Bosnia' had envisaged. Princip could not believe that the assassination had triggered the outbreak of world war in 1914. In general, the extensive practice of assassination in the 20th century seldom had the particular effects for which terrorists hoped.

In the half-century after the World War Two, terrorism broadened well beyond assassination of political leaders and heads of state. In certain European colonies, terrorist movements developed, often with two distinct purposes. The first was obvious: to put pressure on the colonial powers (such as Britain, France, and the Netherlands) to hasten their withdrawal. The second was more subtle: to intimidate the indigenous population into supporting a particular group's claims to leadership of the emerging post-colonial state. Sometimes these strategies had some success, but not always.

India's achievement of independence in 1947 was mainly the result, not of terrorism, but of the movement of non-violent civil disobedience led by Gandhi. In Malaya, communist terrorists launched a major campaign in 1948, but they failed due to a mixture of determined British military opposition and a programme of political reform leading to independence.

Terrorism did not end after the winding-up of the main European overseas empires in the 1950s and 1960s. It continued in many regions in response to many circumstances. In South-East Asia, the Middle East and Latin America there were killings of policemen and local officials, hostage-takings, hijackings of aircraft, and bombings of buildings. In many actions, civilians became targets. In some cases governments became involved in supporting terrorism, almost invariably at arm's length so as to be deniable. The causes espoused by terrorists encompassed not just revolutionary socialism and nationalism, but also in a few cases religious doctrines. Law, even the modest body of rules setting some limits in armed conflict between states, could be ignored in a higher cause.

How did certain terrorist movements come to be associated with indiscriminate killings? When in September 1970 Palestinian terrorists hijacked several large aircraft and blew them up on the ground in Jordan but let the passengers free, these acts were viewed by many with as much fascination as horror. Then in September 1972 11 Israelis were murdered in a Palestinian attack on Israeli athletes at the Olympic Games at Munich. This event showed a determination to kill: the revulsion felt in many countries was stronger than two years earlier.

A justification offered by the perpetrators of these and many subsequent terrorist actions in the Middle East was that the Israeli occupation of the West Bank and Gaza (which had begun in 1967) was an exercise of violence against which counter-violence was legitimate. The same was said in connection with the suicide bombings by which Palestinians attacked Israel in 2001-2. In some of the suicide bombings there was a new element which had not been evident in the Palestinian terrorism of 2 or 3 decades earlier: Islamic religious extremism.

In the 1990s, a new face of terrorism emerged. Osama Bin Laden, son of a successful construction engineer, became leader of a small fanatical Islamic movement called Al-Qaida (The Base). Its public statements were an odd mixture of religious extremism, contempt for existing Arab regimes, hostility to US dominance, and insensitivity to the effects of terrorist actions. Many of its leaders, having helped to free Afghanistan of Soviet occupation in the 1980s, now developed the broader ambition of resisting western dominance, especially in Muslim countries such as Saudi Arabia and Egypt.

In pursuit of these ambitions they killed hundreds in bombings of US embassies in Africa in August 1998. Here was a new kind of terrorist movement that had a cause, and a network, that was not confined to any one state, and whose adherents were willing to commit suicide if they could thereby inflict carnage and destruction on their adversaries, as they did on September 11. Since their aims were vague and apocalyptic, there was little scope for any kind of compromise or negotiation.

There are some common factors that can be detected behind the many changing faces of terrorism. First, it usually has an unofficial character, claiming to be the result of an upsurge of public feeling. Second, terrorism is based on a naïve belief that a few acts of violence, often against symbolic targets representing the power of the adversary, will transform the political landscape in a beneficial way. Third, terrorism has become increasingly involved in attacking innocent civilians—often with the purpose of demonstrating that the state is incapable of protecting its own people. Fourth, terrorists generally underestimate the strong revulsion of ordinary people to acts of political violence.

There is a further common factor—the tendency of terrorism to become endemic in particular countries and regions. Started by the Left, it has been continued by the Right, and vice versa. Started in a nationalist cause, it is then employed in resistance to the resulting state. Started to cleanse society of corruption and external control, it continues in support of the drug trade and prostitution. If violence becomes a habit, its net effect can be to prevent economic development, to provide a justification for official violence, and to perpetuate existing patterns of dominance and submission.

Since there are common factors, it ought to be possible to define terrorism. In the 1960s the UN General Assembly embarked on an attempt to do this. Initially little progress was made, partly because many states were reluctant to go far along the road of outlawing terrorism unless at the same time the 'causes of terrorism' were addressed. Other states saw this approach as implying that terrorism was a response to real grievances, and thereby insinuating that it was justified.

Thus the main emphasis at the UN was on limited practical measures. In a series of 12 international conventions drawn up between 1963 and 1999, particular terrorist actions, such as aircraft hijacking and diplomatic hostage-taking, were prohibited. As the

1990s progressed, and concern about terrorism increased, the UN General Assembly embarked on discussions about defining and outlawing terrorism generally. Its Legal Committee issued a rough draft of a convention, which:

Reiterates that criminal acts intended or calculated to provoke a state of terror in the general public, a group of persons or particular persons for political purposes are in any circumstances unjustifiable, whatever the considerations of a political, philosophical, ideological, racial, ethnic, religious or other nature that may be used to justify them. There are still disagreements between states about this draft convention. Even if it is eventually agreed, there is a difference between agreement on the general principle of outlawing terrorism and its application to particular facts. The labelling of individuals and movements as 'terrorist' will remain complicated and highly political.

In the past there have been strong disagreements about whether certain movements were or were not terrorist: for example, the Jewish extremist group Irgun in Palestine in the 1940s, the Viet Cong in South Vietnam from the late 1950s to the mid-1970s, and the Provisional IRA in Northern Ireland from the late 1960s onwards. Famously, in 1987-8 the UK and US governments labelled the African National Congress of South Africa 'terrorist': a questionable attribution even at the time not because there had been no violence, but because the ANC's use of violence had been discriminate and had constituted only a small part of the ANC's overall strategy.

The extremism of the September 11 attacks has led to a strong international reaction. As a result, none of the 189 member states of the UN opposed the USA's right to take military action in Afghanistan after the events of September 11, and none has offered explicit support for Al-Qaida. While there remain numerous concerns about the direction of the US and international moves against terrorism, and it is too early to say that the new face of terrorism is on the retreat, it is not too early to hazard the guess that, by engaging in crimes against humanity, the new face of terrorism may have contributed to its own eventual demise.

1.1. Influencing Factors of New Terrorism

Today's terrorists are ultimately more apocalyptic in their

perspective and methods. For many violent and radical organisations, terror has evolved from being a means to an end, to becoming the end in itself. Some analysts argue that the evolution of terrorism represents continuity rather than change, that mass-casualty bombings have long been characteristic of terrorist methods, and that radical extremism has always dominated terrorist motivations. Walter Laqueur's most recent book warns against trying to categorise or define terrorism at all because there are "many terrorisms," and he emphasises the particularities of various terrorist movements and approaches.

Various factors have led to the development of this new type of terrorism. Paul Wilkinson pondered the increase in indiscriminateness among terrorists, and he posited several possible reasons accounting for this upsurge. First, the saturation of the media with images of terrorist atrocity has raised the bar on the level of destruction that will attract headline attention. Second, terrorists have realised that civilian soft targets involve lower risk to themselves. Finally, there has been a shift from the politically-minded terrorist to the vengeful and hard-line fanatic.

While Wilkinson's factors accurately describe developments in terrorist strategy and tactics, there are more fundamental forces at work. The world has undergone a variety of changes on several levels. While it is impossible to link all social changes to terrorism today, it is possible to track several distinct factors that have converged to evolve a form of terrorism that is unprecedented in the level of threat it poses around the world. This article will explore these factors from cultural, political, and technological perspectives.

1.1.1. Cultural Factors

Islamic radicalism is the most notorious form of the new culture of terrorism, but it is far from the only variety of cultural trends motivating terrorist activity. Numerous cults, whose emergence in many cases has been synchronised with the turn of the new millennium, have also posed an increasing threat. Finally, the American religious right has been active with escalating and destructive objectives, although law enforcement presence has restrained these groups. It is important to distinguish religious terrorists from those terrorists with religious components, but whose primary goals are political.

Religiously motivated terrorist groups grew sixfold from 1980 to 1992 and continued to increase in the 1990s. Hoffman asserted that "the religious imperative for terrorism is the most important characteristic of terrorist activity today." This may not be as much an entirely new phenomenon as a cyclic return to earlier motivations for terror. Until the emergence of political motives such as nationalism, anarchism, and Marxism, "religion provided the only acceptable justifications for terror." However, terrorism in modern times has not, until recent years, been so dominated by religious overtones. At the time when modern international terrorism first appeared, of the 11 identifiable terrorist groups, none could be classified as religious.

Today's terrorists increasingly look at their acts of death and destruction as sacramental or transcendental on a spiritual or eschatological level. The pragmatic reservations of secular terroristsdo not hold back religious terrorists. Secular terrorists may view indiscriminate violence as immoral. For religious terrorists, however, indiscriminate violence may not be only morally justified, but constitute a righteous and necessary advancement of their religious cause. In addition, the goals of secular terrorists are much more attuned to public opinion, so senseless violence would be counterproductive to their cause, and hence not palatable to them.

As Hoffman observed, the constituency itself differs between religious and secular terrorists. Secular terrorists seek to defend or promote some disenfranchised population and to appeal to sympathisers or prospective sympathisers. Religious terrorists are often their own constituency, having no external audience for their acts of destruction. Aum Shinrikyo has been included in typologies of terrorism that include radical Islamists as part of a group of religiously motivated organisations that attack symbols of the modern state. In many ways, the dynamics of cultist followings make groups such as AumShinrikyo (also known as Aleph) more dangerous than religious terrorists rooted in conventional and broadly based religious traditions or denominations. There is no constituency of more moderate adherents to share common beliefs with the radical group while at the same time posing a restraining influence. For the fundamentalist Islamic or Christian radical, authoritative figures from either of those religions can condemn violence and delegitimise the terrorist, at least in the eyes of the average faithful.

Another feature of religious cults that makes them incredibly dangerous is the personality-driven nature of these groups. Cultist devotion to one leader leaves followers less able to make their own moral decisions or to consult other sources of reasoning. If that leader is emotionally or mentally unstable, the ramifications can be catastrophic. The more dangerous religious terrorist groups from traditional faiths may often share this feature of the cult: a charismatic leader who exerts a powerful influence over the members of the group.

According to many analysts, Aum Shinrikyo demonstrated its comparatively more threatening potential in its sarin attack in the Tokyo subway. As D.W. Brackett wrote, "A horrible bell had tolled in the Tokyo subway. . . . Terrorists do not follow rules of engagement in their operations but they do absorb the lessons to be learned from successful acts of violence." If for no other reason than providing an example to others, Aum Shinrikyo has gained notoriety as one of the more dangerous terrorist elements. Despite setbacks such as the incarceration of key leadership figures, the group continues to pose future threats. The ability of Aum Shinrikyo to recruit individuals with a high level of education and technical knowledge also has been a significant aspect of the threat posed by the cult.

In the past, cults were not viewed as national security threats; they were more dangerous to unwary individuals who might succumb to the cult's influence. Even the emergence of cultist mass suicides did not alter this perception. However, the recent appearance of cults willing and able to adopt destructive political goals has revised the more benign view of the cult phenomenon. Since cults are often fundamentally based on the violence of coercion, they can be accustomed to the mindset necessary to adopt terrorist methods. Although cults more often practice a mental violence with psychological control and extreme invasions of privacy, they do occasionally engage in physical abuse.

The most dangerous cults are also fascinated by visions of the end of the world-which, like radicals from more mainstream religions, cultists often believe that they are instrumental in bringing about. The nature of the cult's mythical figure can also be indicative of the level of threat. A vengeful deity is more threatening than a suffering saviour. This sign is somewhat unpredictable, however, because cults can switch their principal myths as circumstances change. Cults are a particularly dangerous form of religious terrorism because they can appear quickly without warning, have no rational goals, and can become agitated due to the apprehension and hostility with which they are viewed by the society at large. Whether initiated by cultists or by extremists from more established religions, the violence of religious terrorists can be particularly threatening in comparison with that of the political terrorists of earlier years.

As Hoffman notes, "For the religious terrorist, violence is a divine duty . . . executed in direct response to some theological demand . . . and justified by scripture." Religion can be a legitimising force that not only sanctions but compels large-scale violence on possibly open-ended categories of opponents. Terrorist violence can be seen as a divinely inspired end in itself. One explanation that has been proffered to account for violent Islamic extremism views revenge as the principal goal of the terrorists. This reasoning makes political change or conventional political objectives irrelevant, and it is consistent with observations that violence is itself the objective.

Fundamentalist Islam "cannot conceive of either coexistence or political compromise. To the exponents of Holy Terror, Islam must either dominate or be dominated." A recent study that traced the Islamic theological doctrine to the Middle Ages noted recent philosophical developments that explain the preponderance of religious mass-casualty terrorism coming from adherents of Islam.

Steven Simon and David Benjamin noted that many al Qaeda attacks, including the major planning phase of the 9/11 attacks, took place during favourable times for the Palestinians in the Middle East peace process, and that no foreign policy changes by the US government could possibly have appeased the bin Ladenist radical. While Islamic terrorists are the most notorious of today's violent radicals, others such as right-wing Christian extremists also exhibit many characteristics of the new terrorism.

In the past, right-wing Christian terrorists conducted racially motivated or religiously motivated acts of violence discriminately against chosen victims, and confrontation with the state was limited to instances when the state interfered with the political or religious agenda of the terrorist groups. Today, some such groups are directly hostile to the government, which adherents believe is engaged in a widespread conspiracy threatening the existence of the "white Christian way of life."

Christian violence in the United States has been discriminately focused for decades against racial minorities and "immoral" targets, it recently has expanded into attempted bombings and poisoning municipal water supplies. These indiscriminate attacks demonstrate a willingness to tolerate greater levels of collateral damage in efforts to generate mass levels of casualties. The bombing of the Murrah Federal Building in Oklahoma City was the pinnacle of this trend, and although Timothy McVeigh accepted responsibility for that attack, some speculate that there was additional involvement by other conservative militia or Christian terrorists. Effective domestic law enforcement in the United States has largely prevented these groups from achieving widespread violence on the level of Oklahoma City, making that incident a tragic exception among a larger number of foiled plots. While there is certainly no cooperation between foreign Islamist and US-domestic Christian radicals, there is a disquieting similarity in their views.

These aspects include a conception of righteous killing-as-healing, the necessity of total social destruction as part of a process of ultimate purification, a preoccupation with weapons of mass destruction, and a cult of personality where one leader dominates his followers who seek to become perfect clones. These aspects taken together represent a significant departure from the culture of earlier terrorist groups, and the organisations that these characteristics describe represent a serious threat to the civilised world.

1.1.2. Political and Organisational Factors

A number of developments on the international scene have created conditions ripe for mass-casualty terrorism. Gross inequalities in economic resources and standards of living between different parts of the world are a popular reason given for the ardency and viciousness of contemporary terrorists, although governmental collapse in "failed states" as a breeding ground for terrorists presents a more convincing variation on this logic. However, there is no "comprehensive explanation in print for how poverty causes terror," nor is there a "demonstrated correlation between the two." The intrusion of Western values and institutions into the Islamic world through the process of free-market globalisation is an alternative explanation for the growth of terrorism, which is the weaker party's method of choice to strike back.

The process of globalisation, which involves the technological, political, economic, and cultural diminution of boundaries between countries across the world, has insinuated a self-interested, inexorable, corrupting market culture into traditional communities. Many see these forces as threatening their way of life. At the same time that globalisation has provided a motivation for terrorism, it has also facilitated methods for it.

One of the major consequences of globalisation has been a deterioration of the power of the state. The exponential expansion of non-governmental organisations (NGOs), regional alliances, and international organisations has solidified this trend. Although certainly not a conventional humanitarian-based NGO like the Red Cross or Doctors without Borders, al Qaeda has distinguished itself as among the most "successful" of non-governmental organisations in pursuing its privately-funded global agenda. The trend among terrorists to eschew direct connections with state sponsors has had several advantages for the enterprising extremist.

Terrorist groups are more likely to maintain support from "amorphous constituencies," so extreme methods are more acceptable because such methods can be used without fear of alienating political support. Harvey Kushner described this development as a growth of "amateur" groups as direct state sponsorship has declined. Lawrence Freedman pointed out that the Taliban-ruled Afghanistan was not so much a state sponsor of terrorism as it was a "terrorist-sponsored state."

Terrorists do, however, continue to enjoy the benefits of indirect state sponsorship. Although the opportunity for state sponsorship has arguably diminished as a result of the Bush Administration's war on terror that has been prosecuted in the aftermath of the 9/11 attacks, state sponsorship remains widespread. In fact, developments in counterterrorist measures may propagate some dangerous trends of modern terrorism. When terrorists cannot rely on direct state sponsorship, they may become less accountable and harder to track. States must conceal their involvement by exercising less control and thus maintain less-comprehensive intelligence of radical terrorist organisations.

Many states have been on the US government list of state sponsors for more than a decade, including Cuba, Iran, Iraq, North Korea, Libya, and Syria. More recently, Sudan and Afghanistan became government sponsors of terrorism. Many state sponsors cooperate with one another to promote terrorist violence, making terrorist activity further disconnected from the foreign policy of any single state. Iran has funded training camps in Sudan, and the Palestinian Islamic Jihad has received support from both Iran and Syria. Further exacerbating the problem is the method of funding, which often has no measures for accountability. Iran's support for terrorist organisations can include no particular target selection, and it occasionally results, with the funds disappearing, in no terrorist attacks. This unpredictability is tolerated by state sponsors because of the occasional destructive payoff and the obfuscation of evidence connecting the state to the terrorist. Iran has consciously created a decentralised command structure because of these advantages. A further advantage of maintaining arm's length from extremist operatives is for self-protection. The government intelligence organisation of Sudan evidently monitored Osama bin Laden while he lived in that country, apparently to prevent his activists from eventually doing harm to even that extremist government.

While the American operations in Afghanistan and Iraq have diluted the threat from those states, other sponsors have possibly been left off official lists for political reasons. Pakistani intelligence reportedly has been involved in sponsoring violent terrorists, both in Afghanistan and in the contentious Kashmir. Additionally, the Kingdom of Saudi Arabia has been at the center of controversy over sponsorship and proliferation of radicalism and violence.

Another factor of globalisation that benefits terrorism is targeting: "In today's globalising world, terrorists can reach their targets more easily, their targets are exposed in more places, and news and ideas that inflame people to resort to terrorism spread more widely and rapidly than in the past." Among the factors that contribute to this are the easing of border controls and the development of globe-circling infrastructures, which support recruitment, fund-raising, movement of materiel, and other logistical functions.

In addition to international political changes, developments in organisational practice have enhanced the lethality of terrorists. As corporations have evolved organisationally, so have terrorist organisations. Terrorist groups have evolved from hierarchical, vertical organisational structures, to more horizontal, less command-driven groups. John Arquilla, David Ronfeldt, and Michele Zanini note that terrorist leadership is derived from a "set of principles [that] can set boundaries and provide guidelines for decisions and actions so that members do not have to resort to a hierarchy-'they know what they have to do.'"

1.1.3. Technological Factors

In addition to the cultural and religious motivations of terrorists and the political and organisational enabling factors, technology has evolved in ways that provide unprecedented opportunities for terrorists. The collapse of the Soviet Union and the possibility of proliferation of nuclear weapons to non-state users is the primary factor that has significantly increased the danger of nuclear terrorism. However, nonnuclear weapons of mass destruction and information technology also have created opportunities for terrorists that are in many ways more threatening than radiological terrorism because these alternatives are more probable.

Some theorists have argued that weapons of mass destruction do not represent a weapon of choice for most terrorists, even in these changing times. Stern writes that "most terrorists will continue to avoid weapons of mass destruction (WMD) for a variety of reasons," preferring the "gun and the bomb."Brian Jenkins agreed that most terrorist organisations are technologically conservative, but he also noted that the self-imposed moral restraints which once governed terrorist actions are fading away.

Walter Laqueur's New Terrorism emphasises the availability of very powerful weapons of mass destruction as the major current danger facing the industrialised world. Aside from the nuclear variety of WMD, biological and chemical weapons pose serious dangers. Biological weapons are limited because human contact is required to spread the effects, but as the Asian brush with Severe Acute Respiratory Syndrome (SARS) demonstrated, the associated panic and uncertainty can take a large economic and political toll-not to mention the cost in human suffering for those exposed to the pathogen, perhaps without knowing how or even whether they have been infected. Biological weapons can come in a variety of forms, including viruses, bacteria, and rickettsia (bacteria that can live inside host cells like viruses).

Chemical toxins differ from biological weapons in that they are nonliving pathogens and require direct infection and contact with the victim. This negates the continual spread of the weapon, but it entails more direct and possibly more damaging effects. Chemical agents appear in several types: choking agents that damage lung tissue, blood agents that cause vital organs to shut down, blister agents (also known as vesicants) that damage the skin, and-most lethal-nerve agents. Various methods allow the agent to infect its victim, including inhalation, skin absorption, and ingestion into the digestive tract. Exacerbating the danger is the fact that many deadly chemicals, or their components, are commercially available.

The State Department's annual report on terrorism asserted that the events of 11 September 2001 confirmed the intent and capability of terrorist organisations to plan and execute mass-casualty attacks. The report also stated that these unprecedented attacks may lead to an escalation of the scope of terrorism in terms of chemical, biological, radiological, or nuclear methods. Activities of cults such as Aum Shinrikyo and American terrorist plans to poison municipal water facilities provide further evidence of the WMD threat. Another key development is recent advances in communications and information technology. This technology provides both assistance to the terrorists and an opportunity for targeting as industrialised societies place greater reliance on information infrastructures.

Terrorists will likely avoid dismantling the internet because they need the technology for their own communication and propaganda activities. Accordingly, terrorists may be more interested in "systemic disruption" rather than the total destruction of information networks. While the consequences of a major disruption of American or global information infrastructures could be catastrophic financially or socially, terrorists have not shown the inclination or capability to undertake massive strikes in this area. There have been limited attacks along these lines, but the major use of information technology has been as an aid for terrorists rather than as a target of their activity.

The reported use of the internet and e-mail by al Qaeda to coordinate the strikes on the World Trade Center and the Pentagon provides a dramatic example of this sort of coordination. As Paul Pillar noted, "Information technology's biggest impact on terrorists has involved the everyday tasks of organising and communicating, rather than their methods of attack."

Technology also has increased the ability of terrorists to conduct mass-casualty attacks. The worst single terrorist attack before 9/11 claimed the lives of about 380 people. The yield of contemporary radiological, chemical, and biological weapons could dwarf that number, given the goals of today's terrorists as exemplified by the World Trade Center and Pentagon attacks, the Oklahoma City bombing, the sarin gas attack on the Tokyo subway, and other, less-successful attacks of the past decade. Technological developments and their availability as spread by the globalised market economy have unavoidably expanded the dangers of terrorism in the new century.

1.2. Future Challenges

The future of terrorism will depend, in large part, on the use and accessibility of technology. Increasingly destructive weaponry makes terrorism more lethal; advances in transportation increase the reach of terrorists; and cheaper and more secure means of communication make terrorism harder to detect. As these technologies advance, proliferate and become available to a wider range of actors, more and more potential enemies may use terrorism as a strategy and tactic.

The future of terrorism will be affected in part by the mobility of people. Globalisation entails greater mobility in goods, services, and people, as well as money and information. Expanding markets and cheaper, easier, and faster transportation increasingly blur national borders. Whether this trend accelerates or decelerates will have a major impact on the reach of terrorist groups, and the role of national borders in security thinking.

The future of terrorism will be shaped by our actions in defending against terrorism. Our adversaries base their actions in part on our actions—if we harden one target or defend against one means of attack, it pushes them to search for other vulnerabilities, redirecting the threat and displacing risk to a new area to secure.

Understanding the future of terrorism requires our understanding trends and developments in a wide range of areas. It is impossible to predict with precision the future success of our adversaries, but we can evaluate the factors that will contribute to their success or failure.

REFERENCES

Freedman, Lawrence et al., *Terrorism and International Order*, Routledge and Kegan Paul for the Royal Institute of International Affairs, 1986.

Gurr, Nadine, Benjamin Cole, *The New Face of Terrorism: Threats from Weapons of Mass Destruction*, 2002.

Laqueur, Walter, The Age of Terrorism, *Weidenfeld and Nicolson*, 1987.

Wilkinson, Paul, *Terrorism and the Liberal State (2nd edition)*, Macmillan, 1986.

2
Types of Terrorism

Terrorism in the modern sense is violence or other harmful acts committed (or threatened) against civilians for political or other ideological goals. As a form of unconventional warfare, terrorism is sometimes used when attempting to force political change by convincing a government or population to agree to demands to avoid future harm or fear of harm, destabilising an existing government, motivating a disgruntled population to join an uprising, escalating a conflict in the hopes of disrupting the status quo, expressing a grievance, or drawing attention to a cause.

Terrorism has been used by a broad array of political organisations in furthering their objectives; both right-wing and left-wing political parties, nationalistic, and religious groups, revolutionaries and ruling governments. The presence of non-state actors in widespread armed conflict has created controversy regarding the application of the laws of war.

2.1. Definitions of Terrorism

Definitions of terrorism are usually complex and controversial, and, because of the inherent ferocity and violence of terrorism, the term in its popular usage has developed an intense stigma. It was first coined in the 1790s to refer to the terror used during the French Revolution by the revolutionaries against their opponents. The Jacobin party of Maximilien Robespierre carried out a Reign of Terror involving mass executions by the guillotine. Although terrorism in this usage implies an act of violence by a state against its domestic enemies, since the 20th century the term has been applied most frequently to violence aimed, either directly or indirectly, at governments in an effort to influence policy or topple an existing regime.

Terrorism is not legally defined in all jurisdictions; the statutes that do exist, however, generally share some common elements. Terrorism involves the use or threat of violence and seeks to create fear, not just within the direct victims but among a wide audience. The degree to which it relies on fear distinguishes terrorism from both conventional and guerrilla warfare. Although conventional military forces invariably engage in psychological warfare against the enemy, their principal means of victory is strength of arms.

Similarly, guerrilla forces, which often rely on acts of terror and other forms of propaganda, aim at military victory and occasionally succeed (e.g., the Viet Cong in Vietnam and the Khmer Rouge in Cambodia). Terrorism proper is thus the systematic use of violence to generate fear, and thereby to achieve political goals, when direct military victory is not possible. This has led some social scientists to refer to guerrilla warfare as the "weapon of the weak" and terrorism as the "weapon of the weakest."

In order to attract and maintain the publicity necessary to generate widespread fear, terrorists must engage in increasingly dramatic, violent, and high-profile attacks. These have included hijackings, hostage takings, kidnappings, car bombings, and, frequently, suicide bombings. Although apparently random, the victims and locations of terrorist attacks often are carefully selected for their shock value. Schools, shopping centres, bus and train stations, and restaurants and nightclubs have been targeted both because they attract large crowds and because they are places with which members of the civilian population are familiar and in which they feel at ease.

The goal of terrorism generally is to destroy the public's sense of security in the places most familiar to them. Major targets sometimes also include buildings or other locations that are important economic or political symbols, such as embassies or military installations. The hope of the terrorist is that the sense of terror these acts engender will induce the population to pressure political leaders toward a specific political end.

Some definitions treat all acts of terrorism, regardless of their political motivations, as simple criminal activity. For example, in the United States the standard definition used by the Federal Bureau of Investigation (FBI) describes terrorism as "the unlawful use of force and violence against persons or property to intimidate or coerce a government, the civilian population, or any segment thereof, in furtherance of political or social objectives."

The element of criminality, however, is problematic, because it does not distinguish among different political and legal systems and thus cannot account for cases in which violent attacks against a government may be legitimate. A frequently mentioned example is the African National Congress (ANC) of South Africa, which committed violent actions against that country's apartheid government but commanded broad sympathy throughout the world. Another example is the Resistance movement against the Nazi occupation of France during World War II.

Since the 20th century, ideology and political opportunism have led a number of countries to engage in transnational terrorism, often under the guise of supporting movements of national liberation. (Hence, it became a common saying that "One man's terrorist is another man's freedom fighter.") The distinction between terrorism and other forms of political violence became blurred—particularly as many guerrilla groups often employed terrorist tactics—and issues of jurisdiction and legality were similarly obscured.

These problems have led some social scientists to adopt a definition of terrorism based not on criminality but on the fact that the victims of terrorist violence are most often innocent civilians. For example, the U.S. government eventually accepted the view that terrorism was premeditated, politically motivated violence perpetrated against noncombatant targets. Even this definition is flexible, however, and on occasion it has been expanded to include various other factors, such as that terrorist acts are clandestine or surreptitious, that terrorists choose their victims randomly, and that terrorist acts are intended to create an overwhelming sense of fear.

In the late 20th century, the term ecoterrorism was used to describe acts of environmental destruction committed in order to further a political goal or as an act of war, such as the burning of Kuwaiti oil wells by the Iraqi army during the Persian Gulf War. The term also was applied to certain environmentally benign though criminal acts, such as the spiking of lumber trees, intended to disrupt or prevent activities allegedly harmful to the environment.

2.2. History of Terrorism

Terror has been practiced by state and nonstate actors throughout history and throughout the world. The ancient Greek historian Xenophon (c. 431–c. 350 BC) wrote of the effectiveness of psychological warfare against enemy populations. Roman emperors such as Tiberius (reigned AD 14–37) and Caligula (reigned AD 37–41) used banishment, expropriation of property, and execution as means to discourage opposition to their rule.

The most commonly cited example of early terror, however, is the activity of the Jewish Zealots, often known as the Sicarii (Hebrew: "Daggers"), who engaged in frequent violent attacks on fellow Hebrews suspected of collusion with the Roman authorities. Likewise, the use of terror was openly advocated by Robespierre during the French Revolution, and the Spanish Inquisition used arbitrary arrest, torture, and execution to punish what it viewed as religious heresy. After the American Civil War (1861–65), defiant Southerners formed the Ku Klux Klan to intimidate supporters of Reconstruction (1865–77) and the newly freed former slaves.

In the latter half of the 19th century, terror was adopted in western Europe, Russia, and the United States by adherents of anarchism, who believed that the best way to effect revolutionary political and social change was to assassinate persons in positions of power. From 1865 to 1905 a number of kings, presidents, prime ministers, and other government officials were killed by anarchists' guns or bombs.

The 20th century witnessed great changes in the use and practice of terror. It became the hallmark of a number of political movements stretching from the extreme right to the extreme left of the political spectrum. Technological advances, such as automatic weapons and compact, electrically detonated explosives, gave terrorists a new mobility and lethality, and the growth of air travel provided new methods and opportunities. Terrorism was virtually an official policy in totalitarian states such as those of Nazi Germany under Adolf Hitler and the Soviet Union under Stalin. In these states arrest, imprisonment, torture, and execution were carried out without legal guidance or restraints to create a climate of fear and to encourage adherence to the national ideology and the declared economic, social, and political goals of the state.

Terror has been used by one or both sides in anticolonial conflicts (e.g., Ireland and the United Kingdom, Algeria and France, and Vietnam and France and the United States), in disputes between different national groups over possession of a contested homeland (e.g., Palestinians and Israelis), in conflicts between different religious denominations (e.g., Catholics and Protestants in Northern Ireland), and in internal conflicts between revolutionary forces and established governments (e.g., in the successor states of the former Yugoslavia, Indonesia, the Philippines, Nicaragua, El Salvador, and Peru).

In the late 20th and early 21st centuries some of the most extreme and destructive organisations that engaged in terrorism possessed a fundamentalist religious ideology (e.g., Hamas and al-Qaeda). Some groups, including the Liberation Tigers of Tamil Eelam and Hamas, adopted the tactic of suicide bombing, in which the perpetrator would attempt to destroy an important economic, military, political, or symbolic target by detonating a bomb on his person. In the latter half of the 20th century the most prominent groups using terrorist tactics were the Red Army Faction, the Japanese Red Army, the Red Brigades, the Puerto Rican FALN, Fatah and other groups related to the Palestine Liberation Organisation (PLO), the Shining Path, and the Liberation Tigers.

In the late 20th century the United States suffered several acts of terrorist violence by Puerto Rican nationalists (such as the FALN), antiabortion groups, and foreign-based organisations. The 1990s witnessed some of the deadliest attacks on American soil, including the bombing of the World Trade Center in New York City in 1993 and the Oklahoma City bombing two years later, which killed 168 people. In addition, there were several major terrorist attacks on U.S. government targets overseas, including military bases in Saudi Arabia (1996) and the U.S. embassies in Kenya and Tanzania (1998). In 2000 an explosion triggered by suicide bombers caused the deaths of 17 sailors aboard a U.S. naval ship, the USS *Cole*, in the Yemeni port of Aden.

The deadliest terrorist strikes to date were the September 11 attacks (2001), in which suicide terrorists associated with al-Qaeda hijacked four commercial airplanes, crashing two of them into the twin towers of the World Trade Center complex in New York City and the third into the Pentagon building near Washington, D.C.; the fourth plane crashed near Pittsburgh, Pennsylvania. The crashes destroyed much of the World Trade Center complex and a large portion of one side of the Pentagon and killed more than 3,000 people.

Terrorism appears to be an enduring feature of political life. Even prior to the September 11 attacks, there was widespread concern that terrorists might escalate their destructive power to vastly greater proportions by using weapons of mass destruction—including nuclear, biological, or chemical weapons—as was done by the Japanese doomsday cult AUM Shinrikyo, which released nerve gas into a Tokyo subway in 1995. These fears were intensified after September 11, when a number of letters contaminated with anthrax were delivered to political leaders and journalists in the United States, leading to several deaths. U.S. President George W. Bush made a broad war against terrorism the centrepiece of U.S. foreign policy at the beginning of the 21st century.

2.3. Types of Terrorism

Various attempts have been made to distinguish among types of terrorist activities. It is vital to bear in mind, however, that there are many kinds of terrorist movements, and no single theory can cover them all. Not only are the aims, members, beliefs, and resources of groups engaged in terrorism extremely diverse, but so are the political contexts of their campaigns. One popular typology identifies three broad classes of terrorism: revolutionary, subrevolutionary, and establishment terrorism. Although this typology has been criticised as inexhaustive, it provides a useful framework for understanding and evaluating terrorist activities.

Revolutionary terrorism is arguably the most common form. Practitioners of this type of terrorism seek the complete abolition of a political system and its replacement with new structures. Modern instances of such activity include campaigns by the Italian Red Brigades, the German Red Army Faction (Baader-Meinhof Gang), the Basque separatist group ETA, and the Peruvian Shining Path (Sendero Luminoso), each of which attempted to topple a national regime. Subrevolutionary terrorism is rather less common. It is used not to overthrow an existing regime but to modify the existing sociopolitical structure. Since this modification is often accomplished through the threat of deposing the existing regime, subrevolutionary groups are somewhat more difficult to identify. An example can be seen in the ANC and its campaign to end apartheid in South Africa.

Establishment terrorism, often called state or state-sponsored terrorism, is employed by governments—or more often by factions within governments—against that government's citizens, against factions within the government, or against foreign governments or groups. This type of terrorism is very common but difficult to identify, mainly because the state's support is always clandestine.

The Soviet Union and its allies allegedly engaged in widespread support of international terrorism during the Cold War; in the 1980s the United States supported rebel groups in Africa that allegedly engaged in acts of terrorism, such as the National Union for the Total Independence of Angola (UNITA); and various Muslim countries (e.g., Iran and Syria) purportedly provided logistical and financial aid to Islamic revolutionary groups engaged in campaigns against Israel, the United States, and some Muslim countries in the late 20th and early 21st centuries.

The military dictatorships in Chile (1973–90) and Argentina (1976–83) committed acts of state terrorism against their own populations. The violent police states of Joseph Stalin in the Soviet Union and Saddam Hussein in Iraq are examples of countries in which one organ of the government—often either the executive branch or the intelligence establishment—engaged in widespread terror against not only the population but also other organs of the government, including the military.

The persistent element of all forms of establishment terrorism, unlike that of nonstate terrorism, is that of secrecy. States invariably seek to disavow their active complicity in such acts, both to evade international censure and to avoid political and military retribution by those they target.

In the spring of 1975, the Law Enforcement Assistant Administration in the United States formed the National Advisory

Committee on Criminal Justice Standards and Goals. One of the five volumes that the committee was entitled *Disorders and Terrorism*, produced by the Task Force on Disorders and Terrorism under the direction H.H.A. Cooper, Director of the Task Force staff. The Task Force classified terrorism into six categories.

— Civil Disorders
— Political Terrorism
— Non-Political Terrorism
— Quasi-Terrorism
— Limited Political Terrorism
— Official or State Terrorism –

2.3.1. Civil Disorder

Civil disorder, also known as civil unrest, is a broad term that is typically used by law enforcement to describe one or more forms of disturbance caused by a group of people. Civil disturbance is typically a symptom of, and a form of protest against, major socio-political problems. Typically, the severity of the action coincides with public outrage. Examples of civil disorder include, but are not necessarily limited to: illegal parades; sit-ins and other forms of obstructions; riots; sabotage; and other forms of crime. It is intended to be a demonstration to the public and the government, but can escalate into general chaos.

Frequently, participants in a civil disorder are not in agreement about appropriate behaviour. As was the case in the WTO Meeting of 1999, most protesters were peaceful, and a small, highly visible minority of government provocateurs, much like the ones present at the 2007 Security and Prosperity Partneship summit in Quebec, were responsible for most of the damage.

Any civil disorder is a delicate balance of power, and indeed, a political power struggle of some sort is typically the root cause of any such conflict. Often, public demonstrations are viewed as the last resort of political organisations. If the power equation in a civil disorder becomes unbalanced, the result is either oppression or riot. Police brutality is a frequent result of civil disorder, while at other times, civil disorder may develop as a *result* of police brutality.

Citizens not directly involved in a civil disorder may have their lives significantly disrupted. Their ability to work, enjoy recreation and in some cases, obtain necessities may be jeopardised. Disruption of intrastructure may occur during very severe events. Public utilities such as water, fuel and electricity may be temporarily unavailable, as well as public infrastructure for communication.

Occasionally, the disruption of such services may be the original cause of the disorder. More frequently, the cause of such issues is related to economic stagnation, severe inflation, devaluation of currency, severe unemployment, oppression, political scandal, or, in some countries, sporting events.

2.3.2. Political Terrorism

In a trend to the serious breaches of due process and respect for civil liberty that are taking place worldwide under the active promotion of the United States of America, many countries are being pushed, willingly and few unwillingly, on such a path in using terrorism to increase government powers to monitor citizens activities and have powers to intimidate and coerce — in effect destroying the principal that a person is innocent until proven guilty, putting even an innocent citizen in a defensive position, as opposed to having the burdens of such claims on the government.

While governments have legitimate claims for need to be vigilant in protecting citizens from harm, there is no need to having special laws related to terrorism. Terrorism is a crime, and as such, it should be dealt with in the law within this framework. Terrorism, as a political concept, is a different issue. When the politics of this issue begins to interfere with the rights of citizens, it can cause harms to the very citizens, these laws claim to want to help.

Citizens are very likely to support extreme measures, in general they have no understanding of the full ramifications of these laws, or may care less in the heat of the passions that surround tragic events, exceptional events, which also are used by some for political gains. But exceptional events, and fears should not be used to destroy civil liberties in the war of politics.

The damage has become extreme. On the civil side, with noted personalities such as Phil Donuhue being removed from TV programmes, famous personalities that speak out on various issues being demonised and ostracised. This, in a country that prides itself in free speech and its protection. This, from a people, whose passions have been inflamed by politicians to blind them from wanting to hear anything, except, what they want to hear.

Looking at the number of people killed from terrorism, or other related costs, there is simply no logical sense to justify the extreme measures being taken to deal with this issue. These measures, economic, civil, and political assets being spent on this issue are beyond reason, unless of course, in our passion, we have lost reason, or we have other objectives behind these measures. A dose of justice to those who are being oppressed and deprived from basic human and civil rights will go a long way towards dealing with this issue, else, we will be fighting oppression with oppression, a negative cycle that only increases the cause that brings people to such extreme acts.

Terrorism has become a stick that is used to beat domestic political opposition with. On the international level, it is being used as a cover to beat some countries with, and to provide other countries with a cover to beat up their domestic political opposition. Domestically and at the international level, these forces that are promoting the politics of terrorism are being joined for the same purpose, and their goals are not more democracy, but more oppression. And this seems to suit the US fine. It is said that a cat that is burned from sitting on a hot stove, will never sit on a cold one either. Having been hurt by the events of September 11, tragic as they maybe, the US, is using a tragic event to cause more tragedy. The politics of terrorism is very bad politics.

2.3.3. Non-political Terrorism

This category of terrorism includes acts of mass destruction committed with the goal of either financial or personal gain, or ones motivated by sheer mental disorder. A typical criminal motivation is extortion while other personal motivations can include seeking asylum in a third country. Finally, there is the category of terrorist acts performed by the often lone terrorist in a state of mental disorder, such as the highly publicised cases of

California kindergarten shootings and the Unabomber a few years ago.

2.3.4. Quasi-Terrorism

The activities incidental to the commission of crimes of violence that are similar in form and method to genuine terrorism but which nevertheless lack its essential ingredient. It is not the main purpose of the quasi-terrorists to induce terror in the immediate victim as in the case of genuine terrorism, but the quasi-terrorist uses the modalities and techniques of the genuine terrorist and produces similar consequences and reaction. For example, the fleeing felon who takes hostages is a quasi-terrorist, whose methods are similar to those of the genuine terrorist but whose purposes are quite different.

2.3.5. Limited Political Terrorism

Genuine political terrorism is characterised by a revolutionary approach; limited political terrorism refers to "acts of terrorism which are committed for ideological or political motives but which are not part of a concerted campaign to capture control of the State.

2.3.6. Official or State Terrorism

State terrorism is a controversial term, with no agreed on definition, used when arguing that there may be a similarity between terrorism and certain acts done by states. All acts of terrorism, all the outrages which have struck and which strike the imagination of men, have been and are either *offensive* actions or *defensive* actions. If they form part of an offensive strategy, experience has shown for a long time that they are always doomed to fail. If, on the other hand, they form part of a defensive strategy, experience shows that these acts can expect some success, which, however, is only momentary and precarious.

However, it is not only the strategy which changes, according to whether it is a matter of offensive or defensive terrorism, but also *the strategists*. The desperate and the deluded resort to offensive terrorism; on the other hand it is *always and only* States which resort to defensive terrorism, either because they are deep in some grave social crisis, like the Italian State, or else because they fear one, like the German State.

The defensive terrorism of States is practised by them either *directly* or *indirectly*, either with their own arms or with others. All secret terrorist groupuscules are organised and directed by a clandestine hierarchy of veritable militants of clandestinity, which reflects perfectly the division of labour and roles proper to this social organisation: above it is decided and below it is carried out. Ideology and military discipline shield the real summit from all risk, and the base from all suspicion.

Any secret service can invent "revolutionary" initials for itself and undertake a certain number of outrages, which the press will give good publicity to, and after which, it will be easy to form a small group of naive militants, that it will direct with the utmost ease. But in the case of a small terrorist group spontaneously formed, there is nothing in the world easier for the detached corps of the State than to infiltrate it and, thanks to the means which they dispose of, and the extreme freedom of manoeuvre which they enjoy, to get near the original summit, and to substitute themselves there, either by specific arrests activated at the right moment, or through the assassination of the original leaders, which, as a rule, occurs after an armed conflict with the "forces of order," forewarned about such an operation by their infiltrated elements.

From then on, the parallel services of the State find they have, at their disposal, a perfectly efficient organism to do as they please with, composed of naive or fanatical militants, which asks for nothing other than to be directed. The original little terrorist group, born of the mirages of its militants about the possibilities of realising an effective strategic offensive, changes strategists and becomes nothing other than a *defensive* appendage of the State, which manoeuvres it with the utmost agility and ease, according to its own necessities of the moment, or what it *believes* to be its own necessities.

The population, which is generally hostile to terrorism, and not without reason, must then agree that, *at least in this*, it *needs* the State, to which it must thus delegate the widest powers so that it might confront with vigour the arduous task of the common defence against an obscure, mysterious, perfidious, merciless, and, in a word, *chimeric*, enemy. In view of a terrorism always presented as *absolute evil*, evil in-itself and for-itself, all the other evils fade into the background and are even forgotten; since the fight against terrorism coincides with the *common interest*, it already is the *general good*, and the State, which magnanimously conducts it, is good in-itself for-itself. Without the wickedness of the devil, God's infinite bounty could not appear and be appreciated as is fitting.

The State, along with its economy, weakened to the extreme by all the attacks it has been undergoing daily for ten years, from the proletariat on the one hand, and from the incapacity of its managers on the other, can thus silence both in solemnly taking upon itself the staging of the spectacle of the common and sacrosanct defence against the terrorist monster, and in the name of this holy mission, can exact from all its subjects a further portion of their tiny freedom, which will reinforce police control over the entire population. "We are at war," and at war with an enemy so powerful that all other disagreement or conflict would be an act of sabotage or desertion: it is only in order to protest against terrorism that one has the right to resort to a general strike.

Terrorism and "the emergency," a state of perpetual emergency and "vigilance," these are the only existing problems, or at the very least, the only ones with which it is permitted and necessary to be pre-occupied. All the rest does not exist, or is forgotten and in any case is silenced, distanced, repressed in the social unconscious, in the face of the gravity of the question of "public order." And faced with the universal duty of its defence, all are invited to partake of denunciation, baseness, and fear: cowardice becomes, for the first time in history, a sublime quality, fear is always justified, the only "courage" which may not be despicable is that of approving and supporting all the lies, all the abuses, and all the infamies of the State.

Since the present crisis spares no country of the planet, no geographical frontier of peace, war, freedom or truth any longer exists: this frontier lies within every country, and every State is arming itself and declaring war on truth.

REFERENCES

Bruce Hoffman, *Inside Terrorism*, 1999.

Grant Wardlaw, *Political Terrorism: Theory, Tactics, and Counter-Measures*, 2nd ed., rev. and extended, 1989.

Martha Crenshaw (ed.), *Terrorism in Context*, 1995.

Mark Juergensmeyer, *Terror in the Mind of God: The Global Rise of Religion's Violence*, 2000.

Paul Wilkinson, *Terrorism and the Liberal State*, 2nd ed., rev., extended, and updated, 1986.

Richard A. Falkenrath, Robert D. Newman, and Bradley A. Thayer, *America's Achilles' Heel: Nuclear, Biological, and Chemical Terrorism and Covert Attack*, 1998.

Walter Laqueur, *The New Terrorism: Fanaticism and the Arms of Mass Destruction*, 1999.

3
International Terrorism

There are many terrorist states in the world, but the United States is unusual in that it is *officially* committed to international terrorism, and on a scale that puts its rivals to shame. Thus Iran is surely a terrorist state, as Western governments and media rightly proclaim. Its major known contribution to international terrorism was revealed during the Iran-Contra inquiries: namely, Iran's perhaps inadvertent involvement in the US proxy war against Nicaragua. This fact is unacceptable, therefore unnoticed, though the Iranian connection in US-directed international terrorism was exposed at a time of impassioned denunciation of Iranian terrorism.

The same inquiries revealed that under the Reagan Doctrine, the US had forged new paths in international terrorism. Some states employ individual terrorists and criminals to carry out violent acts abroad. But in the Reagan years, the US went further, not only constructing a semi-private international terrorist network but also an array of client and mercenary *states* — Taiwan, South Korea, Israel, Saudi Arabia, and others — to finance and implement its terrorist operations. This advance in international terrorism was revealed during the period of maximal anguish over the plague, but did not enter into the discussion and debate.

The US commitment to international terrorism reaches to fine detail. Thus the proxy forces attacking Nicaragua were directed by their Central Intelligence Agency (CIA) and Pentagon commanders to attack "soft targets," that is, barely defended civilian targets. The State Department specifically authorised attacks on agricultural cooperatives — exactly what we denounce with horror when the agent is Abu Nidal. Media doves expressed thoughtful approval of this stand.

When a Contra supply plane was shot down in October 1986 with an American mercenary on board, it became impossible to suppress the evidence of illegal CIA supply flights to the proxy forces. A few days after they ended, the Central American presidents signed the Esquipulas II peace agreement. The US undertook at once to subvert it. The agreement identified one factor as "an indispensable element to achieving a stable and lasting peace in the region," namely termination of any form of aid "to irregular forces or insurgent movements" on the part of "regional or extraregional" governments.

In response, the US moved at once to escalate the attacks on soft targets in Nicaragua. Right at the moment when indignation over Washington's clandestine operations peaked, Congress and the media kept their eyes scrupulously averted from the rapid increase in CIA supply flights to several a day, while cooperating with the White House program of dismantling the unwanted accords, a goal finally achieved in January 1988; though further steps were required to subvert a follow-up agreement of the Central American presidents in February 1989.

As supply and surveillance flights for the proxy forces increased, so did violence and terror, as intended. This too passed largely unnoticed, though an occasional reference could be found. The *Los Angeles Times* reported in October 1987 that "Western military analysts say the contras have been stashing tons of newly dropped weapons lately while trying to avoid heavy combat... Meanwhile, they have stepped up attacks on easy government targets like the La Patriota farm cooperative...., where several militiamen, an elderly woman and her year-old grandson died in a pre-dawn shelling." To select virtually at random from the many cases deemed unworthy of notice, on November 2, 1987, 150 Contras attacked two villages in the southern province of Rio San Juan with 88-mm mortars and rocket-propelled grenades, killing six children and six adults and injuring 30 others. Even cooperatives of religious pacifists who refused to bear arms were destroyed by the US terrorist forces. In El Salvador too, the army attacks cooperatives, killing, raping and abducting members.

The decision of the International Court of Justice in June 1986 condemning the United States for the "unlawful use of force" and illegal economic warfare was dismissed as an irrelevant pronouncement by a "hostile forum". Little notice was taken when the US vetoed a Security Council resolution calling on all states to observe international law and voted against General Assembly resolutions to the same effect (with Israel and El Salvador in 1986; with Israel alone in 1987). The guiding principle, it appears, is that the US is a lawless terrorist state and *this is right and just*, whatever the world may think, whatever international institutions may declare.

A corollary is the doctrine that no state has the right to defend itself from US attack. The broad acquiescence in this remarkable doctrine was revealed as Reagan administration agitprop floated periodic stories about Nicaraguan plans to obtain jet interceptors. There was some criticism of the media for uncritically swallowing the disinformation, but a more significant fact was ignored: the general agreement that such behaviour on the part of Nicaragua would be entirely unacceptable. When the tale was concocted to divert attention from the Nicaraguan elections of 1984, Senator Paul Tsongas of Massachusetts, with the support of other leading doves, warned that the US would have to bomb Nicaragua if it obtained vintage 1950s MiGs, because "they're also capable against the United States," hence a threat to its security — as distinct, say, from US nuclear missiles on alert status in Turkey, no threat to the USSR since they are purely for defensive purposes.

It is understood that jet interceptors might enable Nicaragua to protect its territory from the CIA supply flights needed to keep the US proxy forces in the field and the regular surveillance flights that provide them with up-to-the-minute information on the disposition of Nicaraguan troops, so that they can safely attack soft targets. Understood, but scarcely mentioned. And it seems that no one in the mainstream released the open secret that Nicaragua would happily accept French planes instead of MiGs if the US had not pressured its allies to bar military aid so that we might cower in fear of "the Soviet-supplied Sandinistas."

The same issue arose in August 1988, when congressional doves effusively supported the Byrd Amendment on "Assistance for the Nicaraguan Resistance." Three days before, the Contras had attacked the passenger vessel *Mission of Peace*, killing two people and wounding 27, all civilians, including a Baptist minister from New Jersey who headed a US religious delegation. The incident was unmentioned in the Senate debate on the Byrd Amendment. Rather, congressional doves warned that if the Nicaraguan army carried out "an unprovoked military attack" or "any other hostile action" against the perpetrators of such terrorist atrocities, then Congress would respond with vigour and righteousness by renewing official military aid to them. Media coverage and other commentary found nothing odd or noteworthy in this stance.

Accordingly, organisation of a terrorist proxy army to subdue some recalcitrant population is a legitimate chore. On the right, Jeane Kirkpatrick explained that "forceful intervention in the affairs of another nation" is neither "impractical" nor "immoral"— merely illegal, a crime for which people were hanged at Nuremberg and Tokyo with ringing declarations that this was not "victor's justice" because, as Justice Robert Jackson proclaimed, "If certain acts and violations of treaties are crimes, they are crimes whether the United States does them or whether Germany does them. We are not prepared to lay down a rule of criminal conduct against others which we would not be willing to have invoked against us."

Countering any such thoughts, Irving Kristol explains that "The argument from international law lacks all credibility." True, "a great power should not ordinarily intervene in the domestic affairs of a smaller nation," but this principle is overcome if "another great power has previously breached this rule." Since it is "beyond dispute" that "the Soviet Union has intervened in Nicaragua" by providing arms and technicians "in both the military and civilian spheres," then the US has the right to send its proxy army to attack Nicaragua. By the same argument, the Soviet Union has a perfect right to attack Turkey or Denmark — far more of a security threat to it than Nicaragua is to the United States — since it is "beyond dispute" that the US provides them with assistance, and would do far more if the USSR were to exercise the right of aggression accorded it by Kristol's logic.

Kristol might, however, counter this argument too by invoking a crucial distinction that he has drawn elsewhere in connection with the right of forceful intervention by the United States: "insignificant nations, like insignificant people, can quickly experience delusions of significance," he explained. And when they do, these delusions must be driven from their minds by force: "In truth, the days of 'gunboat diplomacy' are never over... Gunboats are as necessary for international order as police cars are for domestic order." Hence the US is entitled to use violence against Nicaragua, an insignificant nation, though the USSR lacks this right in the case of Turkey or Denmark.

The overwhelming endorsement for US-directed international terrorism should not be obscured by the wide elite opposition to the Contra war. By 1986, polls showed that 80 percent of "leaders" opposed aid to the Contras, and there was vigorous debate in Congress and the media about the program. But it is important to attend to the terms of the debate. At the dissident extreme, Tom Wicker of the *New York Times* observed that "Mr. Reagan's policy of supporting [the Contras] is a clear failure," so we should "acquiesce in some negotiated regional arrangement that would be enforced by Nicaragua's neighbours" — if they can take time away from slaughtering their own populations, a feature of these terror states that does not exclude them from the role of enforcing regional arrangements on the errant Sandinistas, against whom no remotely comparable charge could credibly be made.

The motivation for the resort to international terrorism has been candidly explained. High administration officials observed that the goal of the attack against Nicaragua was "forcing [the Sandinistas] to divert scarce resources to the war and away from social programs." This was the basic thrust of the 1981 CIA program endorsed by the administration. As outlined by former CIA analyst David MacMichael in his testimony before the World Court, this program has as its purpose: to use the proxy army to "provoke cross-border attacks by Nicaraguan forces and thus serve to demonstrate Nicaragua's aggressive nature," to pressure the Nicaraguan Government to "clamp down on civil liberties within Nicaragua itself, arresting its opposition, demonstrating its allegedly inherent totalitarian nature and thus increase domestic dissent within the country," and to undermine the shattered economy. Discussing the strategy of maintaining a terrorist force within Nicaragua after the huge CIA supply operation was theoretically cancelled by Congress in February 1988 (and the proxy forces largely fled, revealing — though not to articulate opinion — how little resemblance they bore to indigenous guerillas), a Defence Department official explained:

> Those 2000 hard-core guys could keep some pressure on the Nicaraguan government, force them to use their economic resources for the military, and prevent them from solving their economic problems — and that's a plus... Anything that puts pressure on the Sandinista regime, calls attention to the lack of democracy, and prevents the Sandinistas from solving their economic problems is a plus.

Viron Vaky, Assistant Secretary of State for Interamerican Affairs in the Carter administration, observed that the principal argument for the terrorist attack is that "a longer war of attrition will so weaken the regime, provoke such a radical hardening of repression, and win sufficient support from Nicaragua's discontented population that sooner or later the regime will be overthrown by popular revolt, self-destruct by means of internal coups or leadership splits, or simply capitulate to salvage what it can." As a dove, Vaky regards the conception as "flawed" but in no way wrong.

The terrorist forces fully understand their directives, as we learn from one of the most important defectors of the 1980s, the head of intelligence of the main Contra force (FDN), Horacio Arce, whose *nom de guerre* was "Mercenario", — talk of "democrats" and "freedom fighters" is for home consumption. Sandinista defectors are eagerly exploited by the White House and the media, and the Contras generally received extensive coverage. Contra *defectors* are another matter, particularly when they have unwelcome tales to relate.

3.1. International Terrorism During 1980s

During the 1980s, the primary locus of international terrorism has been Central America. In Nicaragua the US proxy forces left a trail of murder, torture, rape, mutilation, kidnapping, and destruction, but were impeded because civilians had an army to defend them. No comparable problems arose in the US client states, where the main terrorist force attacking the civilian population *is* the army and other state security forces.

In El Salvador, tens of thousands were slaughtered in what Archbishop Riveray Damas in October 1980, shortly after the operations moved into high gear, described as "a war of extermination and genocide against a defenceless civilian population." This exercise in state terror sought "to destroy the people's organisations fighting to defend their fundamental human rights," as Archbishop Oscar Romero warned shortly before his assassination, while vainly pleading with President Carter not to send aid to the armed forces who, he continued, "know only how to repress the people and defend the interests of the Salvadorean oligarchy."

The goals were largely achieved during the Reagan administration, which escalated the savagery of the assault against the population to new heights. When it seemed that the US might be drawn into an invasion that would be harmful to its own interests, there was some concern and protest in elite circles, but that abated as state terror appeared successful, with the popular organisations decimated and "decapitated." After elections under conditions of violence and repression guaranteeing victory to privileged elements acceptable to the US, the issue largely passed below the threshold.

Little notice was taken of the significant increase in state terror after the Esquipulas II accords; or of an Amnesty International report entitled *El Salvador: "Death Squads" — A Government Strategy* (October 1988), reporting the "alarming rise" in killings by official death squads as part of the government strategy of intimidating any potential opposition by "killing and mutilating victims in the most macabre way," leaving victims "mutilated, decapitated, dismembered, strangled or showing marks of torture... or rape." Since the goal of the government strategy is "to intimidate or coerce a civilian population" (that is, terrorism, as officially defined in the US Code), it is not enough simply to kill. Rather, bodies must be left dismembered by the roadside, and women must be found hanging from trees by their hair with their faces painted red and their breasts cut off, while domestic elites pretend not to see as they continue to fund, train, and support the murderers and torturers.

In the same years, a massacre of even greater scale took place in Guatemala, also supported throughout by the United States and its mercenary states. Here too, terror increased after the Esquipulas II peace agreement in order to guard against steps towards democracy, social reform, and protection of human rights called for in the accords. As in El Salvador, these developments were virtually ignored; the assigned task at the time was to focus attention on Nicaragua and to express vast outrage when Nicaragua occasionally approached the *lesser* abuses that are regular practices in the US client states. Since the goal is to restore Nicaragua to "the Central American mode" and ensure that it observes the "regional standards" satisfied by El Salvador and Guatemala, terror in client states is of no real concern, unless it becomes so visible as to endanger the flow of aid to the killers.

Notice crucially that all of this is *international* terrorism, supported or directly organised in Washington with the assistance of its international network of mercenary states.

Well after the 1984 elections that were hailed for having brought democracy to El Salvador, the church-based human rights organisation Socorro Juridico, operating under the protection of the archdiocese of San Salvador, described the results of the continuing terror, still conducted by "the same members of the armed forces who enjoy official approval and are adequately trained to carry out these acts of collective suffering," in the following terms:

Salvadoran society, affected by terror and panic, a result of the persistent violation of basic human rights, shows the following traits: collective intimidation and generalised fear, on the one hand, and on the other the internalised acceptance of the terror because of the daily and frequent use of violent means. In general, society accepts the frequent appearance of tortured bodies, because basic rights, the right to life, has absolutely no overriding value for society. The same comment applies to the societies that oversee these operations, or simply look the other way.

International terrorism is, of course, not an invention of the 1980s. In the previous two decades, its major victims were Cuba and Lebanon. Anti-Cuban terrorism was directed by a secret Special Group established in November 1961 under the code name "Mongoose," involving 400 Americans, 2,000 Cubans, a private navy of fast boats, and a $50 million annual budget, run in part by a Miami CIA station functioning in violation of the Neutrality Act and, presumably, the law banning CIA operations in the United States. These operations included bombing of hotels and industrial installations, sinking of fishing boats, poisoning of crops and livestock, contamination of sugar exports, etc.

Several of these terrorist operations took place at the time of the Cuban missile crisis of October-November 1962. In the weeks before, Raymond Garthoff reports, a Cuban terrorist group operating from Florida with US government authorisation carried out "a daring speedboat strafing attack on a Cuban seaside hotel near Havana where Soviet military technicians were known to congregate, killing a score of Russians and Cubans;" and shortly after, attacked British and Cuban cargo ships and again raided Cuba, among other actions that were stepped up in early October.

At one of the tensest moments of the missile crisis, on November 8, a terrorist team dispatched from the United States blew up a Cuban industrial facility after the Mongoose operations had been officially suspended. Fidel Castro alleged that 400 workers had been killed in this operation, guided by "photographs taken by spying planes." This terrorist act, which might have set off a global nuclear war, evoked little comment when it was revealed. Attempts to assassinate Castro and other terror continued immediately after the crisis terminated, and were escalated by Nixon in 1969.

Such operations continued after the Nixon years. In 1976, for example, two Cuban fishing vessels were attacked in April by boats from Miami, the main center of anti-Cuban terrorism worldwide. A few weeks later, the Cuban embassy in Portugal was bombed with two killed. In July, the Cuban mission to the UN in New York was bombed and there were bombings aimed at Cuban targets in the Caribbean and Colombia, along with the attempted bombing of a pro-Cuban meeting at the Academy of Music in New York.

In August, two officials of the Cuban embassy in Argentina were kidnapped and Cubana airlines offices in Panama were bombed. The Cuban embassy in Venezuela was fired upon in October and the embassy in Madrid was bombed in November. In October, CIA-trained Cuban exiles bombed a Cubana civilian airliner, killing all 73 aboard, including Cuba's gold-medal-winning international fencing team. One of the agents of this terrorist operation, Bay of Pigs veteran Luis Posada Carriles, was sprung from the Venezuelan jail where he was held for the bombing; he mysteriously escaped and found his way to El Salvador, where he was put to work at the Ilopango military airbase to help organise the US terrorist operations in Nicaragua. The CIA attributed 89 terrorist operations in the US and the Caribbean area for 1969-79 to Cuban exile groups, and the major one, OMEGA 7, was identified by the FBI as the most dangerous terrorist group operating in the US during much of the 1970s.

Cuba figures heavily in scholarly work on international terrorism. Walter Laqueur's standard work contains many innuendos about Cuban sponsorship of terrorism, though little evidence. There is not a word, however, on the terrorist operations *against* Cuba. He writes that in "recent decades... the more oppressive regimes are not only free from terror, they have helped to launch it against more permissive societies." The intended meaning is that the United States, a "permissive society," is one of the victims of international terrorism, while Cuba, an "oppressive regime," is one of the agents. To establish the conclusion it is necessary to suppress the fact that the US has undeniably launched major terrorist attacks against Cuba and is relatively free from terror itself; and if there is a case to be made against Cuba, Laqueur has signally failed to present it.

Turning to the second major example of the pre-Reagan period, in southern Lebanon from the early 1970s the population was held hostage with the "rational prospect, ultimately fulfilled, that affected populations would exert pressure for a cessation of hostilities" and acceptance of Israeli arrangements for the region. Notice that this justification, offered by a respected Labour party dove, places these actions squarely under the rubric of international terrorism.

Thousands were killed and hundreds of thousands driven from their homes in these attacks. Little is known because the matter was of no interest; PLO attacks against Israel in the same years, barbaric but on a far lesser scale, elicited great indignation and extensive coverage. The Israeli raids and shelling of their villages, their gradual exodus from south Lebanon to the growing slums on the outskirts of Beirut were nothing compared to the lurid tales of the 'terrorists' who threatened Israel, hijacked aeroplanes and seized embassies." The reaction was much the same, he continues, when Israeli death squads were operating in southern Lebanon after the 1982 Israeli invasion. In 1976, Syria entered Lebanon with US approval and helped implement further massacres, the major one at the Palestinian refugee camp of Tel Al-Zaater, where thousands were murdered by Syrian-backed Christian forces with Israeli arms.

In the Middle East, the main center of international terrorism according to the canon, the worst single terrorist act of 1985 was a car-bombing in Beirut on March 8 that killed 80 people and wounded 256. "About 250 girls and women in flowing black chadors, pouring out of Friday prayers at the Imam Rida Mosque, took the brunt of the blast," Nora Boustany reported three years later: "At least 40 of them were killed and many more were maimed." The bomb also "burned babies in their beds, killed a bride buying her trousseau," and "blew away three children as they walked home from the mosque" as it "devastated the main street of the densely populated" West Beirut suburb. The target was the Shi'ite leader Sheikh Fadlallah, accused of complicity in terrorism, but he escaped.

Even under its chosen conventions, then, it seems that the United States wins the prize for acts of international terrorism in the peak year of the official plague. The US client state of Israel follows closely behind. Its Iron Fist operations in Lebanon were without parallel for the year as sustained acts of international terrorism in the Middle East, and the bombing of Tunis (with tacit US support) wins second prize for single terrorist acts, unless we take this to be a case of actual aggression, as was determined by the UN Security Council.

In 1986, the major single terrorist act was the US bombing of Libya — assuming, again, that we do not assign this attack to the category of aggression. This was a brilliantly staged media event, the first bombing in history scheduled for prime-time TV, for the precise moment when the networks open their national news programs. This convenient arrangement allowed anchormen to switch at once to Tripoli so that their viewers could watch the exciting events live. The next act of superbly crafted TV drama was a series of news conferences and White House statements explaining that this was "self-defence against future attack" and a measured response to a disco bombing in West Berlin ten days earlier for which Libya was [allegedly] to blame.

The media were well aware that the evidence for this charge was slight, but the facts were ignored in the general adulation for Reagan's decisive stand against terrorism, echoed across the political spectrum. Crucial information undermining the US charges was suppressed from that moment on. It was later conceded quietly that the charges were groundless, but they nevertheless continued to be aired and the conclusions that follow from this belated recognition were never drawn.

For 1986 too the United States seems to place well in the competition for the prize for international terrorism, even apart from the wholesale terrorism it sponsored in Central America, where, in that year, Congress responded to the World Court call for an end to the "unlawful use of force" by voting $100 million of military aid to the US proxy forces in what the administration gleefully described as a virtual declaration of war.

3.2. Terror and Resistance

Sometimes, nationalist groups are prepared to describe their actions as terrorism, and some respected political leaders decline to condemn acts of terrorism in the national cause. An example is the pre-state Zionist movement. Israel is the source of the 1980s "terrorism industry", as an ideological weapon against the Palestinians. The PLO is anathema in the United States. A special act of Congress, the Anti-Terrorism Act of 1987, "prohibits American citizens from receiving any assistance, funds, or anything of value except informational materials from the PLO," which is not permitted to establish offices or other facilities to further its interests. Palestinian violence has received worldwide condemnation. The pre-state Zionist movement carried out extensive terror against Arab civilians, British, and Jews, also murdering UN mediator Folke Bernadotte.

What the Western democracies considered to be resistance in occupied Europe or Afghanistan, the Nazis and the USSR branded terror — in fact, terror inspired from abroad, therefore international terrorism. The US took the same position towards the South Vietnamese who bore the brunt of the US attack.

On similar grounds, South Africa [during the apartheid years] takes strong exception to the international conventions on terrorism. Specifically, it objects to UN General Assembly

Resolution 42/159 (December 7, 1987) because, while condemning international terrorism and outlining measures to combat it, the General Assembly:

Considers that nothing in the present resolution could in any way prejudice the right to self-determination, freedom and independence, as derived from the Charter of the United Nations, of peoples, forcibly deprived of that right..., particularly peoples under colonial and racist regimes and foreign occupation or other forms of colonial domination, nor... the right of these peoples to struggle to this end and to seek and receive support [in accordance with the Charter and other principles of international law].

While this provision is endorsed by virtually the entire world community, South Africa is not entirely alone in opposing it. The resolution passed 153 to 2, with the United States and Israel opposed and Honduras alone abstaining. In this case, the stand of the US government won wide approval in the United States. Across the spectrum of articulate opinion in the US, it is implicitly taken for granted that the South African position is correct, indeed beyond controversy.

The issue came to a head in late 1988 in connection with the Israel-Palestinian conflict. In November, the Palestinian National Council (PNC) declared an independent Palestinian state alongside of Israel, endorsing the UN terrorism resolution and other relevant UN resolutions. Yasser Arafat repeated the same positions in subsequent weeks in Europe, including a special session of the UN General Assembly convened in Geneva when he was barred from New York, in violation of legal obligations to the United Nations, on the grounds that his presence there would pose an unacceptable threat to the security of the United States. The reiteration by the PNC and Arafat of the UN terrorism resolution was denounced in the United States on the grounds that the Palestinian leadership had failed to meet Washington's conditions on good behaviour, including "Rejection of terrorism in all its forms" without qualification. The qualification in question is the one endorsed by the world community with the exception of the US and Israel (and South Africa).

The reasoning is straightforward. The PLO had refused to join the US, Israel and South Africa off the spectrum of world opinion, and therefore merits either derision (from the hardliners) or encouragement for its limited but insufficient progress (from the dissidents). When the US became isolated diplomatically, by December 1988, Washington moved to a fall-back position, pretending that Arafat had capitulated to US demands, though his position had not changed in any substantive way — for years, in fact. With Arafat's capitulation to US demands now official, by US stipulation, he could be rewarded by discussions with the US Ambassador in Tunis. As was underscored by Israeli Defence Minister Yitzhak Rabin, the US-PLO discussions were designed to deflect diplomatic pressures for settlement and to grant Israel a year or more to suppress the Palestinian uprising (Intifada) by "harsh military and economic pressure" so that "they will be broken."

The issue of terrorism versus resistance arose at once during the US-PLO discussions. The protocols of the first meeting were leaked and published in the *Jerusalem Post*, which expressed its pleasure that "the American representative adopted the Israeli positions," stating two crucial conditions that the PLO must accept: the PLO must call off the Intifada, and must abandon the idea of an international conference. With regard to the Intifada, the US stated it position as follows:

Undoubtedly the internal struggles that we are witnessing in the occupied territories aim to undermine the security and stability of the State of Israel, and we therefore demand cessation of those riots, *which we view as terrorist acts against Israel*. This is especially true as we know you are directing, from outside the territories, those riots which are sometimes very violent.

Once this "terrorism" is called off and the previous conditions of repression restored, the US and Israel can proceed to settle matters to their satisfaction. Again, the resistance of an oppressed population to a brutal military occupation is "terror," from the point of view of the occupiers and their paymaster.

The same issue arose during the 1985 Iron Fist operations of the Israeli army in southern Lebanon. These too were guided by the logic outlined by Abba Eban, cited earlier. The civilian population was held hostage under the threat of terror to ensure its acceptance of the political arrangements dictated by Israel for southern Lebanon and the occupied territories. The threat can be realised at will. To cite only one case, while the eyes of the world were focused in horror on Arab terrorists, the press reported that Israeli tank cannon poured fire into the village of Sreifa in southern Lebanon, aiming at 30 houses from which the Israeli Army claimed they had been fired upon by "armed terrorists," resisting their military actions as they searched for two Israeli soldiers who had been "kidnapped" in the "security zone" Israel has carved out of Lebanon.

Kept from the American press was the report by the UN peace-keeping forces that the IDF "went really crazy" in these operations, locking up entire villages, preventing the UN forces from sending in water, milk, and oranges to the villagers subjected to "interrogation" by the Israeli Defence Forces (IDF) or its local mercenaries. The IDF then left with many hostages including pregnant women, some taken to Israel in further violation of international law, destroying houses and looting and wrecking others. Prime Minister Shimon Peres, lauded in the US as a man of peace, said that Israel's search "expresses our attitude towards the value of human life and dignity."

To the Israeli high command, the victims of the Iron Fist operations were "terrorist villagers;" it was thus understandable that 13 villagers were massacred by militiamen of the Israeli mercenary forces in the incident that elicited this observation. Yossi Olmert of the Shiloah Institute, Israel's Institute of Strategic Studies, observed that "these terrorists operate with the support of most of the local population." An Israeli commander complained that "the terrorist... has many eyes here, because he lives here." The military correspondent of the *Jerusalem Post* (Hirsh Goodman) described the problems faced in combating the "terrorist mercenary," "fanatics, all of whom are sufficiently dedicated to their causes to go on running the risk of being killed while operating against the IDF," which must "maintain order and security" despite "the price the inhabitants will have to pay."

A similar concept of terrorism is widely used by US officials and commentators. The press reports that Secretary of State Shultz's concern over international terrorism became "his passion" after the suicide bombing of US Marines in Lebanon in October 1983, troops that much of the population saw as a military force sent in to impose the "New Order" established by the Israeli aggression: the rule of right-wing Christians and selected Muslim elites. The media did not call upon witnesses from Nicaragua, Angola, Lebanon and the occupied territories, and elsewhere, to testify to Shultz's "passion," either then, or when they renewed their praise for his "visceral contempt for terrorism" and "personal crusade" against it in explaining his refusal to admit Arafat to speak at the United Nations.

Doubtless Syria too regards the Lebanese who resist its bloody rule as "terrorist," but such a claim would evoke the ridicule and contempt it merits. The reaction changes with the cast of characters.

3.3. Concept of Retaliation

Retaliation is a useful device of ideological warfare. Throughout a cycle of violent interaction, each side typically perceives its own acts as retaliation for the terrorism of the adversary. In the Middle East, the Israeli-Arab conflict provides many examples. Israel being a client state, US practice adopts the Israeli conventions. To illustrate, consider the hijacking of the *Achille Lauro* and the murder of Leon Klinghoffer in 1985, doubtless a vile terrorist act. The hijackers, however, regarded their action not as terror but as retaliation for the Israeli bombing of Tunis a week earlier, killing 20 Tunisians and 55 Palestinians with smart bombs that tore people to shreds beyond recognition, among other horrors described by Israeli journalist Amnon Kapeliouk on the scene. Washington cooperated by refusing to warn its ally Tunisia that the bombers were on their way, and George Shultz telephoned Israeli Foreign Minister Yitzhak Shamir to inform him that the US administration "had considerable sympathy for the Israeli action," the press reported.

Shultz drew back from this open approval when the UN Security Council unanimously denounced the bombing as an "act of armed aggression" (the US abstaining). Prime Minister Shimon Peres was welcomed to Washington a few days later, while the press solemnly discussed his consultations with President Reagan on "the evil scourge of terrorism" and what can be done to counter it.

For the US and Israel, the Tunis bombing was not terror or aggression but rather legitimate retaliation for the cold blooded murder of three Israelis in Larnaca, Cyprus. Secretary Shultz termed the Tunis bombing "a legitimate response" to "terrorist attacks," evoking general approbation. The Larnaca killers, as Israel conceded, had probable connections to Syria but none to Tunis, which was selected as a target because it was defenceless; the Reagan administration selected Libyan cities as a bombing target a few months later in part for the same reason.

The perpetrators of the Larnaca atrocity, in turn, regarded their act not as terrorism but as retaliation. It was, they claimed, a response to Israeli hijackings in international waters for many years, including civilian ferries travelling from Cyprus to Lebanon, with large numbers of people kidnapped, over 100 kept in Israeli prisons without trial, and many killed, some by Israeli gunners while they tried to stay afloat after their ship was sunk, according to survivors interviewed in prison. These Israeli terrorist operations are sometimes marginally noted. The Israeli peace organisation Dai l'Kibbush reports that in 1986-7, Israeli military courts convicted dozens of people kidnapped at sea or in Lebanon of "membership in a forbidden organisation" but no anti-Israel activity or plans; the Palestinians kidnapped allegedly belonged to the PLO, and the Lebanese to Hizballah and in at least one case to the major Shi'ite organisation Amal, all legal in Lebanon. By the same logic, British occupying forces could have sent agents to kidnap Zionists in the United States or on the high seas in 1947, placing them in prison camps without charge or convicting them of support for terrorism. These Israeli operations are little discussed and do not fall within the canon.

The concepts of terrorism and retaliation are supple instruments, readily adapted to the needs of the moment.

3.4. International Terrorism in South Asia

In the wake of the September 2001 terrorist attacks on the United States, President Bush launched major military operations in South and Southwest Asia as part of the global U.S.-led anti-terrorism effort. Operation Enduring Freedom in Afghanistan has seen substantive successwith the vital assistance of neighbouring Pakistan. Yet the United States increasingly is concerned that members of Al Qaeda and its Taliban supporters have found haven and been able to at least partially regroup in Pakistani cities and in the rugged Pakistan-Afghanistan border region inhabited by ethnic Pashtuns who express solidarity with anti-U.S. forces. Al Qaeda also reportedly has made alliances with indigenous Pakistani terrorist groups that have been implicated in both anti-Western attacks in Pakistan and terrorism in Indian Kashmir, while also seeking to oust the government of President Gen. Pervez Musharraf. Along with these concerns, the United States expresses an interest in the cessation of "cross-border infiltration" by separatist militants based in Pakistani-controlled areas who cross the Kashmiri Line of Control (LOC) to engage in terrorist activities in Indian Kashmir and in Indian cities.

3.4.1. Al Qaeda, the Taliban, and Pakistani Terrorist Groups

Among the central goals of Operation Enduring Freedom were the destruction of terrorist training camps and infrastructure within Afghanistan, the capture of Al Qaeda and Taliban leaders, and the cessation of terrorist activities in Afghanistan. Most, but not all, of these goals have been achieved. However, since the Taliban's ouster from power in Kabul and subsequent retreat to the rugged mountain region near the Afghanistan-Pakistan border, what the U.S. military calls its "remnant forces" have been able to regroup and to conduct "hit-and-run" attacks against U.S.-led coalition forces, possibly in tandem with suspected Al Qaeda fugitives. These forces are then able to find haven on the Pakistani side of the border.

Al Qaeda founder Osama bin Laden may himself be in a remote area of Pakistan near Afghanistan. The frequency of these attacks has increased throughout 2003 and, in October, U.S. Special Envoy to Afghanistan Zalmay Khalilzad reportedly warned that resurgent Taliban and Al Qaeda forces are presenting a serious threat to Afghani reconstruction efforts. Indigenous Pakistani Terrorist Groups. In January 2002, Pakistan banned five extremist organisations, including Lashkar-e-Taiba (LET), Jaish-e-Mohammed (JEM), and Sipah-e-Sahaba Pakistan (SSP). The United States designates LET and JEM as Foreign Terrorist Organisations (FTOs); SSP appears on the State Departments's terrorism "watch list."

Following Al Qaeda's 2001-2002 expulsion from Afghanistan and ensuing relocation of some core elements to Pakistani cities such as Karachi and Peshawar, some Al Qaeda activists are believed to have joined forces with indigenous Pakistani Sunni militant groups, including LET, JEM, SSP, and Lashkar-i-Jhangvi, an FTO-designated offshoot of the SSP. Al Qaeda reportedly was linked to anti-U.S. and anti-Western terrorist attacks in Pakistan during 2002, although the primary suspects in such attacks have been from indigenous Pakistani groups.

During 2003, Pakistan's domestic terrorism mostly has involved Sunni-Shia conflict. Some analysts believe that, by redirecting Pakistan's internal security resources, this increase in sectarian violence may ease pressure on Al Qaeda and so allow that group to operate more freely. In a landmark January 2002 speech, President Musharraf vowed to end Pakistan's use as a base for terrorism, and he criticised religious extremism and intolerance in the country. In the wake of the speech, about 3,300 extremists were arrested and detained, though perhaps half of these have since been released. These releases included the founders of both Lashkar-e-Taiba and Jaish-e-Muhammad. Though officially banned, these groups continue to operate under new names: LET is now Jamaat al-Dawat; JEM is now Khudam-ul Islam; and Harakat-ul Mujahideen is now Jamiat-ul Ansar.

3.4.2. Pakistan-U.S. Anti-Terrorism Cooperation

According to the U.S. Departments of State and Defence, Pakistan has afforded the United States unprecedented levels of cooperation by allowing the U.S. military to use bases within the country, helping to identify and detain extremists, and deploying tens of thousands of its own security forces to secure the Pakistan-Afghanistan border. Top U.S. officials regularly praise Pakistani anti-terrorism efforts. In the spring of 2002, U.S. military and law enforcement personnel reportedly began engaging in direct, low-profile efforts to assist Pakistani security forces in tracking and apprehending fugitive Al Qaeda and Taliban fighters on Pakistani territory.

The State Department reports that Islamabad has facilitated the transfer of more than 400 captured alleged terrorists to U.S. custody, including several top suspected Al Qaeda leaders. Pakistan also ranks fourth in the world in seizing terrorist assets. Despite Pakistan's "crucial" cooperation, there remain doubts about Islamabad's commitment to core U.S. concerns in the vast "lawless zones" of the Afghani-Pakistani border region where Islamic extremists find shelter. Especially worrisome are indications that the Taliban receive significant logistical and other support inside Pakistan.

Senator Richard Lugar and Senator Joseph Biden reportedly have voiced such worries, including concern that elements of Pakistan's Inter-Services Intelligence agency (ISI) might be helping members of the Taliban and perhaps even Al Qaeda. In August 2003, at least three Pakistani army officers, including a lieutenant colonel, were arrested on suspicion of having ties to Islamic extremists. In late September, Deputy Secretary of State Armitage was quoted as saying he does "not think that affection for working with us extends up and down the rank and file of the Pakistani security community."

In October testimony before the Senate Foreign Relations Committee, Assistant Secretary of Defence for International Security Affairs Peter Rodman said, "There are elements in the Pakistani government who we suspect are sympathetic to the old policy of before 9/11," adding that there still exists in northwestern Pakistan a radical Islamic infrastructure that "spews out fighters that go into Kashmir as well as into Afghanistan." Military Operations. In an effort to block infiltration along the Pakistan-Afghanistan border, Islamabad had by the end of 2002 deployed some 70,000 troops to the region.

In June 2003, in what may have been a response to increased U.S. pressure, Islamabad for the first time sent its armed forces into the traditionally autonomous western Federally Administered Tribal Areas in search of renegade Al Qaeda and Taliban fighters who have eluded the U.S.-led campaign in Afghanistan. By September, Islamabad had up to 25,000 troops in the tribal areas, and a major border operation reportedly took place in coordination with U.S.-led forces on the Afghani side of the border. In early October, Pakistani security forces engaged suspected Al Qaeda fugitives in the South Waziristan district, killing 8 and capturing 18 others. Pakistan has lost at least 12 of its own security personnel in gun battles with Al Qaeda fighters.

The October operations have encouraged U.S. officials, who see in them a positive trend in Islamabad's commitment to tracking and capturing wanted extremists on Pakistani territory.

Still, these officials admit that the Pakistani government finds it more difficult politically to pursue Taliban members who enjoy ethnic and familial ties with Pakistani Pashtuns.

3.4.3. Madrassas and Pakistan Islamists

Anotable development in September 2003 was the arrest by Pakistani security forces of 19 Indonesian and Malaysian nationals at a Karachi madrassa (Islamic school). The men are suspected of running a sleeper cell of the Jemaah Islamiyah (JI) terrorist network in what would be the first indication that JI, a group linked to Al Qaeda, is operating in Pakistan. Among the approximately 10,000 madrassas in Pakistan are some that have been implicated in teaching militant anti-Western, anti-American, and anti-Hindu values.

Many of these madrassas are financed and operated by Pakistani Islamist political parties such as Jamaat-e-Ulema Islam (JUI, closely linked to the Taliban), as well as by multiple unknown foreign entities. While President Musharraf has in the past pledged to crack down on the more extremist madrassas in his country, there is little concrete evidence that he has done so.

The Muttahida Majlis-e-Amal (MMA) -- a coalition of six Islamist opposition parties-holds about 20% of Pakistan's National Assembly seats, while also controlling the provincial assembly in the North West Frontier Province (NWFP) and leading a coalition in the provincial assembly of Baluchistan. Pakistan's Islamists, including the leadership of some of their legal political parties, are notable for their virulent expressions of anti-American sentiment; they have at times called for "jihad" against what they view as the existential threat to Pakistani sovereignty that alliance with Washington entails. In addition to decrying President Musharraf's cooperation with the United States, many also are viewed as opposing the U.S.-supported Kabul government. In September 2003, Afghani President Karzai called on Pakistani clerics to stop supporting Taliban members who seek to destabilise Afghanistan.

3.4.4. Terrorism in Kashmir and India

Separatist violence in the Indian Jammu and Kashmir state has surged in recent months. New Delhi consistently blames Pakistan-based militant groups for lethal attacks on Indian civilians, as well as on government security forces, in both Kashmir and in major Indian cities. India holds Pakistan responsible for providing material support and training facilities to Kashmiri militants. Most often blamed for terrorism in India are FTO-designates Lashkar-e-Taiba, Jaish-e-Mohammed, and Harakat ul-Mujahideen, and Hizbul Mujahideen, the latter identified on the State Department's terrorism watch list. According to the U.S. government, several anti-India militant groups fighting in Kashmir are based in Pakistan and are closely linked to Islamist groups there:

— Harakat ul-Mujahideen, based mainly in Muzaffarabad (Azad Kashmir) and Rawalpindi, is aligned with the Jamiat-i Ulema-i Islam Fazlur Rehman party (JUI-F), itself a constituent of the MMA Islamist coalition in Pakistan's National Assembly;
— Hizbul Mujahideen, believed to have bases in Pakistan, is the militant wing of Pakistan's largest Islamic political party and MMA member, the Jamaat-i-Islami;
— Jaish-e-Mohammed, based in both Peshawar and Muzaffarabad, also is aligned with JUI-F; and
— Lashkar-i-Taiba, based in Muzaffarabad and near Lahore, is the armed wing of a Pakistan-based, anti-U.S. Sunni religious organisation formed in 1989.

Pakistan's powerful and largely autonomous ISI is widely believed to have provided significant support for militant Kashmiri separatists over the past decade in what is perceived as a proxy war against India. In March 2003, the chief of India's Defence Intelligence Agency reported providing the United States with "solid documentary proof" that 70 Islamic militant camps are operating in Pakistani Kashmir.

In May, the Indian Defence Minister claimed that about 3,000 "terrorists" were being trained in camps on the Pakistani side of the LOC. Some Indian officials have suggested that Al Qaeda may be active in Kashmir. Deputy Secretary of State Armitage reportedly received a June 2002 pledge from Pakistani President Musharraf that all "cross-border terrorism" would cease, followed by a May 2003 pledge that any terrorist training camps in Pakistani-controlled areas would be closed. Yet, in September, Indian PM Vajpayee reportedly told President Bush that continued cross-border terrorism from Pakistan was making it difficult for India to maintain its peace initiative, and current infiltration rates are widely believed to be on the rise.

3.5. Countering International Terrorism in Britain

Terrorism is an international phenomenon which takes many forms. The Government's strategy is informed by, and has informed, the counter-terrorism strategies of a number of other countries. Their strategy comprises both open elements, which can be freely publicised and discussed, and classified elements, which are kept secret. There have to be such secret elements, in order to avoid alerting the terrorists themselves either to capabilities we possess for countering their purposes or to vulnerabilities which they could exploit.

The principal terrorist threat is currently from radicalised individuals who are using a distorted and unrepresentative interpretation of the Islamic faith to justify violence. Such people are referred to here as Islamist terrorists. In any response to this threat, it is important to recognise that terrorists using these distorted readings of Islam are a tiny minority within Muslim communities. Muslim communities themselves do not threaten the security - in fact, the huge contribution they make to the economic, cultural, and social life of the UK. Muslims are as much at risk from terrorism as anyone else, as was shown by those who were killed or injured in the attacks on 7 July 2005.

During the 1990s Islamist terrorist groups carried out numerous attacks in a variety of countries. A bomb attack against the World Trade Center in New York in 1993 and the Paris Metro attacks in 1995 were amongst the earliest of these, but later in the decade many more attacks were made in other countries, including in Saudi Arabia, Egypt, Tanzania and Kenya, and Yemen.

In the event, the most serious of these attacks came in September 2001, when four simultaneous actions in the eastern USA killed nearly 3,000 people, including 67 British citizens, making it the worst terrorist incident of modern times. Since then, there have been further significant attacks: in predominantly

Muslim countries such as Pakistan, Tunisia, Morocco, Qatar, Jordan, Indonesia - including the bombing of a nightclub in Bali in October 2002, in which over 190 people were killed, including 28 British citizens - and Turkey; in India; as well as more attacks in Egypt, Saudi Arabia, and Yemen. There have also been significant attacks in Europe: multiple attacks on the Madrid train network in March 2004 and attacks in the United Kingdom in July 2005, when nearly simultaneous explosions on the Underground network and a bus in London killed 52 innocent people and injured over 700 others. Many intended terrorist actions in this period, however, were disrupted or unsuccessful.

3.5.1. Characteristics

Terrorism is not a new phenomenon. For example, the UK experienced repeated domestic terrorist attacks as a result of the long-running troubles in Northern Ireland. Nevertheless, the threat that we currently face does have certain distinctive characteristics.

First, the threat is genuinely international. Compared with earlier terrorist threats, attacks have been carried out, or attempted, against a very wide range of targets in many countries. Sometimes these attacks are carried out by individuals from the country concerned and sometimes by outsiders, so the domestic and international dimensions of this threat are closely interlinked. The terrorists also make maximum use of the freedoms and possibilities of modern life - especially the ease of travel and the ease with which information and money flows across the world.

Second, the threat comes from a variety of groups, networks and individuals. These range from larger groups organised around clear hierarchic and bureaucratic structures, to much looser and smaller groups of like-minded individuals. These different elements often cooperate and assist each other, but often also pursue separate goals. In the past, terrorists have sometimes sought protection or sponsorship from states, as was provided in the 1990s in Sudan and under the Taliban regime in Afghanistan. They continue to seek out places where governments and security forces are weak as 'havens' for training and other activities. These terrorists are, however, essentially non-state actors - they do not need state support to operate.

Third, these terrorists intend to cause mass casualties. They are indiscriminate: aiming to cause the most death and destruction that they can, regardless of the age, nationality, or religion of their victims. Whilst they do aim at governmental targets, such as embassies and units of the armed forces, or those with symbolic value, such as the twin towers of the World Trade Center in New York, one distinctive feature of their attacks is that these often deliberately strike at ordinary people going about their lives. Other terrorist groups have done this in the past, but not on such a scale. And these terrorists are often prepared to kill themselves as a means of killing many others. This is not unique to these groups, but it has not been a feature of previous threats that the UK has faced.

Fourth, the people involved in these terrorist attacks are driven by particular violent and extremist beliefs. A common thread connecting many of the planned or successful terrorist attacks in the UK, the rest of Europe, the Middle East, South Asia, and North America over the past decade has been that those involved have claimed to be acting in defence of Islam. However, the great majority of Muslims in the UK and abroad reject both extremism and violence. What the terrorists in fact draw on is a particular and distorted form of Islam, sometimes referred to as Islamist extremism, which they say encourages or obliges its adherents to carry out acts of violence against those that they identify as their enemies.

The threat to the UK comes from different quarters. In the tragic events of 7 July 2005, terrorists inspired by Islamist extremism may come from within British communities -the bombers were British citizens brought up in this country. However, those charged in connection with the incidents on 21 July 2005 are of African origin. In recent years, terrorist suspects investigated in the UK have come originally from countries as diverse as Libya, Algeria, Jordan, Saudi Arabia, Iraq, Somalia, and elsewhere - as well as those who have lived most or all of their lives in the UK.

The Government assesses that the current threat in the UK from Islamist terrorism is serious and sustained. British citizens also face the threat of terrorist attacks when abroad. The UK has achieved some significant successes in dealing with potential attacks by Islamist terrorists, since before 2001. A number of credible plans to cause loss of life have been disrupted; in many cases the individuals involved have either been successfully prosecuted and imprisoned or are awaiting trial. However, as the tragic attacks of 7 July 2005 have shown, it is not possible to eliminate completely the threat of terrorist attacks in this country.

Since early 2003, the United Kingdom has been implementing a long-term strategy for countering international terrorism and the extremism that lies behind it. The aim is: to reduce the risk from international terrorism, so that people can go about their daily lives freely and with confidence.

To achieve this, the Government has put in place a comprehensive programme of action, against both short and long term objectives and involving activity both at national and local level here in the UK and overseas. The strategy and the programme to implement it are divided into four principal areas:

— preventing terrorism by tackling the radicalisation of individuals;
— pursuing terrorists and those that sponsor them;
— protecting the public, key national services, and UK interests overseas; and _ preparing for the consequences.

3.5.2. Principles

The Government believes that respect for international law and human rights standards must be an integral part of its efforts to counter terrorism. The promotion of good governance and human rights internationally is also a key element of wider efforts to combat terrorism and extremism. Similarly, the drive for equality, social inclusion, community cohesion and active citizenship in Britain strengthens society and its resistance to terrorism here in the UK. Successful delivery of this counter-terrorism strategy depends upon partnerships between all parts of Government; the public, private, and voluntary sectors; and all of us as individuals and as members of communities.

3.5.2.1. Counter radicalisation

The first area of action to counter radicalisation lies in addressing structural problems in the UK and elsewhere that may contribute to radicalisation. In the UK, this forms part of the Government's broader equality agenda and they are working with communities and the public and private sectors to address these wider issues. Many Government programmes that are not specifically directed at tackling radicalism nevertheless help to build cohesion in communities across the country - for example, Sure Start.

The second area of action to counter radicalisation is by changing the environment in which the extremists and those radicalising others can operate; deterring those who facilitate terrorism and those who encourage others to become terrorists.

Sometimes particular places can also be sources of radicalising influences. The influence of particular mosques has already been mentioned, but there is also evidence that individuals can become radicalised whilst in prison. The Government will be working with local communities to identify other areas where radicalisation may be taking place and to help communities protect themselves and counter the efforts of extremist radicalisers.

Speaking on 21 March 2006, the Prime Minister said: "This terrorism will not be defeated until its ideas, the poison that warps the minds of its adherents, are confronted, head-on, in their essence, at their core". The third area of action to counter radicalisation is therefore a battle of ideas, challenging the ideological motivations that extremists believe justify the use of violence.

The Government has been working with communities for many years to help shape policy and determine its objectives. The Home Office has supported Muslim and other faith communities and encouraged their contribution to social cohesion and interfaith activities (work now being taken forward by the Department of Communities and Local Government). This has included establishing a Ministerial and Officials visits programme in January 2003 to listen to the concerns of Muslim communities; working with media organisations to improve perceptions of Muslim communities; working with the Police on protecting the Muslim community; and consulting with all faith communities on the Anti-Terrorism, Crime and Security Act 2001.

Similarly, the Foreign and Commonwealth Office (FCO) has been working with Muslim communities on a range of generic and country specific issues. Typical examples include setting up the

British Hajj Delegation (providing consular support to British Hajj pilgrims) seven years ago, and regular Ministerial involvement in community events, such as Mike O'Brien's speech at the inaugural meeting of the Association of London Mosques in 2005. Following the attacks in London last July, Home Office ministers visited nine towns and cities with large Muslim populations to consult them about how government could work with communities to prevent extremism. 1,000 British Muslims took part in these consultations and seven community-led working groups were set up under the banner of 'Preventing Extremism Together' (PET). The working groups produced 64 recommendations: 27 of these were for the Government to lead on, while the remainder were for communities themselves to work on, supported by Government where necessary.

Progress on the three principal recommendations, where the Government is supporting communities - a national grassroots-led campaign targeted at Muslim youth; Muslim Forums on Extremism and Islamophobia, and a Mosques and Imams National Advisory Board - is outlined below.

Action has been agreed on all 27 of the recommendations for the Government. At the time of writing, action on three of the recommendations had already been completed - consultation on the Department for Education and Skills (DfES) 'Youth Matters' Green Paper; extending Equal Opportunities legislation to cover discrimination on the grounds of faith; and expanding the Muslim Ethnic Achievement project to improve the achievement levels of Muslim students. In a further 17 cases the Government has accepted the recommendation and work is in progress to implement it. For three recommendations the Government is still considering its response; for two more an alternative outcome has been put in place; and the remaining two recommendations are not being taken forward.

A key outcome of the PET initiative has been that representatives of many differing views within the British Muslim communities have worked with Government towards a single goal. This approach is continuing. Within the PET framework, a cross-government forum has been established to consider how to tackle extremism on campuses; outside PET, the Government is working with Muslim communities to improve their approach to tackling extremism - for example, funding the charity Forward

Thinking to run a series of workshops across England with young Muslims on the role of Islam in a pluralistic society.

The Foreign Office is doing more to explain that the foreign policy is based upon striving for UK interests in a safe, just and prosperous world and to counter extremists' allegations that it has an anti-Islamic agenda. This means explaining better the reasons why, for example, we supported and continue to support action in Iraq and Afghanistan. Many disagreed with the decisions to take military action in those countries. However, the UK Government intervened because of wider issues and not because these are Muslim countries.

3.5.2.2. Pursuing terrorists

The pursue strand of contest is concerned with reducing the terrorist threat to the UK and to UK interests overseas by disrupting terrorists and their operations.

3.5.2.3. Intelligence

By their nature, terrorists operate in secret. Intelligence is therefore vital to defeating terrorism. All disruption operations depend upon the collection and exploitation of information and intelligence that helps identify terrorist networks, including their membership, intentions, and means of operation. The Security Service (MI5), the Secret Intelligence Service (SIS), and the Government Communications Headquarters (GCHQ) - known collectively as the security and intelligence agencies - are therefore critical to the work on PURSUE, as is the work of the police, both special branches and neighbourhood policing alike, for UK-based terrorist networks.

Since September 2001 there has seen a significant shift of Government resources into the business of gathering and analysing information on the threat and configuring departments and agencies in the most effective way to address it.

Public safety is the top priority for the Government, the police, and the intelligence agencies. The Government fully support the police and Security Service in the difficult decisions they must make when faced with the current terrorist threat. Operational decisions on whether and how to conduct counter terrorist operations are a matter for the police. There may be situations where the police believe they have no choice but to take action on the basis of the specific intelligence they have received. The difficulties in assessing intelligence about terrorist activity were highlighted in the Government's response to the Intelligence and Security Committee's Report into the London Terrorist Attacks on 7 July 2005:

"... many pieces of intelligence are received by the [Security and Intelligence] Agencies on a weekly basis on potential terrorist threats and intentions. Terrorists make great efforts to ensure that intelligence about their intentions is difficult to obtain and analyse. Intelligence is generally fragmentary, of varying reliability and difficult to interpret. Complex and challenging investigative judgements have to be made on the basis of often incomplete data. There is always a difficult balance to strike between investigating those known to be a current threat and working to discover other possible threats."

3.5.2.4. Disruption

Covert operational counter-terrorist activity in the United Kingdom is conducted by the Security Service in close collaboration with police forces across the country and the Anti-Terrorist Branch of the Metropolitan Police. The police are responsible for taking executive action, such as arrests, and conducting the investigation against those suspected of involvement in terrorism. The SIS and GCHQ, in collaboration with intelligence and security partners overseas, operate covertly in support of the Security Service to disrupt terrorist threats.

The Government continues to strengthen its co-ordinated, multi-agency, and international approach to the disruption of terrorist activity. Prosecution remains the preferred way of responding to persons involved in terrorist activity, but other options for taking disruptive action include deportation on grounds of national security or unacceptable behaviour, control orders under the Prevention of Terrorism Act 2005, freezing and seizing financial assets, and proscription of organisations.

In addition, where individuals are being prosecuted for terrorist offences, the Government obviously cannot discuss specific cases until the legal processes are complete. Many disruptions of terrorist networks lead to prosecutions for other, non-terrorist offences - sometimes major offences such as crimes of violence, and sometimes lesser offences such as fraud - or to actions for deportation, or to impose control orders.

Successful prosecution in the courts, based on gathering the necessary evidence and apprehending those involved in planning acts of terrorism before they can carry out their intentions, is of course the preferred way of disrupting terrorist activity.

Where the person concerned is a foreign national, and is a threat to the UK, deportation will usually be an appropriate means of disrupting terrorist activity. This is important in terms of ensuring public safety, as well as sending a strong signal that foreign nationals who threaten the national security cannot expect to be allowed to remain in the UK.

The Prevention of Terrorism Act 2005 enables the Secretary of State to make a "nonderogating" control order against an individual who he has reasonable grounds for suspecting is involved in terrorism-related activity and where he considers it necessary for the protection of the public. These measures can be applied to any individual, irrespective of nationality, and whatever the nature of the terrorist activity. A control order is a last resort measure, to address the threat from an individual where prosecution is not possible and, in the case of a foreign national, where it is not possible to deport him or her due to the international human rights obligations (in particular, where there is a real risk of torture).

Control orders are preventative. They place one or more obligations upon an individual in order to prevent, restrict or disrupt involvement in terrorism-related activity. A range of obligations can be imposed to address the risk posed by the individual concerned, including a curfew, restrictions on the use of communication equipment, restrictions on the people that the individual can associate with, and travel restrictions. The legislation requires that control orders made by the Secretary of State must be compatible with the individual's right to liberty under Article 5 of the European Convention on Human Rights (ECHR). Although there is a procedure in the legislation for Parliament to agree to derogate from Article 5 of the ECHR, so the Secretary of State can apply to a court to make a "derogating" control order, this has currently not been exercised.

The 2005 Act contains strong safeguards to protect the rights of the individual, including requirements for judicial oversight and review of control orders. The legislation and its operation have recently been challenged in the courts. The Government is appealing both judgements in the Court of Appeal. All existing control orders remain in force (including the six cases in the second High Court ruling which remain in force pending the outcome of the appeal), and the Secretary of State will continue to make new control orders where he considers it necessary to do so.

Whenever terrorists come into contact with the financial system, they can generate vital clues that can lead to their disruption and apprehension. To maximise the impact of this financial intelligence, and make it harder for terrorists to operate, the UK's money laundering and terrorist finance measures require financial institutions to 'know their customer', keep proper records, and report suspicious activity. Irrespective of any final charges, every terrorist suspect is subject to financial investigation. Enquiries following the attacks of 7 July and attempted attacks of 21 July demonstrated the critical role of terrorist finance investigation in progressing specific enquiries and establishing an enhanced intelligence picture.

A major challenge for law enforcement is to disrupt terrorists' ability to raise, move and use funds. Experience has shown the costs of carrying out bombing incidents to be relatively low but terrorist networks also need more significant funding to support the rest of their activities, including recruitment, training and welfare payments to the families of those killed. This is often achieved through ordinary criminal activity such as identity fraud, cheque fraud and misuse of charities.

Various powers now exist to challenge terrorist fund-raising. For example, the UK's terrorist asset freezing powers publicly identify suspected individuals and groups linked to terrorism. These also freeze any existing assets and disable terrorists' ability to raise or move further funds. An effective and collaborative partnership between specialist law enforcement officers, government and the private financial sector in the UK has raised awareness of the vulnerabilities and has helped develop solutions.

In accordance with UN Security Council Resolutions, countries are required to freeze the assets of individuals who are involved with terrorism and stop them receiving payments directly or indirectly. To ensure that these sanctions do not contravene basic human rights, the Government is required to make payments under licence to meet basic expenses. The Government has announced to Parliament that state benefits paid to individuals sharing the same household with a listed person will only be paid under strict licence conditions, providing safeguards to ensure funds are not diverted to terrorism.

The proscription of terrorist organisations also contributes towards making the UK a hostile environment for terrorists and sends a strong message that the UK totally rejects such organisations and any claims to legitimacy. Proscription is a tough power as it has the effect of outlawing previously lawful activity. Once an organisation is proscribed it is a criminal offence to belong to, support, or display support for a proscribed organisation. The Terrorism Act also allows the police to seize all property of a proscribed organisation.

3.5.3. Protecting the Public

The protect strand of contest is concerned with reducing the vulnerability of the UK and UK interests overseas to a terrorist attack. This covers a range of issues such as borders, the critical national infrastructure, and crowded places. For security reasons, this paper does not provide any information about the extent to which there are currently concerns in relation to specific risks or vulnerabilities relating to any particular sector or area.

3.5.3.1. Borders

The Border Management Programme (BMP) is a cross-government initiative aimed at developing and implementing closer and more effective joint working in order to strengthen border security whilst minimising the impact on legitimate traffic.

The strategic objectives of the programme are to:

— improve intelligence sharing in support of border operations;
— jointly identify and manage risks;

- provide a more effective border control; and
- minimise the impact on legitimate traffic and business partners.

Risks are assessed and identified through a national process which considers the probability of the event and especially its impact on the UK. This helps to identify the priorities for protection, the aim of which is to reduce the vulnerability to and likelihood of a terrorist attack through proportionate security measures and technological advances.

The contribution of the private sector is crucial in protecting the UK and UK interests overseas against terrorism. This involves the public sector working closely with key utilities, such as energy and water, and with key services, such as transport and finance, within a framework of advice and regulation that aims to help these businesses operate safely.

3.6. Changing International Terrorism

There are dramatically fewer international terrorist incidents than in the mid-eighties. Many of the groups that targeted America's interests, friends, and allies have disappeared. The Soviet bloc, which once provided support to terrorist groups, no longer exists. Countries that once excused terrorism now condemn it. This changed international attitude has led to 12 United Nations conventions targeting terrorist activity and, more importantly, growing, practical international cooperation. However, if most of the world's countries are firmer in opposing terrorism, some still support terrorists or use terrorism as an element of state policy. Iran is the clearest case.

The Revolutionary Guard Corps and the Ministry of Intelligence and Security carry out terrorist activities and give direction and support to other terrorists. The regimes of Syria, Sudan, and Afghanistan provide funding, refuge, training bases, and weapons to terrorists. Libya continues to provide support to some Palestinian terrorist groups and to harass expatriate dissidents, and North Korea may still provide weapons to terrorists. Cuba provides safehaven to a number of terrorists. Other states allow terrorist groups to operate on their soil or provide support which, while falling short of state sponsorship, nonetheless gives terrorists important assistance.

The terrorist threat is also changing in ways that make it more dangerous and difficult to counter. International terrorism once threatened Americans only when they were outside the country. Today international terrorists attack Britain on their own soil. Just before the millennium, an alert U.S. Customs Service official stopped Ahmad Ressam as he attempted to enter the United States from Canada-apparently to conduct a terrorist attack. This fortuitous arrest should not inspire complacency, however. On an average day, over one million people enter the United States legally and thousands more enter illegally.

Terrorist attacks are becoming more lethal. Most terrorist organisations active in the 1970s and 1980s had clear political objectives. They tried to calibrate their attacks to produce just enough bloodshed to get attention for their cause, but not so much as to alienate public support. Groups like the Irish Republican Army and the Palestine Liberation Organisation often sought specific political concessions. Now, a growing percentage of terrorist attacks are designed to kill as many people as possible.

In the 1990s a terrorist incident was almost 20 percent more likely to result in death or injury than an incident two decades ago. The World Trade Center bombing in New York killed six and wounded about 1,000, but the terrorists' goal was to topple the twin towers, killing tens of thousands of people. The thwarted attacks against New York City's infrastructure in 1993-which included plans to bomb the Lincoln and Holland tunnels-also were intended to cause mass casualties. In 1995, Philippine authorities uncovered a terrorist plot to bring down 11 U.S. airliners in Asia.

The circumstances surrounding the millennium border arrests of foreign nationals suggest that the suspects planned to target a large group assembled for a New Year's celebration. Overseas attacks against the United States in recent years have followed the same trend. The bombs that destroyed the military barracks in Saudi Arabia and two U.S. Embassies in Africa inflicted 6,059 casualties. Those arrested in Jordan in late December had also planned attacks designed to kill large numbers. The trend toward higher casualties reflects, in part, the changing motivation of today's terrorists. Religiously motivated terrorist groups, such as Usama bin Ladin's group, al-Qaida, which is believed to have bombed the U.S. Embassies in Africa, represent a growing trend toward hatred of the United States. Other terrorist groups are driven by visions of a postapocalyptic future or by ethnic hatred. Such groups may lack a concrete political goal other than to punish their enemies by killing as many of them as possible, seemingly without concern about alienating sympathisers. Increasingly, attacks are less likely to be followed by claims of responsibility or lists of political demands.

The shift in terrorist motives has contributed to a change in the way some international terrorist groups are structured. Because groups based on ideological or religious motives may lack a specific political or nationalistic agenda, they have less need for a hierarchical structure. Instead, they can rely on loose affiliations with like-minded groups from a variety of countries to support their common cause against the United States.

Al-Qaida is the best-known transnational terrorist organisation. In addition to pursuing its own terrorist campaign, it calls on numerous militant groups that share some of its ideological beliefs to support its violent campaign against the United States. But neither al-Qaida's extremist politico-religious beliefs nor its leader, Usama bin Ladin, is unique. If al-Qaida and Usama bin Ladin were to disappear tomorrow, the United States would still face potential terrorist threats from a growing number of groups opposed to perceived American hegemony.

Moreover, new terrorist threats can suddenly emerge from isolated conspiracies or obscure cults with no previous history of violence. These more loosely affiliated, transnational terrorist networks are difficult to predict, track, and penetrate. They rely on a variety of sources for funding and logistical support, including self-financing criminal activities such as kidnapping, narcotics, and petty crimes. Their networks of support include both front organisations and legitimate business and nongovernment organisations. They use the Internet as an effective communications channel.

Guns and conventional explosives have so far remained the weapons of choice for most terrorists. Such weapons can cause many casualties and are relatively easy to acquire and use. But some terrorist groups now show interest in acquiring the capability to use chemical, biological, radiological, or nuclear

(CBRN) materials. It is difficult to predict the likelihood of a CBRN attack, but most experts agree that today's terrorists are seeking the ability to use such agents in order to cause mass casualties. Still, these kinds of weapons and materials confront a non-state sponsored terrorist group with significant technical challenges.

While lethal chemicals are easy to come by, getting large quantities and weaponising them for mass casualties is difficult, and only nation states have succeeded in doing so. Biological agents can be acquired in nature or from medical supply houses, but important aspects of handling and dispersion are daunting. To date, only nation states have demonstrated the capability to build radiological and nuclear weapons.

The 1995 release of a chemical agent in the Tokyo subway by the apocalyptic Aum Shinrikyo group demonstrated the difficulties that terrorists face in attempting to use CBRN weapons to produce mass casualties. The group used scores of highly skilled technicians and spent tens of millions of dollars developing a chemical attack that killed fewer people than conventional explosives could have. The same group failed totally in a separate attempt to launch an anthrax attack in Tokyo. However, if the terrorists' goal is to challenge significantly Americans' sense of safety and confidence, even a small CBRN attack could be successful.

Moreover, terrorists could acquire more deadly CBRN capabilities from a state. Five of the seven nations the United States identifies as state sponsors of terrorism have programs to develop weapons of mass destruction. A state that knowingly provides agents of mass destruction or technology to a terrorist group should worry about losing control of the terrorists' activities and, if the weapons could be traced back to that state, the near certainty of massive retaliation. However, it is always difficult and sometimes dangerous to attempt to predict the actions of a state.

Moreover, a state in chaos, or elements within such a state, might run these risks, especially if the United States were engaged in military conflict with that state or if the United States were distracted by a major conflict in another area of the world. The Commission was particularly concerned about the persistent lack of adequate security and safeguards for the nuclear material in the former Soviet Union (FSU). A Center for Strategic International Studies panel chaired by former Senator Sam Nunn concluded that, despite a decade of effort, the risk of "loose nukes" is greater than ever. Another ominous warning was given in 1995 when Chechen rebels, many of whom fight side-by-side with Islamic terrorists from bin Ladin's camps sympathetic to the Chechen cause, placed radioactive material in a Moscow park.

Certainly, terrorists are making extensive use of the new information technologies, and a conventional terrorist attack along with a coordinated cyber attack could exponentially compound the damage. While the Commission considers cyber security a matter of grave importance, it also notes that the measures needed to protect the United States from cyber attack by terrorists are largely identical to those necessary to protect us from such an attack by a hostile foreign country, criminals, or vandals. Not all terrorists are the same, but the groups most dangerous to the United States share some characteristics not seen 10 or 20 years ago:

— They operate in the United States as well as abroad.

— Their funding and logistical networks cross borders, are less dependent on state sponsors, and are harder to disrupt with economic sanctions.

— They make use of widely available technologies to communicate quickly and securely.

— Their objectives are more deadly.

This changing nature of the terrorist threat raises the stakes in getting American counterterrorist policies and practices right.

REFERENCES

AbuKhalil, As'ad, *Bin Laden, Islam, and America's New 'War on Terrorism'*, Open Media Pamphlet Series, New York: Seven Stories Press, 2002.

Raymond L. Garthoff, *Reflections on the Cuban Missile Crisis*, Brookings Institution, 1987.

Robert O. Slater and Michael Stohl, "States, Terrorism and State Terrorism," *Current Perspectives on International Terrorism*, Macmillan, 1988.

Rosalyn Higgins and Maurice Flory, eds., *Terrorism and International Law*, London, Florence, KY Routledge, 1997.

4
State Sponsored Terrorism

State sponsorship of terrorism is one of the most important factors in fostering international terrorism. A number of governments afford terrorists safehaven, travel documents, arms, training, and technical expertise. To support for terrorist groups, some governments engage directly in terrorism as a tool of their foreign and domestic policies. Other governments, though not direct sponsors of terrorist groups, contribute to such groups' capabilities by allowing them unimpeded transit, permitting them to operate commercial enterprises, and allowing them to carry out recruitment and other support activities. Any type of government support for terrorist groups makes law enforcement efforts to counter terrorism much more difficult.

The United States and its allies in the fight against terrorism have focused on raising the costs for those governments who support, tolerate, and engage in terrorism. The United States currently lists Cuba, Iran, Iraq, Libya, North Korea, and Syria as state supporters of terrorism. This and related U.S. statutes impose trade and other restrictions on countries determined by the secretary of state to have repeatedly provided support for acts of international terrorism. The People's Democratic Republic of Yemen was dropped from the list in 1990 after it merged with its northern neighbour to form the Republic of Yemen. Iraq was added to the list because of its renewed support for terrorist groups in 1990.

The international effort to eliminate state support for terrorism has achieved some notable results. International public opinion and cooperation among like-minded governments have generated great pressure on governments to change their behaviour or, at a minimum, make significant efforts to hide their involvement in terrorism. This is reflected in the number of terrorist incidents attributable to governments on the U.S. list of state supporters of terrorism. The totals have declined from 176 in 1988 to 58 in 1989 and finally to 54 in 1990. Indeed, the continuing danger posed by state sponsorship was demonstrated in 1990 by two developments. First, the 30 May abortive seaborne attack by the Palestine Liberation Front (PLF) on crowded Israeli beaches was made possible by Libyan government support for the training, provision, and transportation of the PLF terrorists.

While the operation was foiled without civilian casualties, the attack significantly raised tensions in the region and resulted in the termination of the U.S.-PLO dialogue. Had the operation succeeded, it could have led to numerous casualties among bathers on the crowded Tel Aviv public beaches. Second, after Iraq's August invasion of Kuwait, the world saw Iraq assemble an impressive array of terrorist groups aimed at intimidating the international coalition opposed to the invasion.

Libya's involvement in terrorism during 1990 went beyond support for the 30 May attack on Israel. Tripoli continued to shelter and aid the notorious Abu Nidal organisation (ANO), to fund other radical Palestinian groups such as the Popular Front for the Liberation of Palestine-General Command (PFLP-GC), and to support terrorist groups elsewhere in Africa, Latin America, and Asia.

Iran continued its use of and support for terrorism in 1990, targeting and assassinating Iranian dissidents overseas, attacking Saudi officials and interests, continuing to support the holders of the American and other Western hostages in Lebanon, and supporting radical Palestinian groups such as the Palestine Islamic Jihad (PIJ) and the PFLP-GC. Syria continued to give refuge and support to Lebanese, Palestinian, Turkish, Japanese, and Iranian terrorists while maintaining that all attacks on Israel and the occupied territories are legitimate "national liberation" efforts. North Korea continued to harbour some Japanese Red Army (JRA) terrorists and to provide some support to the New People's Army in the Philippines. Cuba continued to supply and support groups that use terrorism in El Salvador, Colombia, Peru, Honduras, and Chile, among others.

4.1. Cuba

Cuba continues to serve as a haven for regional revolutionaries and to provide military training, weapons, funds, and guidance to radical subversive groups that use terrorism. The island today remains a major training centre and transit point for Latin subversives and some international groups.

El Salvador's Farabundo Marti National Liberation Front (FMLN) has been the primary beneficiary of Cuba's clandestine support network over the last several years. Havana has been the point of origin for most of the weapons used by the FMLN for insurgent and terrorist operations in El Salvador. Other Central American groups, notably in Honduras and Guatemala, have also received Cuban aid. In South America, Chilean radical leftist groups have been the favoured recipients of Cuban support, but their aid may have declined since Chile's peaceful transition to civilian rule in March 1990.

Several rebel organisations have offices and members stationed in Havana. Wounded rebels are often treated in Cuban hospitals. With the demise of the pro-Cuban governments in Panama and Nicaragua, Cuba's support has become even more important to radical groups.

4.2. Iran

Iran's extensive support for terrorism continued during 1990, although the number of terrorist acts attributed to Iranian state sponsorship dropped to 10 in 1990 from 24 in 1989. Iran has used its intelligence services extensively to facilitate and conduct terrorist attacks, particularly against regime dissidents. Intelligence officers in embassies have used the diplomatic pouch for conveyance of weapons and finances for terrorist groups. Iran continued to strengthen its relationship with Muslim extremists throughout the world, often providing them with advice and financial assistance. Over the past year, Iranian support for terrorism has included:

— Repeating the call for the death of the author of *The Satanic Verses*, Salman Rushdie.
— Assassinations of four antiregime dissidents — in Pakistan, Switzerland, Sweden, and France.

— Supporting radical Shia attacks on Saudi interests, including the assassinations of three Saudi diplomats, in retaliation for the execution of the Hajj bombers.
— Extensive support for Hizballah, the PFLP-GC, the PIJ, and other groups, including provision of arms, funding, and training.

Iranian-backed Shia groups are believed to be in control of Western hostages in Lebanon, and most observers believe that the key to releasing the hostages rests with Iran. One such group, Hizballah, is believed to hold all of the remaining American hostages. Iranian President All Akbar Hashemi-Rafsanjani, whose domestic political strength increased during 1990, is thought to favour a pragmatic approach to foreign policy and improved relations with the West, which would require resolution of the hostage problem. For example, The Tehran Times, a newspaper considered to reflect Rafsanjani's views, editorialised on 22 February that the hostages should be freed without preconditions. Two months later, U.S. hostages Robert Polhill and Frank Reed were released. The hostage releases received some criticism from hardline elements both in Iran and within Hizballah who questioned whether Iran or the hostage holders had received any benefit for their actions in terms of a good will gesture from the West. No more U.S. hostages were freed in 1990, and press reports indicated that Iran was seeking rewards before any further movement on the hostages was possible.

Major terrorist figures, including Ahmad Jabril of the PFLP-GC and various prominent members of Hizballah, frequently visit Iran. Iran hosted a World Conference on Palestine in Tehran in December in an effort to gain increasing influence over Islamic affairs, in general, and over the Palestinian movement, in particular. Leaders of several radical Palestinian and Lebanese groups including Saïqa, Hamas, Hizballah, and the Palestinian Islamic Jihad attended.

4.3. Iraq

Iraq was returned to the terrorist list in September 1990 because of its increased contact with, and support for, terrorist groups. After the formation of an international coalition against the invasion of Kuwait, Iraqi officials issued public statements endorsing terrorism as a legitimate tactic.

Following its invasion of Kuwait on 2 August, the government of Iraq systematically seized the citizens of the United States and many other nations. This occurred in both Kuwait and Iraq and continued for several months. Many of the hostages were moved to strategic sites in Iraq, including armaments factories, weapons research facilities, and major military bases. This mass act of hostage taking was condemned by nations throughout the world, and the U.N. Security Council adopted Resolution 664, demanding that Iraq release these hostages.

Saddam Hussein eventually released the hostages, starting with women and children. By December, all the Western hostages were freed, but many Kuwaitis remained in captivity.

Hostage taking on the scale undertaken by Iraq is unprecedented in recent history. Saddam Hussein's operation represented a cynical and futile attempt to terrorise both foreign nationals and their governments and to weaken international resolve to oppose his occupation and annexation of Kuwait.

During 1990, and particularly after 2 August, the press reported increasing movement of terrorists to Baghdad, signaling the deepening relationship between these groups and Iraq. Even before the invasion of Kuwait, Iraq provided safehaven, training, and other support to Palestinian groups with a history of terrorist actions. The Arab Liberation Front (ALF) and Abu Abbas's PLF, responsible for the 1985 Achille Lauro hijacking and the terrorist attack on Israel beaches in May, are among these groups. The ANO is also reported to have restablished its presence in Iraq in the first half of 1990. Abu Ibrahim, leader of the now-defunct 15 May terrorist organisation and famed for his skill as a bombmaker, is also reportedly based in Baghdad.

With the end of the Iran-Iraq war, Iraq reduced its support for anti-Iranian dissident groups including the Mujahidin-e-Khaiq (MEK). Speculation continues regarding increased Iraqi support for the terrorist Kurdish Worker's Party (PKK) in Turkey. This is coupled with the worsening of Turkish-Iraqi relations over Turkey's enforcement of U.N. mandated trade sanctions after the invasion of Kuwait and disputes over water rights.

Senior Iraqi government officials, including Foreign Minister Tariq Aziz, made public statements justifying terrorism as a legitimate Iraqi response in the event of hostilities between Iraq and the multinational force deployed in the region. There were reports that Iraq planned to put these words into effect and that Iraqi officials, as well as Baghdad's Palestinian surrogates, conducted surveillance against various coalition targets.

4.4. Libya

In 1990, Libya demonstrated its continued support for terrorism by supporting the Palestine Liberation Front's failed 30 May seaborne attack on crowded Israeli beaches. Tripoli helped the PLF plan, train for, supply, and carry out the seaborne operation. Since 1986, Libyan leader Muammar Qadhafi has made public disclaimers about his support for terrorist groups. He continued to provide money, training, and other support to his terrorist clients. Qadhafi's claims of having expelled certain terrorist groups — the PLF, ANO, and PFLP-GC — remained unsubstantiated as of the end of 1990. Libya also resumed funding to the PFLP-GC, and possibly other Palestinian terrorist groups, in 1990.

Libya also continues its support for a variety of terrorist/insurgent groups worldwide. In the Philippines, Libya has supported the NPA, which carried out terrorist attacks against Americans that killed five persons in 1990. Costa Rican officials believe that all 15 members of the Santamaria Patriotic Organisation (OPS) arrested in Costa Rica in February for grenade attacks against U.S. facilities had undergone terrorist training in Libya. The group that attacked the Trinidad and Tobago Parliament on 27 July in a coup attempt, which killed several persons, received training and financial support from Libya, among others.

In April, Ethiopia expelled two Libyan diplomats for alleged involvement in the 30 March bombing at the Hilton Hotel in Addis Ababa. Throughout 1990, indications of Libya's previous involvement in acts of terrorism emerged. According to German press reports, German officials uncovered evidence in the files of the now-defunct East German secret police, the Stasi, that demonstrated Libyan responsibility for the 1986 bombing of the La Belle Disco in West Berlin.

In addition, according to press reports, the investigation into the September 1989 bombing of the French UTA Flight 772 — which killed 170 persons, including seven Americans — indicates that the bomb was brought into Congo in the Libyan diplomatic pouch and delivered to three Libyan-trained Congolese terrorists by an official of the Libyan Embassy in Brazzaville. African and French press reports state that both the Congolese and Zairians are holding suspects who have implicated Libya in the bombing.

Press reports in late 1990 also laid much of the responsibility on the Libyans for the bombing in December 1988 of Pan Am Flight 103. According to American, British, and French press, investigators discovered that the detonator used in the Pan am Flight 103 bombing was identical to one carried by two Libyan agents arrested in Dakar, Senegal, in February 1988. The official investigation into both of these cases was continuing through the end of 1990.

4.5. North Korea

North Korea is not known to have sponsored a terrorist attack since members of its intelligence service planted a bomb on a South Korean airliner in 1987. However, it continues to provide safehaven to a small group of Japanese Red Army (JRA) members who hijacked a JAL airliner to North Korea in 1970. North Korea has provided some support to the New People's Army in the Philippines. It has not renounced the use of terrorism. Syria

There is no direct evidence of Syrian government involvement in terrorist attacks outside Lebanon since 1987, although Syria continues to provide support and safehaven to groups that engage in international terrorism. Syria has made some progress in moving away from support for some terrorist groups. Syria has also cooperated with Iran and others to obtain the release of Western hostages held by terrorist groups in Lebanon, including the successful release of American hostages Polhill and Reed in the spring of 1990. The government-controlled media has described the Abu Nidal organisation as a terrorist organisation, but the Syrian government has failed to take concrete measures against the ANO in Syrian-controlled areas of Lebanon.

At the same time, Syria publicly supports the Palestinians' right to armed struggle for their independence. President Assad has publicly defended and supported Palestinian attacks in Israel and the occupied territories. Syria continues to provide political and material support for Palestinian groups who maintain their headquarters in Damascus and who have committed terrorist acts in the past, most notably the PFLP-GC whose propaganda radio station, al Quds, broadcasts from Syrian soil. It also hosts the Abu Musa group, the Popular Struggle Front (PSF), the Popular Front for the Liberation of Palestine (PFLP), and Democratic Front for the Liberation of Palestine (DFLP). The leader of the PFLP had publicly stated that he would carry out attacks against U.S. targets and others opposed to Iraq in the event of a military clash in the Gulf. At year's end, no such attacks had occurred.

The United States continued to express its serious concern to the Syrian government — both publicly and privately — about terrorist groups supported by Syria. The Syrian government has taken some positive steps, particularly since the beginning of the Gulf crisis in August 1990, to rein in terrorist groups based in Syria. The did not, however, take steps to close down these groups or expel them from Syria. Syria has taken no steps to disband or eliminate the presence of other terrorist organisations, such the Kurdish Worker's Party (PKK), the Armenian Secret Army for the Liberation of Armenia (ASALA), and the Japanese Red Army. A number of these groups have camps in Lebanon's Bekaa Valley, which is under the control of Syrian forces. Syria also tolerates the presence of a faction of the Palestinian Islamic Jihad that took responsibility for the massacre in February of nine Israeli civilians on a tour bus in Egypt. The PIJ statement was broadcast on the PFLP-GC-controlled radio station in southern Syria.

In 1990, and particularly since the Iraqi invasion of Kuwait, Syria has attempted to minimise its public association with terrorist activities and groups in the international arena, apparently in an attempt to improve its standing with the West. Syrian officials have said that Syria is committed to bring to justice and punish those individuals within Syria's jurisdiction accused of acts of terrorism, if given supporting evidence of their crimes. They have also repeated that any organisation that is involved in terrorist crimes will have to bear the consequences. Following the September visit by Secretary of State James Baker, Syrian Foreign Minister Shara' stated publicly that Syria condemned all forms of terrorism, including hijacking and hostage taking. However, Syria continues to draw a distinction between "legitimate struggle against the occupation troops" and acts of terrorism — a fundamental difference between U.S. and Syrian news.

4.6. International Economics and State Sponsored Terrorism

A nation as a whole is better off by integrating with the global economy and following a policy of free trade in all goods and services. However, another well-known conclusion of standard trade models is that not all individuals and/or groups within a country benefit from free trade, even though the country as a whole unambiguously benefits. The usual explanation for this result is based on the Stolper-Samuelson Theorem. The transition from no trade to free trade redistributes income within a country away from the scarce factor to the abundant factor. Logically, owners of the scarce factor would be opposed to free trade, because for them free trade is welfare reducing.

Most economists favour open economies and free trade, as the benefits of exchange of goods and services among countries are perceived to greatly offset associated costs of movement to more open economies. The crux of the argument is that individuals, companies and countries should specialise in and exchange activities in which they are relatively more efficient. The principle of trade evolved from Adam Smith's absolute advantage in 1776 to David Ricardo's comparative advantage

Comparative advantage is the catalyst in the push toward open economies and free trade. Countries benefit when they specialise in production of goods and services in which they have a comparative advantage and exchange for goods and services from other countries that specialise and have a comparative advantage in those other goods and services. This process leads to an improvement in global income as sets of goods and services can be produced less expensively. However, the mix of goods and services produced in various countries will likely change as trade occurs, resulting in some winners and losers. The degree of losers and winners varies from country to country but income redistribution can occur from the winners to the losers if losers can be compensated monetarily. However, there appear to be cases where losers have characteristics that the standard trade model fails to capture, and where monetary compensation doesn't seem to be an issue. Altruistic segments within a society may experience disutility and create extreme divergences from the standard trade model assumption of similar preferences.

A later alternative explanation of comparative advantage is the Heckscher-Ohlin model of international trade. Their argument was that comparative advantage is due to differences in factor endowments among countries. Countries differ from each other in terms of not only productive resources but how goods are produced using different proportions of those factors of production. A country is able to produce a product at a lower cost if its production uses a relatively larger proportion of a more abundant factor in that country. This model suggests therefore that a country will tend to export those products that make intensive use of factors that are locally abundant while importing those products that make intensive use of factors that are locally scarce. This model implies that the observed pattern of trade is determined by differences in factor endowments, as opposed to differences in productivity that underlie Ricardo's comparative advantage version. The Heckscher-Ohlin model is intuitively appealing but Wassily Leontief raised questions about the model's validity. This model, like the previous one, does not necessarily capture the dimensions of the losers from increased trade.

However both versions of comparative advantage provide strong theoretical support to open economies and free trade. A limitation of comparative advantage is that it suggests countries tend to export and import unique types of goods, and one should not expect countries to be importing and exporting the same or similar goods. However 57 percent of U.S. trade in 1996 occurred within the same four-digit industrial classification as opposed to between industrial classifications. Intra-industry numbers for Japan and Europe were 20 percent and 60 percent respectively. Japan has less intra-industry trade since its factor endowments are very different from those of the U.S. and Europe.

Recent theoretical developments better explain intra-industry trade and further strengthen the case for open economies and free trade. New trade theory argues that specialisation may lead to increasing returns to scale instead of the constant returns assumption used in prior trade models. A country specialising in production of a good may encounter economies of scale as production is increased, with lower unit costs and increases in productivity. This leads to increasing returns to specialisation, not diminishing returns.

In economic sectors in which significant output levels are required to reach meaningful scale economies, it may only require a few firms to produce the necessary output for the world economy. New trade theory suggests that in particular sectors, countries having first movers could have a sizeable advantage if large output levels are necessary to reach scale economies. Factor endowments assume less importance in this environment, as first mover advantages may be a deciding factor. An implication of first mover advantages is that government intervention may occur in attempting to assist companies to achieve first mover advantages in sectors expected to experience scale economies at high levels of output.

Government intervention can conflict with the ideals advanced of open economies and free trade. In certain circumstances new trade theory could lead to sizable changes in the mix of goods produced in various countries with major winners and losers. The modifications by this model likewise don't appear to adequately address the dimensions of losers. Exchange of goods among countries can also create dynamic growth gains. Economic growth occurs due to increases in factor endowments and technological improvement. More open economies increase competitive pressures which may lead to positive impacts such as efficiency gains, increases in domestic saving, real income

The income of an individual or group after taking into consideration the effects of inflation on purchasing power. For example, if you received a 2% salary rise over the previous year and inflation for the year was 1%, then your real income only rose 1%. Conversely, if you received a 2% raise in salary and inflation stood at 3%, then your real income would have shrunk 1%. Also known as "real wages", gains, access to capital goods and technology, technology diffusion, reduction of market power of domestic firms and access to larger markets in the global economy. Dynamic growth gains became more apparent the past twenty years as developing countries entered the globalisation process.

It is generally accepted that policies limiting movement toward free trade are likely to result in actual per capita income failing to achieve potential per capita income. The reverse also holds that moves toward globalisation generally reduce poverty. There is strong evidence that specialisation, exchange and transfer of technology lead to improvement in global income. Trade policy outcomes in the aggregate are clearly positive and the textbook analysis using community indifference curves demonstrates that. But non-monetary aspects may be of critical importance to the general public and various demographic segments around the globe such as in the Middle East.

But it is clear that benefits of trade are not as universally accepted as the theoretical and empirical support for free trade might suggest. This is understandable as many people perceive and evaluate issues such as trade in their own self-interest and perceived interest of others. There are many dimensions of trade such as employment and income concerns, environmental concerns, social issues and cultural concerns that may not be adequately incorporated in the aggregate outcomes. The Stolper-Samuelson theorem illustrates for instance that when a country imports labour-intensive goods, a segment of the country's labour force—the lower skill level workers—tend to be losers.

Both current factor income as well as asset values influence preferences in standard trade models. Cultural and social dimensions adversely impacted by movement to open economies, however, may be utility-reducing on particular segments of a society and that net loss in welfare may not be easily compensated for. Demographic segments that perceive this utility loss appear to be capable of creating sizeable adverse economic impacts on the global economy and trade.

4.6.1. International Trends

Cultural differences among countries in the current period of globalisation are much more prevalent than in the preceding one. The first globalisation period, in perspective, was from 1870 to 1914. The second globalisation wave that occurred from 1945 to 1980 was primarily, according to the, among developed rich countries. In the second wave, institutional frameworks such as the IMF and GATT evolved toward the end of WWII and the years immediately following and served primarily developed countries. Reduction of trade barriers among these rich countries was very successful, leading to the rapid expansion in exchange of manufactured goods and gains in scale economies and productivity. In comparison, developing countries had trade barriers that limited trade with each other and also limited trade with developed countries.

Developing countries as a result did not participate in the growth of global manufacturing and services trade. The 1945-1980 period of globalisation was among rich countries of similar heritage. The cultures are very distinct but the dimensions of the heritage of Western cultures are similar. Japan's culture, in comparison, was substantially different from that of the U.S. and Western Europe, but Japan's location, and its ability to separate the economic dimension from the religious dimension allowed Japan to fully benefit from trade in that period. This time frame of globalisation happened to coincide with the time frame of income redistribution and social safety nets in the three geographic areas. Potential adverse implications of trade on cultures and people's way of life didn't surface during this trade period, as major cultural groups didn't feel threatened by more open economies.

There were winners and losers in the employment and income categories but the massive move toward income redistribution and the building of social safety nets helped alleviate concerns. Rodrik suggests there is evidence of a strong, positive relationship between openness and size of government. But there are differing opinions on that assessment. The current or third globalisation wave according to the started around 1980 and had three major characteristics:

i) a group of developing countries that came into the global marketplace such as China, India, Mexico, Malaysia, Thailand, Hungary and the Philippines,

ii) a major increase in capital flows including human capital and

iii) a group of developing countries that fell further behind, which includes most of Africa, some Middle Eastern countries and various former Russian satellite countries.

4.6.2. Economic Performance of Country Groupings

A method of viewing differences in economic performance of countries is through three groupings: 1) rich Christian, 2) poor Christian and 3) Muslim countries. Does the standard of living in Muslim countries, taken as a whole, differ from Christian countries? Does their economic performance over time differ as well? The answer is yes to both questions and could provide a reason why many fundamentalist Muslims reject globalisation and trade with the West.

A grouping of 24 predominantly Muslim countries, stretching from Morocco to Indonesia, is compared to two groups of Christian countries. The population total of the Muslim countries is approximately 900 million so it includes most Muslims. The rich Christian countries, 22 in all, consist of countries in Western Europe, plus the U.S., Canada, Australia, and New Zealand. The 29 poor Christian countries comprise of Latin America, Eastern Europe, plus the Philippines. Major areas excluded from this analysis are the former Soviet Union, India and sub-Saharan Africa. These three areas include substantial numbers of both Muslims and Christians, but cannot be easily classified as exclusively one or the other. Other major areas such as China and Japan are, of course, excluded. The result is that this three-grouping classification scheme excludes a major portion of the world's population.

The grouping of 24 Muslim countries is not only poorer than the rich Christian countries but they are also poorer than the poor Christian countries. GDP/capita in the rich Christian countries is higher than the Muslim countries by a factor 7.7 while GDP/capita in the poor Christian countries is above the Muslim countries by a factor of approximately 1.9. The current wave of globalisation starting in 1980 incorporates developing countries, and standard trade theory suggests that countries reducing trade barriers would have likely participated in the benefits of more open economies and free trade.

An idea of the degree of participation by Muslim countries in the current globalisation wave can be approximated by the trend in GDP/capita over this 20-year time frame. Reformists in many Muslim countries have attempted to modify existing Islamic institutions, to make them more closely resemble those in the rich

Christian countries. Perhaps the best historical example of such a reformist was Mustafa Kemal Ataturk, the founder of modern Turkey. In the 1920s and 1930s, Ataturk deliberately suppressed many Islamic institutions in Turkey, and imported political, legal, and economic institutions from Western Europe.

Corrupt and un-Islamic governments in Muslim countries have allowed the West to exploit and impoverish Muslim populations. The solution, in the mind of the fundamentalist, would be to limit or end trade with the West, and eliminate the corruptive Western influences. As Sayyid Qutb argued, "The Muslims concede defeat in the first round whenever they seek to renew their own life by borrowing Western ways of thought, life, and custom ".

On the other hand, the view of many Western economists in explaining the relatively poor economic performance of the Muslim countries is the fact that non-Muslim countries, on average, are significantly freer than Muslim countries. Approximately 85 percent of the Muslim population lives in countries that are in the lower half of economic freedom out of the 156 countries ranked by the Index of Economic Freedom,

Non-Muslim countries are more open to positive economic impacts of trade and have more market oriented domestic economies. No doubt there are a number of economic and non-economic issues involved as to why Muslim countries have not fully participated in globalisation. Muslim countries, like China during the Qing dynasty, may take the view that foreign ideas, concepts and products generated externally are not wanted or needed. Plus Islam makes no distinction between the spiritual life and political or economic life, in the view of fundamentalists.

Additionally, the lower level of income in Muslim countries may itself be part of the explanation for the rise of fundamentalism in Islam. The extensive poverty, the failure of corrupt and undemocratic governments to deal with it, and the discrediting of Western-oriented reforms in Muslim countries have undoubtedly led many devout Muslims to seek alternative answers, of which fundamentalism is one. Social problems in Western countries such as drug abuse, crime, sexual promiscuity and illegitimacy may lead many Muslims to reject Western liberalism as the wrong path for their countries to take.

4.6.2.1. Fundamentalist muslim model

Fundamentalist Muslims appear to believe that globalisation is a threat to the ethical values passed down to them by God through their prophet Mohammed. In America, people who oppose a policy or set of policies can organise politically and create special action groups or committees to lobby for or against a particular issue or position. In Muslim countries freedom is often limited and the form of government does not appear to allow for such political organisations. For that reason and perhaps many others, Osama bin Laden decided to create an organisation outside of state entities with the intent of slowing or stopping the globalisation process. In particular to slow, stop or reverse the American influence in Muslim countries.

The idea in this model is that individuals are motivated by factors other than selfishness or material gain. Becket makes the point that individuals maximise welfare as they conceive it, whether they are selfish, altruistic, loyal, spiteful, etc. Their behaviour is forward-looking but their actions are constrained by limited resources such as income, time and calculating capacities.

Al Qaeda leaders have made public statements suggesting that their utility would be enhanced by removal of the U.S. influence from Islamic nations. Osama bin Laden said:

> "We declared jihad against the US government, because the US government is unjust, criminal and tyrannical. It has committed acts that are extremely unjust, hideous and criminal whether directly or through its support of the Israeli occupation of the Prophet's Night Travel Land (Palestine).... So, the driving-away jihad against the US does not stop with its withdrawal from the Arabian Peninsula, but rather it must desist from aggressive intervention against Muslims in the whole world".

Al Qaeda leaders oppose the Western influence and decided to directly challenge America via the terrorist channel implemented by suicide attackers. It does appear that al Qaeda leaders appear to be maximising a utility function by their actions.

Fundamentalist Muslims are taught not to be consumers of the Western influence and therefore oppose the idea of movement toward free trade and believe it is wrong for any Muslim to be a consumer of the Western influence. But consumption of the

Western influence may not be opposed by modernising Muslims. This means the consumption of Western goods by modernising Muslims enters the utility function of the fundamentalist Muslim and reduces utility of the fundamentalist Muslim. The assumption is that the fundamentalist Muslim is altruistic and cares not only about his consumption but also that of the modernising Muslim. In comparison the modernising Muslim is egoistic in nature.

4.6.2.2. *Terrorist suicide model*

Al Qaeda implemented their brand of terrorism on 9/11 in the U.S. via the channel of suicide attackers. An economic approach to this issue involves fundamental assumptions of maximising behaviour and equilibrium. The suicide model may have been selected by al Qaeda because of al Qaeda's resource limitations. Al Qaeda is able to operate only with support from state sponsors as al Qaeda has no tax base, no GDP and no permanent location from which to stage attacks on Western interests. In comparison, the U.S. is a $10 trillion economy with the dominant military force in the world. The al Qaeda resource constraint may have led al Qaeda to adopt a decentralised transnational organisational concept to challenge America and the open economy concept. The al Qaeda organisation appears to follow a concept of multiple sleeper cells in multiple countries with each cell potentially consisting of a self-directed team. Recruits for the cells were apparently trained as terrorists in Afghanistan training camps during the 1990s.

Al Qaeda leadership followed this asymmetrical concept in its attack on the U.S. on 9/11. A total of 19 hijackers were able to create large economic costs on the U.S. and global economy. Out-of-pocket costs to the terrorist organisation for the 9/11 operation were estimated to be at most a few million dollars and perhaps as little as under $1million. But the U.S. in response has and is spending billions of dollars domestically and globally in an attempt to find and destroy the al Qaeda organisation. The horizontal nature of the al Qaeda organisation is difficult for the pyramid structure of the U.S. military and intelligence organisations to demolish.

Had resource constraints of al Qaeda been more similar to the U.S., it is possible that al Qaeda may have chosen to follow more conventional or accepted methods of political negotiation and not resort to the use of suicide attackers. Some proportion of the people who went through al Qaeda training camps during the 1990s evolved into suicide attackers, Suicide attackers create extreme negative utility for Westerners because of internalisation of moral principles and ethical rules. The 9/11 attack was repulsive to most Americans as it was an attack on innocent civilians by a group of people intent on committing suicide to further their cause.

References

Cosgrove, Michael, "Terrorist Strategy and Global Economic Implications", *Journal of Business and Economics Research*, Vol. 1 (6), 2003.

Daniel Byman, *Deadly Connections: States That Sponsor Terrorism*, University Press, 2005.

Laqueur, Walter, "Postmodern Terrorism", *Foreign Affairs*, Vol.75 (5), 1996.

Lerner, Brenda Wilmoth & K. Lee Lerner, eds., *Terrorism: Essential primary sources*, Thomson Gale, 2006.

5

Domestic Terrorism

Domestic terrorism is probably a more widespread phenomenon than international terrorism. The number of international terrorist incidents has fallen, from a peak of 665 in 1987, to 296 in 1996, a 25-year low. Moreover, about two-thirds of these attacks were minor acts of politically motivated violence against commercial targets, which caused no deaths and few casualties.

Yet while the incidence of international terrorism has dropped sharply in the last decade, the overall threat of terrorism remains very serious. The death toll from acts of international terrorism rose from 163 in 1995 to 311 in 1996, as the trend continued toward more ruthless attacks on mass civilian targets and the use of more powerful bombs. The threat of terrorist use of materials of mass destruction is an issue of growing concern, although few such attempts or attacks have actually occurred. Finally, domestic terrorism, in countries such as Algeria, India, Sri Lanka, and Pakistan, appears to be growing and is more serious, in gross terms, than international terrorism.

5.1. Domestic Terrorism in the United States

In the United States, acts of domestic terrorism are generally considered to be uncommon. The statutory definition of domestic terrorism in the United States has changed many times over the years; also, it can be argued that acts of domestic terrorism have been occurring since long before any legal definition was set forth.

Under current United States law, set forth in the USA PATRIOT Act, acts of domestic terrorism are those which: "(A) involve acts dangerous to human life that are a violation of the criminal laws of the United States or of any State; (B) appear to be intended—

(i) to intimidate or coerce a civilian population; (ii) to influence the policy of a government by intimidation or coercion; or (iii) to affect the conduct of a government by mass destruction, assassination, or kidnapping; and (C) occur primarily within the territorial jurisdiction of the United States."

5.1.1. Organisations Associated with Domestic Terrorism

5.1.1.1. Ku Klux Klan

From Reconstruction at the end of the civil war to the end of the civil rights movement, the Ku Klux Klan used threats, violence, arson, and murder to further its white-supremacist, anti-semitic, anti-Catholic agenda.

5.1.1.2. Weatherman (organisation)

The Weathermen were a U.S. radical left organisation active from 1969 to 1975. Its members referred to themselves as a "revolutionary organisation of communist women and men." Their goal was the revolutionary overthrow of the U.S. government. Toward this end, and to change U.S. policy in Vietnam, they bombed a number of police and military targets. The group collapsed shortly after the U.S. withdrawal from Vietnam in 1975.

5.1.1.3. Alpha 66

Alpha 66 is a paramilitary group funded by the US government, formed by Cuban exiles in Puerto Rico opposed to the Cuban government. The group trained during the 1960s and 1970s in the Everglades for an eventual armed invasion of Cuba. The Cuban government, among others, has long considered the group to be a terrorist organisation.

In 1976 Miami Police Lieutenant Thomas Lyons and Detective Raul J. Diaz testified that groups including Alpha 66 had international terrorist ties and had sold $100 "bonds" in Miami to help finance their causes. The group were linked to a spate of bombings and assassinations in Miami during the 1970s, directed at moderate community leaders intolerant of the terrorist methods of certain anti-Castro groups. A week before Lyons and Diaz's testimony, broadcaster Emilio Milian had both his legs blown off in a car bomb outside his workplace.

5.1.1.4. Army of God

The Army of God (AOG) is a loose network of individuals and groups connected by ideological affinity and the determination to use violence to end the legal practice of abortion in the United States. Its affiliates consist of right-wing Christian militants who have committed violent acts against abortion providers. Acts of anti-abortion violence increased in the mid-1990s culminating in a series of bombings by Eric Rudolph, whose targets included two abortion clinics, a gay and lesbian night club, and the 1996 Olympics in Atlanta. Letters Rudolph sent to newspapers claiming responsibility in the name of the Army of God focused attention on the problem of right-wing extremism.

5.1.1.5. Earth Liberation Front

The Earth Liberation Front (ELF) is a group associated with environmental extremism and advocates direct action against high polluters. Several fire bombings of SUV dealerships have been attributed to ELF.

5.1.1.6. Black Liberation Army

A splinter group made up of the more radical members of the Black Panther Party, the BLA sought to overthrow the US government in the name of racial separatism and Marxist ideals. The Fraternal Order of Police blames the BLA for the murders of 13 police officers. According to a Justice Department report on BLA activity, the Black Liberation Army was suspected of involvement in over 60 incidents of violence between 1970 and 1976.

5.1.2. Acts of Domestic Terrorism

5.1.2.1. Draft Riots (1863)

The Civil War Draft Riots (1863) — the worst riots in American history; by far outstripping anything in Oakland, Watts, Attica, etc., with hundreds dead, maimed and injured. Under the definition provided by Brian Jenkins ("Terrorism is the use or threatened use of force designed to bring about political change"), the Irish Draft Riots in NYC (1863) could be seen as qualifying as domestic terrorism given that, as per writer Pete Hamill: "...after the Riots the Irish ran Tammany Hall."

5.1.2.2. Bombing of Los Angeles Times building

The bombing of the Los Angeles Times on October 1, 1910, which killed 21 people. The brains of this crime were The McNamara Brothers (James and John McNamara), two Irish-American brothers who wanted to "unionise" the paper, and who were only caught after a dogged, relentless search by a private investigator using his own funds.

5.1.2.3. Wall Street bombing

The Wall Street bombing was a terrorist incident that occurred on September 16, 1920, in the Financial District of New York City, and it was considered the worst politically-motivated one until the Oklahoma City bombing. A horse-drawn wagon filled with 100 pounds (45 kg) of dynamite was stationed across the street from the headquarters of the J.P. Morgan Inc. bank. The explosion killed 38 and injured 400. Even though no one was found guilty, it is believed that the act was carried out by anarchist followers of Luigi Galleani.

5.1.2.4. UNABOMBER Attacks

From 1978 to 1995, anti-industrial radical and former mathematics professor Theodore Kaczynski—known by the codename "UNABOMBER" until his identification and arrest by the FBI—carried out a campaign of sending letterbombs to academics and various individuals particularly associated with modern technology. The attacks ceased with his capture.

5.1.2.5. Oklahoma City Bombing

This truck bomb attack by right-wing extremists Timothy McVeigh and Terry Nichols killed 168 people – the deadliest domestic terrorist attack in US history.

5.1.2.6. Centennial Olympic Park Bombing

The first of four bombings carried out by right-wing Christian fundamentalist Eric Robert Rudolph.

5.1.2.7. 2001 Anthrax Attacks

Beginning on September 18, 2001, a number of media organisations and American politicians received, through the United States Postal Service, envelopes which contained weaponised anthrax. Although as of late 2005, no charges have been filed with regards to these attacks, the matter is widely believed to be an act of domestic terrorism.

5.2. Domestic Terrorism in India

Since its independence in 1947, India has been facing the problem of insurgency and terrorism in different parts of the country. India has faced exclusively terrorist movements in Punjab and Jammu and Kashmir, bordering Pakistan, and part insurgent-part terrorist movements in the northeast, bordering Myanmar and Bangladesh; in Bihar, bordering Nepal; and in certain interior states like Andhra Pradesh, Madhya Pradesh and Orissa that do not have international borders.

India has also faced terrorism of an ephemeral nature, which sprang suddenly due religious anger against either the government or the majority Hindu community or both and petered out subsequently. Examples of this would be the simultaneous explosions in Mumbai on March 12, 1993, which killed about 250 civilians, and the simultaneous explosions in Coimbatore, Tamil Nadu, in February 1998. Tamil Nadu has also faced the fallout of terrorism promoted by the Liberation Tigers of Tamil Eelam in Sri Lanka in the form of attacks by LTTE elements on its political rivals living in the state and in the assassination of former prime minister Rajiv Gandhi in May 1991.

India had also faced, for some years, Hindu sectarian terrorism in the form of the Anand Marg, which, in its motivation and irrationality, resembled to some extent the Aum Shinrikiyo of Japan. The Marg, with its emphasis on meditation, special religious and spiritual practices and use of violence against its detractors, had as many followers in foreign countries as it had in India. Its over-ground activities have petered out since 1995, but it is believed to retain many of its covert cells in different countries. However, they have not indulged in acts of violence recently.

5.2.1. Causes

The causes for the various insurgent/terrorist movements include:

Political causes: This is seen essentially in Assam and Tripura. The political factors that led to insurgency-cum-terrorism included the failure of the government to control large-scale illegal immigration of Muslims from Bangladesh, to fulfil the demand of economic benefits for the sons and daughters of the soil, etc.

Economic causes: Andhra Pradesh, Madhya Pradesh, Orissa and Bihar are prime examples. The economic factors include the absence of land reforms, rural unemployment, exploitation of landless labourers by land owners, etc. These economic grievances and perceptions of gross social injustice have given rise to ideological terrorist groups such as the various Marxist/Maoist groups operating under different names.

Ethnic causes: Mainly seen in Nagaland, Mizoram and Manipur due to feelings of ethnic separateness.

Religious causes: Punjab before 1995 and in J&K since 1989.

In Punjab, some Sikh elements belonging to different organisations took to terrorism to demand the creation of an independent state called Khalistan for the Sikhs. In J&K, Muslims belonging to different organisations took to terrorism for conflicting objectives. Some, such as the Jammu & Kashmir Liberation Front, want independence for the state, including all the territory presently part of India, Pakistan and China. Others, such as the Hizbul Mujahideen, want India's J&K state to be merged with Pakistan. While those who want independence project their struggle as a separatist one, those wanting a merger with Pakistan project it as a religious struggle.

There have also been sporadic acts of religious terrorism in other parts of India. These are either due to feelings of anger amongst sections of the Muslim youth over the government's perceived failure to safeguard their lives and interests or due to Pakistan's attempts to cause religious polarisation.

The maximum number of terrorist incidents and deaths of innocent civilians have occurred due to religious terrorism. While the intensity of the violence caused by terrorism of a non-religious nature can be rated as low or medium, that of religious terrorism has been high or very high. It has involved the indiscriminate use of sophisticated Improvised Explosive Devices, suicide bombers, the killing of civilians belonging to the majority community with hand-held weapons and resorting to methods such as hijacking, hostage-taking, blowing up of aircraft through IEDs, etc.

Certain distinctions between the modus operandi and concepts/beliefs of religious and non-religious terrorist groups need to be underlined, namely:

— Non-religious terrorist groups in India do not believe in suicide terrorism, but the LTTE does. Of the religious terrorist groups, the Sikhs did not believe in suicide terrorism. The indigenous terrorist groups in J&K do not believe in suicide terrorism either; it is a unique characteristic of Pakistan's pan-Islamic jihadi groups operating in J&K and other parts of India. They too did not believe in suicide terrorism before 1998; in fact, there was no suicide terrorism in J&K before 1999. They started resorting to it only after they joined Osama bin Laden's International Islamic Front in 1998. Since then, there have been 46 incidents of suicide terrorism, of which 44 were carried out by bin Laden's Pakistani supporters belonging to these organisations.

— Non-religious terrorist groups in India have not resorted to hijacking and blowing up of aircraft. Of the religious terrorists, the Sikh groups were responsible for five hijackings, the indigenous JKLF for one and the Pakistani jihadi group, the Harkat-ul-Mujahideen (which is a member of the IIF), for one. The Babbar Khalsa, a Sikh terrorist group, blew up Air India's *Kanishka* aircraft off the Irish coast on June 23, 1985, killing nearly 200 passengers and made an unsuccessful attempt the same day to blow up another Air India plane at Tokyo. The IED there exploded prematurely on the ground. The Kashmiri and the Pakistani jihadi groups have not tried to blow up any passenger plane while on flight. However, the JKLF had blown up an Indian Airlines aircraft, which it had hijacked to Lahore in 1971, after asking the passengers and crew to disembark.

— All terrorist groups — religious as well as non-religious — have resorted to kidnapping hostages for ransom and for achieving other demands. The non-religious terrorist groups have targeted only Indians, whereas the religious terrorist groups target Indians as well as foreigners. The Khalistan Commando Force, a Sikh terrorist group, kidnapped a Romanian diplomat in New Delhi in 1991. The JKLF kidnapped some Israeli tourists in J&K in 1992. HUM, under the name Al Faran, kidnapped five Western tourists in 1995 and is believed to have killed four of them. An American managed to escape. Sheikh Omar, presently on trial for the kidnap and murder of American journalist Daniel Pearl in Karachi in January last year, had earlier kidnapped some Western tourists near Delhi. They were subsequently freed by the police.

— Non-religious terrorist groups in India have not carried out any act of terrorism outside Indian territory. Of the religious terrorist groups, a Sikh organisation blew up an Air India plane off the Irish coast and unsuccessfully tried to blow up another plane at Tokyo the same day, plotted to kill then prime minister Rajiv Gandhi during his visit to the US in June 1985 (the plot was foiled by the Federal Bureau of Investigation), attacked the Indian ambassador in Bucharest, Romania, in October 1991, and carried out a number of attacks on pro-government members of the Sikh diaspora abroad. The JKLF kidnapped and killed an Indian diplomat in Birmingham, England, in 1984. In the 1970s, the Anand Marg had indulged in acts of terrorism in foreign countries.

— None of the non-religious terrorist groups advocate the acquisition and use of Weapons of Mass Destruction. Of the religious groups, the Sikh and the indigenous Kashmiri terrorist groups did/do not advocate the acquisition and use of WMD. However, the Pakistani pan-Islamic groups, which are members of the IIF and which operate in J&K, support bin Laden's advocacy of the right and religious obligation of Muslims to acquire and use WMD to protect their religion, if necessary.

The Sikh terrorist groups did not cite their holy book as justification for their acts of terrorism, but the indigenous

Kashmiri groups as well as the Pakistani jihadi groups operating in India cite the holy Koran as justification for their jihad against the government of India and the Hindus.

The Sikh and the indigenous Kashmiri groups projected/ project their objective as confined to their respective state, but the Pakistani pan-Islamic terrorist groups project their aim as extending to the whole of South Asia — namely the 'liberation' of Muslims in India and the ultimate formation of an Islamic Caliphate consisting of the 'Muslim homelands' of India and Sri Lanka, Pakistan and Bangladesh.

The Sikh terrorist groups demanded an independent nation on the ground that Sikhs constituted a separate community and could not progress as fast as they wanted to in a Hindu-dominated country. They did not deride Hinduism and other non-Sikh religions. Nor did they call for the eradication of Hindu influences from their religion. The indigenous Kashmiri organisations, too, follow a similar policy. But the Pakistani pan-Islamic jihadi organisations ridicule and condemn Hinduism and other religions and call for the eradication of what they describe as the corrupting influence of Hinduism on Islam as practised in South Asia.

The Sikh and indigenous Kashmiri terrorist organisations believed/believe in Western-style parliamentary democracy. The Pakistani jihadi organisations project Western-style parliamentary democracy as anti-Islam since it believes sovereignty vests in people and not in God.

Religious as well as non-religious terrorist groups have external links with like-minded terrorist groups in other countries. Examples: The link between the Marxist groups of India with Maoist groups of Nepal, Sri Lanka and Bangladesh; the link between the indigenous Kashmiri organisations with the religious, fundamentalist and jihadi organisations of Pakistan; the link between organisations such as the Students Islamic Movement of India with jihadi elements in Pakistan and Saudi Arabia; and the link between the Pakistani pan-Islamic jihadi organisations operating in India with bin Laden's Al Qaeda and the Taliban.

5.2.2. Role of the Diaspora

Religious as well as non-religious terrorist groups draw moral support and material sustenance from the overseas diaspora. The Khalistan movement was initially born in the overseas Sikh community in the UK and Canada and spread from there to Punjab in India. The indigenous Kashmiri organisations get material assistance from the large number of migrants from Pakistan-occupied Kashmir, called the Mirpuris, who have settled in Western countries. The Marxist groups get support from the Marxist elements in the overseas Indian community.

5.2.3. Funding

The following are the main sources of funding for terrorist and insurgent groups:

— Clandestine contributions from Pakistan's Inter-Services Intelligence.

— Contributions from religious, fundamentalist and pan-Islamic jihadi organisations in Pakistan.

— Contributions from ostensibly charitable organisations in Pakistan and Saudi Arabia.

— Contributions from trans-national criminal groups, such as the mafia group led by Dawood Ibrahim who operates from Karachi, Pakistan.

— Extortions and ransom payments for releasing hostages.

— Collections — voluntary or forced — from the people living in the area where they operate.

— Narcotics smuggling.

The funds are normally transmitted either through couriers or through the informal hawala channel. Rarely are funds transmitted through formal banking channels.

5.2.4. Sanctuaries

Religious terrorist organisations have their main external sanctuaries in Pakistan and Bangladesh, while non-religious terrorist organisations look to Nepal, Bhutan and Myanmar. Some northeast non-religious terrorist groups also operate from Bangladesh, while certain religious groups get sanctuary in Nepal.

Since 1956, Pakistan has been using its sponsorship of and support to different terrorist groups operating in India as a strategic weapon to keep India preoccupied with internal security problems. Before the formation of Bangladesh in 1971, the then East Pakistan was the main sanctuary for non-religious terrorist groups operating in India. Since 1971, the present Pakistan, called West Pakistan before 1971, has been the main sanctuary for all Sikh and Muslim terrorist groups.

Pakistan has given sanctuary to 20 principal leaders of Sikh and Muslim terrorist groups, including hijackers of Indian aircraft and trans-national criminal groups colluding with terrorists. Despite strong evidence of their presence in Pakistani territory and active operation from there, its government has denied their presence and refused to act against them. It has also ignored Interpol's notices for apprehending them and handing them over to India.

For some years after 1971, the Bangladesh authorities acted vigorously against Indian groups operating from their territory. This has gradually diluted due to the collusion of the pro-Pakistan elements in Bangladesh's military-intelligence establishment with Pakistan's military-intelligence establishment, the collusion of Bangladesh's religious fundamentalist parties with their counterparts in Pakistan and the unwillingness or inability of successive governments in Dhaka to act against these elements.

In Nepal, Bhutan and Myanmar, there is no collusion of the governments with the Indian terrorist groups operating from their territory. Their authorities have been trying to be help India as much as they can. However, their weak control over the territory from which the terrorists operate and their intelligence and security establishment does not allow for effective action against the terrorists.

5.2.5. Al Qaeda in India

Pakistan has been the main source of arms, ammunition and training for religious terrorist groups which operated in the Punjab in the past and for those which are operating presently in J&K and other parts of India. The training is given by the ISI, either directly or through religious fundamentalist and pan-Islamic jihadi organisations, in various makeshift camps located in PoK, the Northern Areas (Gilgit and Baltistan) and the North-West Frontier Province.

Before September 11, 2001, the ISI had located the training camps of the Pakistani jihadi organisations, which are members of the IIF, in Afghan territory, but have since shifted them to PoK and the Northern Areas. Five Pakistani jihadi organisations are members of bin Laden's IIF — HUM, Harkat-ul-Jihad-al-Islami, Lashkar-e-Toiba, Jaish-e-Mohammad and Lashkar-e-Jhangvi. The first four operate in India. LEJ, which is an anti-Shia organisation, operates only in Pakistan.

Under US pressure, President Musharraf has banned the activities of LET, JEM and LEJ in Sindh, Punjab, the NWFP and Balochistan, but not in PoK, the Northern Areas and the Federally-Administered Tribal Areas. The activities of HUM and HUJI, which are closest to Pakistan's military-intelligence establishment, have not been banned anywhere.

In a recent judgement against some Pakistani doctors accused of providing sanctuaries and medical assistance to Al Qaeda members, the Pakistani supreme court pointed out that the Pakistan government has not, till now, declared Al Qaeda a terrorist organisation and banned its activities in Pakistan as required under the Anti-Terrorism Act.

5.2.6. Role of Pakistani Mercenaries

Between 1989 and 1993, terrorism in J&K was mainly due to the activities of indigenous Kashmiri organisations. When they were unable to succeed, the ISI started infiltrating trained jihadi cadres of the Pakistani pan-Islamic organisations, who had fought against the Soviet troops in Afghanistan in the 1980s, into J&K for beefing up indigenous organisations. Since 1999, the Pakistani jihadi organisations have taken over the leadership of the anti-government of India movement and have been operating in Indian territory under the guise of Kashmiris.

Out of the 46 suicide terrorist attacks reported since 1999, 44 have been by Pakistanis belonging to these jihadi organisations. The principal leaders of these organisations are Pakistani Punjabis and the majority of their cadres are Pakistani nationals. These Pakistani jihadi organisations project J&K as the gateway to India and say that, after 'liberating' J&K from the control of the Hindus, they will 'liberate' the Muslims in other parts of India and set up two more independent 'homelands' for Muslims — one in north

India and the other in south India. As part of this long-term aim, they have been setting up clandestine cells in other parts of India and have launched some major operations such as the attack inside the Red Fort in New Delhi in January 2001, the attack on the Indian Parliament in December, 2001, and the attack on Hindu worshippers in a temple in Gandhinagar, Gujarat, in September 2002.

There have also been a number of terrorist incidents in other parts of India such as the attack on the security guards outside the US consulate in Kolkata in January 2002, the four explosions in Mumbai in 2002-03 — the latest on March 13, 2003, killed 12 innocent train passengers — and the explosion in a Hindu religious place in Hyderabad last year.

Till now, Al Qaeda's Arab members have not operated in Indian territory. Some Arabs were arrested in J&K during counter-terrorism operations, but they were members of Pakistani pan-Islamic jihadi organisations and not of Al Qaeda as such. However, HUM, HUJI, LET and JEM, the Pakistani jihadi organisations which are members of bin Laden's IIF along with Al Qaeda and the Taliban, have been responsible for most of the religious terrorist incidents in J&K and other places in India.

India has a little over 140 million Muslims — the second largest Muslim community in the world after Indonesia. Only a very small section of the community has taken to terrorism due to various grievances and instigation by the ISI and Pakistan's religious, fundamentalist and jihadi organisations. The overwhelming majority of Indian Muslims are loyal, law-abiding citizens. They have not allowed their anger against the Indian government or the Hindus for any reason to drive them into the arms of terrorist organisations. India has the most modern, peaceful and forward-looking Muslim community in the world.

5.2.7. Domestic Counter-terrorism Policies

India's counter-terrorism policies are based on the following principles:

— A genuine and well-functioning democracy, good governance, responsiveness to public grievances, effective policing and economic development are the best antidotes to terrorism.

- India has not allowed the intimidatory violence of terrorism to come in the way of the electoral process. In the 1990s, elections were held in Punjab at the height of terrorist violence. Elections were held in J&K in September last year despite instructions from the ISI to the Pakistani jihadis to disrupt the process. Foreign diplomatic missions in New Delhi were encouraged to send their observers to the state to satisfy themselves that the elections were free and fair. All of them have certified this. Elections to the Nagaland assembly were held last month.
- The government has not allowed terrorists to disrupt the economic development of the affected areas. Even at the height of terrorism, Punjab continued to be the granary of India, producing a record wheat crop year after year. In J&K, the fall in revenue due to a decline in foreign tourists arrival is being sought to be remedied by encouraging greater domestic tourism.
- In the 1990s, when terrorists prevented the holding of examinations in Srinagar, the government flew the students to Jammu at its cost to take the examination.
- When they prevented businessmen from the rest of India from going to the valley to purchase their requirements of handicrafts and dry fruits, the government flew the vendors to New Delhi to enable them to dispose of their stocks.
- The government has announced many packages for the economic development of the affected areas and has been trying to implement them despite the terrorist violence.
- The government has refused any kind of concessions to terrorists resorting to intimidation tactics such as hijacking, hostage-taking, etc.
- The government has refused to hold talks with terrorists until they give up violence, but began to search for a political solution through talks once the terrorists give up violence.

In the 1970s, a large section of the Naga hostiles and the Mizo National Front gave up violence and entered into talks with the government, which led to a political solution. But the National

Socialist Council of Nagaland, led by Isaac Swu and T Muivah, has been holding on without reaching an agreement. It has, however, been observing a cease-fire for the last two years and holding talks with the government.

The government is maintaining an open mind to suggestions coming from all sections of J&K for improving the political and administrative set-up. It has recently appointed former home secretary N N Vohra to enter into a dialogue with all the elected representatives of the state on their demand for greater autonomy.

5.2.8. External Counter-terrorism Policies

India has been the victim of Pakistan-sponsored terrorism since the 1950s. In those years, Pakistan's ISI had supported the insurgent/terrorist groups in India's northeast region and provided them sanctuaries, training, arms and ammunition in the Chittagong Hill Tracts of the then East Pakistan. India's anxiety to stop this played an important role in its assistance to the people of East Pakistan to liberate themselves.

Since 1980, the ISI has been providing sanctuaries, training, arms and ammunition in Pakistan to religious terrorist groups operating in Punjab, J&K and other parts of India. It is also infiltrating the mercenaries of the Pakistani pan-Islamic jihadi organisations into India to promote cross-border terrorism.

India has taken up this issue with the US since 1992 and wants Pakistan declared a State sponsor of international terrorism under US laws and have punitive action taken against it. In 1993, the Clinton administration placed Pakistan on a watch list of suspected State sponsors of international terrorism for six months and forced Nawaz Sharif, who was then in power, to sack Lieutenant General Javed Nasir, then ISI's director-general, and other senior officers. This did not have any effect on the use of terrorism by the ISI.

Since 9/11, Pakistan's military-intelligence establishment has been collaborating with the US in taking action against Al Qaeda elements posing a threat to US nationals and interests. But it has not taken any action against cross-border terrorism directed against India and to destroy terrorist infrastructure in PoK and the Northern Areas.

After the attack by terrorists belonging to LET and JEM on the Indian Parliament in December 2001, India mobilised and deployed its Army on the border in response to public pressure for action against the terrorist infrastructure in Pakistani territory. In response to appeals from the US, UK and other friendly governments, India refrained from action against Pakistan. Under US pressure, Pakistan banned LET and JEM, but not HUJI and HUM, and arrested some of their leaders and cadres. They have since been released.

US officials themselves admit Pakistan has not implemented its assurances to the US that it would put a stop to cross-border terrorism in J&K. Despite this, the US is reluctant to act against Pakistan because of its cooperation in assisting the US in neutralising Al Qaeda elements who have taken shelter in Pakistan.

India has made it clear that there will be no question of any talks with Pakistan on the normalisation of bilateral relations till it stops cross-border terrorism, winds up the terrorist infrastructure in its territory and gives up the use of terrorism as a weapon against India.

India has also been greatly concerned over the use of Bangladesh territory by religious and non-religious terrorists operating against India. The non-religious terrorist groups continue to enjoy sanctuaries in the CHT. Of the religious terrorist organisations, HUJI has an active branch in Bangladesh. Some Al Qaeda elements, who escaped into Pakistan from Afghanistan, have found their way into Bangladesh, where they have been given shelter by HUJI.

There is active complicity between the ISI and its counterpart in Dhaka in this matter. The Bangladesh authorities have not been co-operating with India in taking effective action against the large-scale illegal immigration into India. However, keeping in view the otherwise good relations with Bangladesh, India has been trying to have these problems sorted out bilaterally at the political and diplomatic levels. But the progress so far has been disappointing.

5.2.9. Counter Terrorism Strategy

India's counter-terrorism set-up consists of the following:

- *The state police and its intelligence set-up:* Under India's federal Constitution, the responsibility for policing and maintenance of law and order is that of the individual states. The central government in New Delhi can only give them advice, financial help, training and other assistance to strengthen their professional capabilities and share with them the intelligence collected by it. The responsibility for follow-up action lies with the state police.

- *The national intelligence community:* This consists of the internal intelligence agency (the ministry of home affairs' Intelligence Bureau), the external intelligence agency (the Cabinet secretariat's Research and Analysis Wing), the Defence Intelligence Agency that was set up a year ago, and the intelligence directorates general of the armed forces.

  The IB collects terrorism-related intelligence inside the country and RAW does it outside. The DIA and the intelligence directorates general of the armed forces essentially collect tactical intelligence during their counter-terrorism operations in areas such as Jammu and Kashmir, Nagaland, etc, where they are deployed.

- *Physical security agencies*: These include the Central Industrial Security Force, responsible for physical security at airports and sensitive establishments; the National Security Guards, a specially trained intervention force to terminate terrorist situations such as hijacking, hostage-taking, etc; and the Special Protection Group, responsible for the security of the prime minister and former prime ministers.

- *Paramilitary forces*: These include the Central Reserve Police Force and the Border Security Force, which assist the police in counter-terrorism operations when called upon to do so.

- *The Army:* Their assistance is sought as a last resort when the police and paramilitary forces are not able to cope with a terrorist situation. But in view of Pakistan's large-scale infiltration in Jammu and Kashmir and the presence and activities of a large number of Pakistani mercenaries, many of them ex-servicemen, the army has a more active, permanent and leadership role in counter-terrorism operations here. What India is facing in J&K is not just terrorism, but a proxy war being waged by the Pakistani Army through its *jihadi* surrogates.

In recent months, there have been two additions to the counter-terrorism set-up:

— A multi-disciplinary centre on counter-terrorism, headed by a senior IB officer, within the IB, expected to be patterned on the CIA's counter-terrorism centre. Officers of various agencies responsible for intelligence collection and counter-terrorism operations will work under a common umbrella and be responsible for joint analysis of the intelligence flowing in from different agencies and co-ordinated follow-up action.

— A counter-terrorism division in the ministry of external affairs, expected to be patterned after the counter-terrorism division of the US state department. It will be responsible for co-ordinating the diplomatic aspects of counter-terrorism, such as briefing other countries on Pakistan's sponsorship of terrorism against India, processing requests for extradition and mutual legal assistance, servicing the work of various joint working groups on counter-terrorism which India has set up with a number of countries, etc.

5.2.10. Counter-terrorism Techniques

The techniques followed by India stress the following:

— The importance of a good grievances detection, monitoring and redressal machinery so that the build-up of grievances in any community is detected in time and the political leadership alerted and advised to take prompt action to redress them. The intelligence agencies have an important role to play as the eyes and ears of the government in different communities to detect feelings of anger and alienation which need immediate attention.

— The importance of good, preventive human intelligence. This is easier said than done because of the difficulties in penetrating terrorist organisations, particularly of the religious kind.

— The importance of timely technical intelligence, which is generally more precise than human intelligence.

— The importance of objective and balanced analysis to avoid over-assessing the strength and capabilities of the terrorists, which could lead to over-reaction by counter-terrorism agencies, thereby aggravating the feeling of alienation within the affected community, driving more people into the arms of terrorists. Such analysis is particularly difficult in the case of human intelligence. For every genuine source who gives correct intelligence, there are often two or three spurious sources who, out of greed to make more money or at the instance of the terrorists themselves, give false information. This tends to make security forces over-react or take wrong action.

— The importance of reverse analysis so that one is trained to analyse possible scenarios not only as a good intelligence analyst, but also as an irrational terrorist.

— The importance of prompt and co-ordinated follow-up action on well-assessed intelligence from all agencies, without allowing inter-agency jealousies and rivalries to come in the way.

— The importance of effective physical security measures so that even if intelligence fails, security agencies are able to prevent acts of terrorism.

— The importance of an effective crisis management apparatus so that if both intelligence and physical security measures fail, one is able to deal effectively with the resulting crisis or disaster.

— The importance of good investigative machinery, specially trained to investigate terrorism-related cases.

— The importance of not over-projecting the personality and capabilities of terrorist leaders, so that they do not become objects of idolisation in their community.

— The importance of constantly underlining to the public that just because some people of a particular community or religion have taken to terrorism, the entire community or religion should not be looked upon with suspicion.

— The importance of highlighting the positive aspects of the affected community or religion to prevent the build-up of a negative image of the community or religion in the eyes of the public.

— The importance of active interaction with the media to ensure that they do not make terrorist leaders appear like heros or prejudice the minds of the public about the affected community or religion or create problems for effective counter-terrorism operations.

— The importance of well-designed psychological war operations to project the terrorists for what they are — irrational killers.

— The importance of observing human rights during counter-terrorism operations.

— The importance of periodic refresher training of all those involved in counter-terrorism operations through special classes, seminars, opportunities for interaction with those who have distinguished themselves in counter-terrorism operations, etc.

5.2.11. Intelligence-sharing on Terrorism

Even before 9/11, arrangements for intelligence-sharing on terrorism amongst the agencies of different countries existed. 9/11 brought the realisation that terrorism is an absolute evil whatever be the cause and that unless the intelligence agencies of the world network themselves as effectively as the terrorist organisations, they might not be able to eradicate this menace. This has improved intelligence-sharing.

India's success in bringing Sikh terrorism in Punjab under control before 9/11 might not have been possible but for the valuable intelligence inputs received from agencies of many countries. Some of the significant successes in different countries against Al Qaeda were apparently possible due to increased intelligence-sharing without reservations.

While this is welcome, one has to remember that political considerations peculiar to each country influence their perceptions of terrorism and this is bound to have an effect on intelligence-sharing. Hence, while continuing to benefit from increased intelligence-sharing, the important task of strengthening one's national intelligence collection capability should not be neglected.

5.2.12. Regional cooperation in South Asia

Regional cooperation in the battle against terrorism has not been as successful in south Asia as it has been in the southeast Asian region. This is largely because of Pakistan's policy of using terrorism as a weapon to keep the Indian security forces bleeding and pre-occupied with internal security duties and Bangladesh's tolerance of the activities of terrorists from its territory. Unless these two countries realise the folly of their policies and actions, which have made their own territories playgrounds for terrorist groups of different hues and irrationalities, there is very little scope for any meaningful co-operation.

India has been facing the problem of Pakistani state-sponsored terrorism for over 40 years and nearly 40,000 civilians and 3,500 members of the various security forces have been killed. This has not prevented India from becoming self-sufficient in agriculture, emerging as a major manufacturing country, developing educational, particularly technological, institutions of excellence the like of which no other Asian country can boast of, becoming the leading information technology software power of the region, and building up a foreign exchange reserve of US $72 billion, which, at this rate, should cross the US $100 billion mark in a couple of years.

India can continue to fight Pakistan-sponsored terrorism for another 40 years and yet move forward on its path of development as a major power in the region. Pakistan, on the other hand, has not had the required funds for educational and social development and for the economic advancement of its people because of its obsessive urge to keep India bleeding through terrorism. In its attempt to lift a big boulder and throw it at India, it is dropping it on its own feet.

5.3. DOMESTIC TERRORISM IN PAKISTAN

Pakistan is facing the menace of terrorism in multiple forms. Pakistan at present is facing the most unique, difficult and gruesome faces of terrorism. No other country in the world is so deeply entangled in this problem as the Pakistan of today. All text book categories of terrorism confront Pakistan. Pakistan had the first taste of ethnicity in the very early period of its being when the whole eastern wing agitated on the question of one national language - Urdu. The discontent established itself into a political movement and led ultimately to the unfortunate events of 1971 resulting in dismemberment of the state.

The political struggle organised on ethnic lines gave a harrowing display of ethnic terrorism when militant organisation like Mukti Bahni started eliminating West Pakistanis and specially the Punjabis. In the recent history of 'New' Pakistan, ethnicity emerged again in the wake of language riots. This time in the province of Sindh where Urdu speaking urbanites of Karachi and Hyderabad clashed with native Sindhis. The quest of Mohajirs - migrants in the wake of partition - for a parallel political identity as the fifth sub nationality along with the native Punjabi, Sindhi, Pashtuns and Balochs lead to large scale bloodshed and terrorist activities.

The ethnic terrorism took hold of major urban cities for nearly a decade in late 80s and 90s but it has subsided for the time being partly due to rejuvenated economic activity and mainstreaming of the ethnic groups but mostly due to political stability giving enough economic and political space to the major players. Sub nationalists who like to call themselves nationalists have been fighting for a proper identity and recognition within the federation.

Their main fears and apprehensions emanate from the predominant role of Punjab in military and civil bureaucracy. They are frustrated by the prospects of facing permanently the majority of one province. They feel threatened about their value system, traditions and culture. They also agitate against the use of their resources by other regions at cheaper costs. The poverty around them frustrates them and the advantaged amongst them successfully point their fingers to the other provinces to turn their gaze that way. The centre and its power corridor on the other hand take this insistence on rights as a kind of revolt against the centre and the rejection of federation. These strained relations have led the extremists amongst the nationalists/sub nationalists to take up arm against the centre quite regularly and sometimes against the state itself. The sub nationalists terrorism has been emerging intermittently since military operations in Pakistan in 1960s.

Governments of the day have been pointing at the external backing of both these types of terrorism. Pakistan on the whole has done fairly well to withstand the ethnic and sub nationalist terrorism even when fanned by external hands and the state structures have been able to work regularly and formally even in the face of these threats. Another major form of terrorist threat facing Pakistan emanates from the sectarian terrorism. Since long, Pakistan has been a victim of the violence by sectarian motives, the recent years have witnessed a high rise in both the frequency and lethality of the sectarian violence.

Domestic terrorism in Pakistan, much of it associated with Islamist sectarianism, has become an increasingly serious problem affecting major Pakistan's cities. Sectarian terrorism in Pakistan has been an off shoot of some historical and some regional rivalries. There are four different schools of thought in Muslims of Pakistan i.e. Brailvi, Deobandi, Ahle Hadith and Shias. The first three are commonly grouped as Sunni but their thinking and its expressions are wide apart. The difference between Sunni and Shia thinking and intra Sunni faction have been historical but they have generally co-existed peacefully.

The prolonged Iraq-Iran war and then post Afghan Jehad rivalries between Northern Alliance, pre-dominantly Shia and orthodox Sunni backed by Saudi Arabia and Pakistan, had adverse impact on sectarian harmony in Pakistan. The main source of recruitment for Jehad in Afghanistan had been Deo Bund and Ahle Hadith madrasas which got undue patronage from Zia govt. and finances from Saudi Arabia and some international agencies. These two groups aligned themselves with anti Shia forces in Afghanistan in late 1980s, and all along in 1990s. The battle in Afghanistan raged in the towns of Pakistan as well when there was pointless and ruthless killings of Shia's and then by Shias in large number. The country virtually had a blood bath on this account during the period 1985-1990.

Sectarian terrorism has affected all parts of the country in varying degrees at different points in time. The northern areas and southern Punjab were the worst sufferers with sporadic strikes in major urban centres as well. The decade of 1990s has been the worst on this account. It did pose a serious threat to the internal security of the country but it has lost its sting due to two major reasons; one the people of Pakistan refused to get divided on sectarian lines and the fissure remained restricted to the fanatics and the extremists with the vast majority remaining detached, unsympathetic and rather antagonist to this approach. Secondly, the emergence of a far grave phenomenon of Jehadi terrorism overshadowed rather watering down the sectarian terrorism. Taking it as a national security concern the government of Pakistan need to overcome and address the genuine grievances of these sectarian groups. The groups involved in terrorist activities should be banned by the government, other groups to be brought into dialogue with government.

It is the emergence of Jehadi terrorism, which is posing a real threat to the national security of Pakistan. The epicenter of Jehadi terrorism is Afghanistan. Initially, it was directed towards infidles and occupation forces but gradually it had to turn towards Pakistan, because of its alliance with the West in the War on Terrorism. The Jehad of 1980s, against the Soviet occupation of Afghanistan degenerated first into in fighting on ethnic lines and ethnic terrorism and then to sectarian terrorism with the arrival of Taliban on the scene. The Taliban took upon themselves the so called divine duty of enforcing Islamic order with the force of arms. Their narrow, myopic and ultra orthodox view of Islam is a force of regression and decadence.

When the resistance moment against American occupation of Afghanistan started engulfing Pakistan also, the perpetrators of Jehadi terrorism were out to chastise the Muslims of Pakistan. The march of Jehadi terrorism towards Pakistan has refueled the sectarian terrorism as well and we have been witnessing the most lethal combination of these two evil forces. "The scene in Pakistan resembled a jungle in which every one was fighting at times everyone else. The terrorists were making money by drug trafficking and gun running, so they were heavily armed. Their operations endangered the very existence of the state, and no one put an estimate even remotely how many people were killed in this fighting".

Military means cannot be the only solution to eradicate terrorism as causes of terrorism can be social, political and economic. The roots of Jehadi terrorism can also be found in social, economic and political factors. Looking at the present economic, social and political conditions in Pakistan it is inconceivable that there are going to be no Jehadi elements in the country. The Jehadi terrorism and its combination is threatening the national security of Pakistan on both the external and internal fronts. 'The acquisition of nuclear war heads by India and Pakistan threatened to make their resolved conflict over Kashmir go ballistic'.

On the external front the vital freedom movement in Kashmir has been undermined. Though the freedom movement in Kashmir is essentially different from the Jehadi terrorism as it is against the occupation forces of India and not to enforce a particular doctrine, but Indians have got a golden chance to malign it by drawing analogies with the Jehadi terrorism. Resultantly forcing Pakistan to be more flexible than it is due on the issue of Kashmir.

Today the most challenging issue emanates from the Islamic militancy. Pakistan has become a hot bed of various militant organisations, resorting to violence in the name of religion. Since the Afghan jihad against the Soviet Union, the militant Islamic organisations have flourished and have been supported by the governments in Pakistan. Therefore their growth was not controlled. One of the most major damages of the 1980s United States - Afghan War was the support provided to anti modern, extremist and intolerant forces of this region. To defeat the Soviet, the US and Pakistan government provided official support to militant and fundamentalist Islamic groups, which eventually led to religious extremism and sectarianism. This religious radicalism spread out in the other parts of the world also. Those forces became influential which rejected tolerance and secularism.

With the changed regional and global environment, Pakistan drastically needs to change its approach towards the militant organisations. 'Sponsoring terrorism is like riding a tiger. Pakistan has to pay a heavy price for its support for Taliban. Even though Musharraf demonstrated wisdom by supporting US war on Terror against Taliban in neighboring Afghanistan, the country continues to be caught in a very complex web of terrorist activity, with greater radicalisation of extremists groups'. The bases of this militant challenge operates in the Tribal areas of west of Pakistan and North West Frontier Province and Federally Administered Tribal Area (FATA). These areas mostly comprise of the Pushtuns and ethnic groups which are conservative, have close religious and tribal links with Pushtoon in Afghanistan and anti western. 'The Pushtun tribal areas have long been a heaven for displaced

Afghans and refugees'. The hilly and difficult terrain of this region has turned out to be a heaven for militant organisations both foreign and national. The foreign militants over here mainly are Uzbek, Chechens and Pushtun Afghanis.

After 9/11 incident and also when Pakistan Govt. realised the gravity of the threat posed by the uncontrolled militant elements, the govt. decided to establish the writ of the state in these areas. Pakistan military initiated operations against these forces and had to face stiff resistance. Wana operation which was started by the military became very controversial and has brought about heavy losses to the government forces and has also resulted in heavy criticism of the government.

In Pakistan, minority and separatist movements are common. In the south west of Pakistan is the province of Balochistan which is mostly a tribal area, over there, intermittent gorilla war has been a feature since last two decades. This is another major form of terrorist threat to Pakistan which is of the separatist nature. The largest but the most underdeveloped area of Balochistan currently is the centre of this threat. It is the ethno-nationalist conflict between the government and the separatists for long that these separatists comprising of tribal militants have been indulged in violent acts for more political and economic authority in Balochistan.

In Balochistan the various insurgents have adopted various violent tactics to sabotage the system. This problem if not resolved in time has the potential to challenge the national integrity of the state. Another new form of terrorism which has started to challenge the state is the takeover by the students, of religious seminaries in the capital city Islamabad of a children's library. The students and administration of madrasa lately took over law in their hands abducting women, police men and Chinese nationals on various charges thus creating state within the state. This brought great embarrassment to the government at both national and international level.

President Musharaf has on a number of occasions reteriated that serious efforts are required to 'combat this modern day evil, which threatens to destabilise our societies'. Unlike terrorist groups in other countries, the groups in Pakistan involved in terrorist activities and violence are also active in political arena in Pakistan. Internally, the latest ultra orthodox combine preaches a distorted, tribalistic, ritualistic and dark version of Islam with no light of tolerance, peaceful coexistence, human rights and finer things of life. This deadly combine seeks to impose their version with the use of arms.

The most dangerous part is that they can allure the law, befool the young, hoodwink the questioner, and over the skeptic in the garb of divine authority. They are against every institution and manifesto of modern age. Their special focus and victims are the women. They want them to be frightened within home: good only for domestic chores and child rearing. They are moving forward as they see a real chance of seizing power in this country and with their march the whole process of development, all institutions of the country, the way of life, religious beliefs and the state structure are under threat, forcing us to think what else constitutes the national security.

5.4. Suicide Terrorism in Sri Lanka

Suicide bombings have emerged as 'deadly weapons' in the arsenal of terrorism. Terrorist organisations are increasingly relying on suicide attacks to achieve major political objectives.For example, spectacular suicide terrorist attacks have recently been employed by Iraqi hardliner groups in attempts to force US and allied forces to abandon the mainland Iraq, by the Liberation Tigers of Tamil Eelam to compel the Sri Lankan government to accept an independent Tamil homeland, by Palestinian groups in attempts to force Israel to abandon West Bank and Gaza, and by Al Qaeda to pressurise the United States to withdraw from the Saudi Arabian Peninsula.

Before the early 1980s, suicide terrorism was rare but not unknown. However, since the attack on the U.S. embassy in Beirut in April 1983, there have been at least 300 separate suicide terrorist attacks worldwide, in Iraq, Lebanon, Israel, Sri Lanka, India, Pakistan, Afghanistan, Yemen, Turkey, Russia and the United States,the most recent being the Uzbekistan suicide bombing in July 31 2004. Thus the numbers have increased from 31 in the 1980s to 104 in the 1990s to 153 in 2000- August 2004, increasing both in tempo and location.

The emerging trend in terrorism over the past three decades has contradicted the conventional thinking that terrorists are averse to using deadly weapons or WMDs. When the conventional terrorist groups of the early 1970s are compared with terrorists in the early 1990s, a trend can be seen i.e., a transition towards nationalistic feeling and religious fervor. The increased threat level, in the form of terrorist actions aimed at achieving a larger scale of destruction through the choice of their targets, which are often symbolic or representative in the targeted nation was dramatically demonstrated with the suicide bombing of the WTC, or the 9/11 attack.

According to Robert Pape, 'the total number of terrorist incidents of all kinds had been falling - from a peak of 666 in 1987 to a low of 274 in 1998. But, in contrast, suicide attacks are proliferating'. There were 98 suicide attacks in the past four years, as compared to 212 attacks during 1983 - 2000. This sharp increase can be attributed to the change in terrorist mindset in engaging their opponents; however, the employment of suicide attacks as a terrorist technique is not a new phenomenon. 'With the invention of dynamite in the late 19century, the use of bombs in terrorist attacks became a generally favored method, and this applies to suicide attacks also'. But with the development of better explosives and means of detonating them, suicide attacks became less common. Later, 'due to the increase in counter terrorism measures, the terrorist organisations began to reintroduce suicide attacks'.

The terrorist organisations arrange suicide attacks to coerce the state into conceding its demands and to punish members of the targeted state for any harm done to their community or religion. Thus they use suicide attacks not only 'as a weapon of protest, but also as a weapon of intimidation and weapon of reprisal'. Subsequently, terrorist organisations venerate these individual acts of suicide terrorism to create a desire among the fellow members to follow suit.

Suicide terrorism must be differentiated from other form of terrorisms. Pape has defined the different forms of terrorism as demonstrative, destructive, and suicide terrorism. However this differentiation is not clear cut. Suicide terrorism cannot be compared with demonstrative and destructive terrorism. It can be argued that the suicide terrorism is merely an instrument or modus operandi, compared to demonstrative or destructive terrorism which are mostly objectives.

Suicide terrorism as an instrument, seeks both objectives to some extent, often aiming at enemy targets and, in some cases, mobilising support for the terrorists' cause. This is explicit in the 9/11 suicide attack; though the attack inflicted civilian causalities, its main objective was to demonstrate that the US is vulnerable to terrorists. However, suicide terrorism can be differentiated from suicidal terrorism. In suicidal terrorism, 'a terrorist undertakes a high risk operation, in which though he does not consciously kill himself in order to kill others, the chances of his surviving the operation and returning alive are very low.' But in the case of suicide terrorism, a terrorist kills others by killing himself.

Schweitzer defines suicide terrorism as a politically motivated violent attack perpetrated by a self-aware individual (or individuals) who actively and purposely causes his own death through blowing himself up along with his chosen target. The perpetrator's ensured death is a precondition for the success of his mission. Suicide terrorism is an act that 'reintroduces an irreducible singularity in a generalised exchange system. It aims to radicalise the world through sacrifice, while the system aims to realise world through force'.The acts of suicide terrorism particularly where the actor accepts his/her demise as certainty assault our notion of human rationality to the core.

5.4.1. Suicide Terror Organisations

Suicide terrorism has confounded governments since it made its modern debut on 23 October 1983, when two explosions destroyed the barracks of the US and French contingents of the multinational peacekeeping force in Beirut, Lebanon. Two centuries of experience had suggested that terrorists, 'though ready to risk their lives, wished to live after the terrorist act in order to benefit from its accomplishments'. Suicide terrorism denies that belief. Despite the complexity of suicide terrorism operations, it remains an 'attractive choice for terror groups due to five main reasons - tactical advantage and success, cost-effective operations, personal rewards for perpetrator, the utility of women and the psychological victory'. For states, 'air power and economic sanctions are often the preferred coercive tools' to engage the enemy.

For terrorist groups, suicide attacks are becoming the coercive instrument of choice, to retaliate against the defending government. Many argue that for most of the organisations that have used these tactics, 'the common denominator is their success in causing large scale casualties and negatively influencing public morale', while entirely failing to change regimes or force their governments to surrender to their strategic demands. The common feature of all suicide terrorist campaigns is that 'they inflict punishment on the opposing society, either directly by killing civilians or indirectly by killing military personnel in circumstances that cannot lead to meaningful battlefield victory'.

On the basis of their deployment, there are three levels of organisations that use suicide attacks. 'At the simplest level, there are groups such as Egyptian Islamic Group, the Egyptian Islamic Jihad, the Kuwaiti Dawa, and the Algerian Armed Islamic Group that neither practice suicide terrorism on a regular basis nor approve of its use as a tactic'. Local members or affiliates of such organisations may initiate it on their own for a variety of reasons, such as imitating the glorious acts of others, responding to perceptions of enormous humiliation and distress, avenging the murder of comrades and relatives, or being presented with a special opportunity to strike.

At the higher level, 'there are groups like the Hizbullah and Kurdistan Worker's Party (PKK) that formally adopt suicide terrorism as a temporary tactic'. Their leaders obtain ideological or theological legitimisation for its use from an authority, recruit and train volunteers, and then send them into action with a specific objective in mind. At the highest level, there are groups like the Liberation Tigers of Tamil Eelam (LTTE), Palestinian Islamic Jihad (PIJ) and Hamas that adopt suicide terrorism 'as a legitimate and permanent strategy'. Currently, suicide battalions of the Liberation Tigers of Tamil Eelam (LTTE) - or Black Tigers - are the leaders of this phenomenon.

The Black Tigers launched their first attack in July 1987, and since then suicide bombings have become an enduring feature of the LTTE's struggle. The Black Tigers offer significant proof that suicide terrorism is not merely a religious phenomenon and that, 'under certain extreme political and psychological circumstances, secular volunteers are fully capable of martyrdom'. While it is difficult to make generalisations about why and at what stage some terrorist organisations, but not others, decide to use suicide attacks, it is necessary to dispel some misconceptions about such operations. For example, it is often claimed that suicide attacks are a product of strategic desperation, 'carried out only when all military and other means have been exhausted'. It is true that groups like Chechen fighters have conducted suicide operations to overcome their entrenched military inferiority.

Indeed, for a terrorist group, 'the practical attractions of suicide attacks are manifold'. The 'weapon' is mobile and, given sufficient guidance, increases targeting possibilities beyond the normal range, as the proximity guaranteed by a suicide attacker greatly heightens the probability of successes. In the West Bank and Gaza Strip, this advantage has proven useful against tight Israeli security checks. Similarly, 'the value of an accurate human guidance system has been evident in the assassination attacks of the LTTE or the September 2001 al-Qaeda killing of Afghan Northern Alliance leader Ahmad Shah Massoud'.

All the suicide terrorist groups have support infrastructures in Europe and in North America. Suicide-capable groups differ in form, size, orientation, goal and support. 'In terms of military and economic power, Hizbullah and the LTTE lead the list of suicide operations. In terms of numbers, the LTTE has conducted the largest volume of suicide attacks, followed by Hamas and the PKK. In terms of range, only some of the groups have operated beyond their territories. The LTTE has conducted one suicide operation in India. It is the only group to have killed two world leaders - the former prime minister of India, Rajiv Gandhi, and the President of Sri Lanka, Ranasinghe Premadasa.

The vast spread of suicide terrorism over the last two decades suggests that there may not be a single profile of a suicide bomber, although the study of the personal characteristics of suicide attackers may help identify individuals whom the terrorist organisations are likely to recruit for this purpose. Until recently, the leading experts in psychological profiling of suicide terrorists characterised them as uneducated, unemployed, socially isolated, single men in their late teens and early 20s.

Now, it is recognised that suicide terrorists can be college educated or uneducated, married or single, men or women, socially isolated or integrated, from ages 13 to 47. In other words, although only a tiny number of people become suicide terrorists, they come from a broad cross section and lifestyles, and it would be impossible to pick them out in advance. Even if many suicide attackers are irrational or fanatical, the leadership groups that recruit and direct them are not. A suicide bomber carries minimal security risks for the organisation sponsoring them.

Should the attacker be captured prior to detonation, it is quite common for him/ her to detonate the explosives regardless, simply to destroy evidence. In Sri Lanka, 'the LTTE's 'Black Tigers are equipped with cyanide pills in the name of security'. Similarly, 'Hamas suicide attackers often remove their fingerprints by burning or scraping away skin tissue, so as to prevent tracing and thus protect the attack's ultimate organisers'. In most cases, however, the attacker is deliberately uninvolved in planning and has little information to give even if captured alive.

Viewed from the perspective of the terrorist organisation, suicide attacks are designed to achieve specific political purposes: to coerce a target government to change policy, to mobilise additional recruits and financial support, or both. This is true in the case of LTTE in Sri Lanka.

5.4.2. Suicide Attacks

In South Asia, three countries have been the principal victims of suicide terrorism: Sri Lanka, India - in Jammu and Kashmir and Pakistan.The terrorist organisations such as the LTTE, JeM, and LeT have been responsible for a relatively high number of suicide attacks and resultant casualties in South Asia. Some attacks by the terrorist groups, such as the 15 October 1997 bombing of the Colombo World Trade Center in Sri Lanka by the Liberation Tigers of Tamil Eelam which killed 18 and injured more than 100 persons, are as shocking as they are destructive. Out of 118 suicide attacks in South Asia between 1990 - 2000, Sri Lanka alone suffered 88 attacks. The island country is vulnerable to such attacks since 1987. The recent suicide attack on Kollupitiya Police station in Colombo on 7 July 2004, the first attack after two years, suggests that the LTTE is back in action.

The LTTE leads the global list of groups that have carried out suicide attacks such as the Palestine Islamic Jihad (PIJ) and the Hamas in Palestine, the Hezbollah in Lebanon, the Kurdistan Workers' Party (PKK) in Turkey, the Groupe Islamique Armee (GIA or the Armed Islamic Group) of Algeria and the Islamic Group of Egypt. The LTTE is the deadliest group that has successfully infused the suicide bomb syndrome into Sri Lanka. It is the only group to have assassinated two world leaders, both assassinations being carried out using the suicide body-suit.

On 5 July 1987, the first suicide attack was launched by Captain Miller, by ramming a truck packed with explosives into a military camp in northern Sri Lanka, which marked the beginning of this dreadful retaliation. The suicide killings formed a 'deadly weapon for which Sri Lanka had no anti'. Other than the loss of leaders, the country's national, political, economic and cultural infrastructure has been severely damaged by suicide attacks.The LTTE deployed suicide bombers with deadly accuracy to destroy the Joint Operations Command, the nerve-centre of the Sri Lankan security forces; the Central Bank; the World Trade Centre; the Temple of the Tooth Relic, the most hallowed Buddhist shrine; and the oil storage installations in Kolonnawa.

The LTTE used suicide bombers to kill a number of service personnel, apart from political leaders and outstanding intellectuals such as Neelan Thiruchelvam. The Sri Lankan Navy chief Admiral Clancy Fernando was killed by a suicide bomber on a motor cycle soon after he returned from India after discussing Indo-Sri Lankan naval cooperation. The LTTE singled out and targeted individuals who were at the forefront of counter-insurgency operations to paralyse the security apparatus.It is interesting to note that unlike other terrorist organisations that target the civilians, the LTTE has mostly targeted the governmental machines. A brief review of the suicide threat from the LTTE to targets in Sri Lanka is therefore in order.

5.4.3. Women Suicide Bombers

History is not short of examples of women terrorists. One of the better-known is Leila Khaled, who, on behalf of the Popular Front for the Liberation of Palestine, hijacked a plane in 1969. In the LTTE, the presence of women cadres in the Black Tigers is a distinct phenomenon. Nearly one-third of the Black Tigers are composed of women. The presence of women in the suicide squad asserts the gender equality that the LTTE preaches.

The Vituthalai Pulikal Makalir Munani (Women's Front of the Liberation Tigers) was formed in 1983, which had begun as a support group and was later absorbed into the fighting formations. The first group of Women Tigers had their training in Tamil Nadu camps by 1985, and had their first taste of combat in July 1986. In October 1987, Prabhakaran set up a training camp exclusively for women in Jaffna for the second and successive batches. By 1989, this unit secured its own leadership structure. In the same year they were recruited for the Sea Tigers, which was then in an embryonic stage.

The female cadres were restricted in numbers till about the early-1990s, at which point there was an expansion brought about by the nature of military engagements and the needs of the LTTE. The women's squad operates from six divisions - Jaffna, Wanni, Mannar, Mullaitivu, Vavunia and Batticaloa. Some criticism has been leveled against the LTTE for using women only as implementers and not the initiators of policy; in other words, they were only used in suicide bombing and to carry out specific military tasks and nothing more. However, of the LTTE's central committee of 12, five are women, but it is not known how much influence they carry on decision-making and determining policy.

As in the case of selecting males for Black tiger operations, the LTTE central military command selects, rather accepts, volunteer women for suicidal missions. The women reportedly undergo the same tough training as men, and like them, are broken up into fighting, intelligence gathering, political and administrative units. The Tigers' conduct political classes and the aspects of female liberation and feminist ideology are taught along with nationalist politics. Tasks are assigned that break taboos such as riding bicycles, driving motor vehicles, swimming and sea faring that have given women a sense of empowerment that could stand them in good stead even outside their military roles. In her book *Women Fighters of Liberation Tigers*, Adele Ann, the Australian-born wife of Anton Balasingham, LTTE theoretician, described the decision by a Tamil woman to join the organisation as a message to society "that they are not satisfied with the social status quo;

it means they are young women capable of defying authority; it means they are women with independent thoughts; young women prepared to lift up their heads." Death, not life, is celebrated. The greatest feat for a woman is to die a martyr. This celebration of heroic death is an aspect of most nationalist movements, but in the LTTE it is a major factor which determines and conditions the life of women who have dedicated themselves to the cause.

LTTE chief Prabhakaran, in an address to women cadres on International Women's Day on March 8, 1996, described the liberation of the Tamil woman as "the fervent child" that was born out of the Tamil "national liberation movement." Women in the LTTE are allegedly forced to suppress their femininity and sexuality, which is regarded as a crime and an evil force that could sap their strength. Marriage is not allowed for women cadres up to the age of 25 and for men up to the age of 28.

5.4.4. Black Sea Tigers

Sea Tigers are the naval wing of LTTE. They are exclusively designated to carry out attacks on the Sri Lankan Naval forces. The Sea Tigers deploy squadrons of heavily armed gunboats and speedboats. Jane's International Defence Review, in a report on Sri Lanka, published a few years ago, pointed out that the Sea Tigers "have taken on the Sri Lankan navy with unprecedented success." Sri Lankan and foreign intelligence agencies estimate the strength of the Sea Tigers at 2,000 to 3,000 cadres.

The Black Sea Tigers, the suicide squad of the naval wing comprising highly motivated young men and women, was formed in 1990. 'Mr. Prabakaran wanted to challenge the supremacy of the Sri Lankan Navy and for this effectively used the dedication of the Sea Tigers. The Black Sea Tigers made use of small boats, packed with large quantities of explosives, and generally under cover of darkness hit their target, triggering off explosions. In the process, they naturally sacrificed their lives. In the first Black Sea Tiger attack off Valvettiturai on July 10, 1990, the guerrillas badly damaged a Sri Lankan naval ship Edithara. On May 4, 1991, they sank the Sri Lankan command ship, Abitha'. Till now there have been 22 such suicide attacks that have led to large scale destruction of ships, naval vessels and containers of the government.

At least 88 persons have been killed, that includes naval forces and security personnel. These Black Sea Tigers go as a squad and attack the enemy forces. Boats laden with explosives and ferries laden with explosives were used. These Black Sea Tigers have specialised in scuba diving by which they penetrate enemy targets. Footage of such attacks has shown them speeding toward Sri Lankan Navy crafts in explosive-ridden crafts, waving and acknowledging the cheers of cadres on other boats. The Triconamalee and Kankesanthurai coastal commands get affected. This explains why suicide terrorists, once launched on a mission, go like a homing pigeon towards their targets and do not develop any fears or second thoughts on the way to their objective or abandon their mission. Their decision to undertake suicide missions is not an impulsive action, but carefully-thought out.

REFERENCES

Eaton, David J., ed. *Weapons of Mass Destruction: Foreign and Domestic Options for Containment: Proceedings of a Conference May 6, 1998,* Austin, TX: Lyndon B. Johnson School of Public Affairs, The University of Texas at Austin, 1999.

Falkenrath, Richard, "Problems of preparedness: US readiness for a domestic terrorist attack", *International Security,* 25 (4): 147-186, 2001.

Lenzy Kelley, *Combat Terrorism: Foreign and Domestic; Steps and Procedures to Protect Yourself, Your Family, and Your Employees Against the Next Wave,* Paperback - February 2001.

Mullins, Wayman C., *A Sourcebook on Domestic and International Terrorism: An Analysis of Issues, Organizations, Tactics, and Responses,* 2nd ed. Springfield, IL: Charles C. Thomas, 1997.

Nadine Gurr, Benjamin Cole, *The New Face of Terrorism: Threats from Weapons of Mass Destruction,* Paperback - November 2000.

United States, Department of State, *Patterns of Global Terrorism,* 2000.

Vohryzek-Bolden, Miki, Gayle Olson-Raymer, and Jeffrey O. Whamond, *Domestic Terrorism and Incident Management: Issues and Tactics,* Springfield, IL: Charles C. Thomas, 2001.

Walter Laqueur, *The Age of Terrorism,* Little Brown, 1987.

6
Religious Terrorism

Religious terrorism refers to terrorism justified or motivated by religion and is a form of religious violence. All major religions can justify violence, and religion has long been associated with terrorism. Ever since there was good and evil, religious people have pondered whether using evil to fight evil is good in the name of justice or self-defence. There may be some kind of connection between attachment to the idea of God and a proclivity toward violence. The most common resort to violence occurs when a religious group feels threatened and thinks of itself as a chosen people. Less common is the compulsion to slaughter others in the name of a deity, and even less common (although not insignificant) is the role of sexuality in the mindset of religious fundamentalists who kill.

Religions also spawn sects, cults, and alternative religions, and religious terrorism (terrorism in the name of religion) likewise tends to spawn offshoots and factions. A sect is an offshoot of an established religion (Mormons, for example), and most either die off or expand into a major denomination like the Mormons did. A sect-based religious group is more likely to play the role of the victim, not the aggressor. A cult, on the other hand, is a more dangerous, spiritually innovative group (the Branch Davidians, for example) headed by a charismatic leader who usually has other aims than to become a major denomination. Many cults are harmless, but others are into mind control and some are into mass suicide. Still other cults have a doomsday orientation, and these tend to be ones which engage in religious terrorism (such as Aum Shinri Kyo).

Any sect or cult can become involved in religious terrorism or it can just worship terrorism (a terrorism cult). The motives can be wide-ranging, from engaging in psychic warfare to expressive behaviours that are homicidal, suicidal, or both. Cults are usually more dangerous than sects. There are four warning signs of a dangerous religious group:

i) apocalyptic thinking, or eschatology, that the world is coming to an end, and true believers will enjoy unique rewards at endtime;

ii) charismatic leadership where the leader dominates the followers spiritually, emotionally, and sexually;

iii) paranoia and demonisation of outsiders, accompanied by intentional isolation within a cloistered community; and

iv) preparations of a defensive nature, usually indicated by a buildup of guns, poisons, and/or weapons of mass destruction.

Many terrorist experts regard apocalyptic thinking as the first and most important danger sign. Professor Huntington in his book *Clash of Civilisations* makes the argument that religion determines culture and that at least eight separate culture clashes are occurring in the world today. The Middle East, of course, goes without saying, and he points to the Balkan (Yugoslavian) region as a place where clashes between Christianity, Orthodox Christianity and Islam often erupt into violence. Japan is another area ripe for conflict, as is the Indian subcontinent and Hindu region. Latin America and Africa will have emerging clashes, mostly Christian in-fighting, or in the case of Africa (which is 40% Christian and 40% Muslim), an ultimate battle clash.

Religion often provides a mantle or cloak of respectability for terrorism. *The Just War Doctrine* is a religious precept, and as old as war itself. Parts of the Bible hint at it, and St. Thomas Aquinas synthesised it in *Summa Theologicae*. The nuclear weapons have made the doctrine outmoded, it might be illustrative with the following basic principles:

i) A just war is only a last resort; all non-violent options must have been exhausted

ii) A just war is carried out by an authority with legitimacy; some society must sanction it

iii) The only permissible reason for a just war is to redress an injury or wrong suffered
iv) A just war should only be fought if there is a reasonable chance of success
v) The ultimate goal of a just war is to re-establish peace
vi) Violence in a just war must be proportional to the violence of the injury suffered
vii) The weapons of a just war must discriminate between combatants and non-combatants

Equally as important as just war theory is in understanding religious terrorism, there is a need to understand the morality of religious warfare, which in many ways is like the *morality of asymmetric warfare*. Martin Luther, founder of the Protestant Reformation in Christianity quoted,

> It is both Christian and an act of love to kill the enemy without hesitation, to plunder and burn and injure him by any method until he is conquered, except that one must beware of sin and not to violate wives and virgins.

There are always moral constraints to religious warfare. They may not be the same kind of constraints reflected in just war principles, but they are constraints nonetheless, and represent a particular kind of restraint (e.g., not violate wives and virgins) which reflects a moral superiority against overpowering odds (asymmetric power situation). Religious terrorists may cross the boundaries of fair play, but they are almost always convinced in their own minds of the moral superiority of their actions.

6.1. MOTIVATION

Half of the world's thirty most dangerous terrorist groups claim religion as their motivation. This motivation involves believing that their religion mandates acts of terror as sacred duty in an endless, cosmic struggle for the best way to please God. Religious terrorism has no military objective. A holy war, or jihad, is endless because it has a spiritual objective. No one ever knows when God is pleased enough, and when the situation in heaven matches the situation on earth. Nobody cares who or how many get killed in spiritual warfare. It for this reason that experts say religious terrorism might not be the world's most dangerous type, but it certainly is the most dedicated and unpredictable. While some are, most religious terrorists are not part of a sect or cult. Instead, most religious terrorists are devout, fundamentalist, "true" believers in their mainstream religion.

The divine mandate for destruction is regarded as the "neglected duty" within the mainstream religion, and implied, directly or indirectly, in the sacred texts, or at least their interpretation of those sacred texts. Religious terrorists also do not consider themselves terrorists, since they say they do not enjoy violence for the sake of violence. They regard themselves as religious activists or militants. Religious terrorists always seem to be spiritually "prepared" for violence, and they have long past the point of having second thoughts or doubts about it.

Religious terrorism is not countered by the same factors that counter other forms of terrorism. Neither military nor diplomatic solutions seem to work. Cease fires and negotiations also don't work, for example, with organisations containing no "secular" wing. Only a few religious organisations maintain a secular, or political front. Hoffman argues that even groups with secular wings will act unconstrained because they are playing to God and no one else. It's also plausible to argue that religious terrorists don't want to win, since religion is at base an underdog philosophy which needs an overpowering demonised enemy, or Great Satan.

In many ways, religious terrorism wants to fail because it adheres to some martyrdom notion of being the world's "loser." This kind of losing ideology is called fatalistic suicide, and is more common that egoistic and altruistic suicide. The greatest fear that most analysts have is if weapons of mass destruction get in the hands of religious terrorists — they have no fear of destroying themselves and everybody else in the process.

6.2. Irish Terrorism

The model known as Irish terrorism is also a model for nationalistic terrorism, but here, we will only consider the religious elements of it, and patterns that have emerged between the Catholics and Protestants. Historically, most Catholics were republicans living in the South, and Protestants were unionists (also landlords and industrialists) living in the North. Each side had been arguing and arming themselves since the 19th century. The first major conflict erupted on Easter in 1916 when the unionists called in British help, and the town of Dublin was demolished by British artillery. The Irish Republican Army (IRA) was formed that day, and led by Michael Collins, a student of Russian anarchism and terrorism. Murder and mayhem followed until a brief peace came after creation of independent Southern Ireland (the Republic of Ireland) in 1921.

The struggle then shifted to Northern Ireland, where the British tightened their hold by creating the Royal Ulster Constabulary (RUC), a sort of semi-military police force, which became the favourite target of the Provisional IRA (a Northern Ireland spin-off group affiliated with the Sinn Fein party — another spin-off group being the Irish Continuity Army, dedicated to international terrorism, not just within Ireland). The Provisional IRA committed sporadic acts of terrorism until 1994 when peace talks began, and a cease-fire was agreed to. During the cease-fire (which some see as surrender), another spin-off group emerged - the *Real IRA*, which is the group officially recognised as the present foreign terrorist organisation although there are still active elements of the Continuity IRA.

There are many theories of the Irish conflict, but any understanding must admit that religion, politics, and economics are inseparably mixed. The three main denominations in Ireland are Catholic, Church of England, and Presbyterian - all religions of providence that emphasise the need for God's approval of secular affairs. Competition for political influence runs high, and people vote along religious lines. Economic discrimination (for jobs) also tends to revolve around religion. Everyone wants to control the state for reasons of deeply felt religious and economic deprivations, and this desire permeates all aspects of everyday life. Religion may not be the root cause of Irish conflict, but it is definitely the fuel that flames the passions.

Most Irish terrorism is in the name of retaliation or retribution, and this kind of retaliation is driven by spiritual conceptions of vengeance. The *Christains* believe they are protecting their homeland from human rights abuses at the hands of an illegitimate British government which is unaccountable under any rule of law. The *Protestants* believe they are being betrayed by a peace-seeking British government and must retaliate for more lethal, indiscriminate, and evil terrorism.

6.3. Religious Terrorism in South Asia

Very often, religious terrorism is mixed with ethnic conflict. That is the situation on the Indian subcontinent and throughout much of South Asia where one identifies as speaking, believing. Sri Lanka, a poor island south of India formerly known as Ceylon, is a good example. There, about 75% of the people are Sinhalese-speaking, Buddhist-believing, 12% of the people are Tamil-speaking, Hindu-believing, and 8% of the people are Arab-speaking, Muslim-believing. The Tamils have long hated the Sinhalese practice of infusing Buddhist philosophy into politics, but there are moderate factions within the Tamils who believe that the Sinhalese can be bargained with.

South Asia (which includes India, Pakistan, Afghanistan, Bangladesh and Nepal) has the highest population densities in the world, there are dozens of languages, low life expectancies, and not enough food to go around (people believing more children means better chance of growing food). After Mohandas Gandhi led a non-violent war of independence in 1947, North India (which was primarily Islamic) became partitioned off from South India (which was primarily Hindu), and Pakistan was born out of a mass migration.

In 1971, a ethnic conflict centered in Pakistan led to another mass migration, this time forming Bangladesh. Since 1975, the Sikhs have controlled the "emergency zone" Punjab region. India has experienced domestic terrorism at the hands of groups like Assam (United Liberation Front of Assam) in the Bengali region. The result is a region with scattered ethno-religious groups, all trying to exercise political clout or self-determination in one way or another. The Kashmir conflict is a good example of this kind of struggle or conflict.

Adherents of different religions often claim they cannot live with one other in the same area. Buddhism tends to be practiced by people living in highland areas, Hindu by lowland people, and Islam by city folk. In Buddhism, everything and everyone is equal. In Hinduism (as well as Confucianism), everything is born unequal - some people are born noble, others are not. Islam and Christianity tend to fuel the mix by adding elements of fundamentalism, most notably in the notion of martydom, which is highly attractive to the Asian region because it has the highest suicides rates of anywhere in the world. Ethno-religious terrorism in the region baffles most experts. It is difficult to distinguish religious and nonreligious motivation, and South Asian terrorism tends to be heavily mixed with a criminal element, both organised and unorganised.

6.4. Religious Terrorism in Balkan Provinces

The Yugoslavia region and the neighbouring Balkans (Albania, Bosnia, Bulgaria, Croatia, Hungary, Macedonia, and Romania) have long been a region of ethnic and religious conflict. There are over 10 million Balkan Muslims (Kosovo, Bosnia, and Bulgaria have over 2 million each), and anti-Muslim hatred runs high as does anti-Christian hatred (the Serbs are Christian). Balkan Muslims are not your average Muslims. They drink, smoke, celebrate Easter and Christmas, and are the descendants of Christians who converted to Islam in the 15-16th century to avoid persecution by the Ottoman Empire. Their sworn enemies are those of Serbian and Slavic descent who happen to be decended from Orthodox Christianity who see their job as protecting Europe from Muslim invasion. In the words of the Serb leader, Slobodan Milosevic, they're "dirty rotten Turks who breed like rabbits, run drugs, flood Slav lands with their alien offspring, and deserve to be sent back to Mecca where they belong."

6.5. Religious Terrorism in Eurasia

The former Russia (Russian Federation) and its Caucasus region have long experienced terrorism which escalated in 1999 with the start of Russia's war on terrorism in Chechnya. The Chechens are a Muslim people (again not your average Muslims) who hate the Russians, declared their independence in 1991, and beat the Russians in a ground war from 1994-1996. Their cause has become the cause of Muslims everywhere. In fact, the idea of an international *mujahidin* can be traced to the Chechnya conflict. There is evidence of a Chechen connection to an al-Qaeda terrorist network, and Chechen militants fought alongside al-Qaeda forces in Afghanistan and Iraq.

Chechen terrorism has spread throughout the region into Georgia, Azerbaijan, Kyrgyzstan, Uzbekistan, and Moscow itself. One of the groups involved in spillover violence is the Islamic Movement of Uzbekistan (IMU), but Chechnya produces plenty of its own militant groups. The region is used as a base for financial and logistic assistance to terrorist groups worldwide. The Islamic charity organisation known as the Global Relief Foundation had a headquarters in Chechnya, and is a known front for financing terrorist groups. Russian organised crime is also heavily active in the region and involved in arms smuggling. The Arab news network *al-Jazeera* frequently broadcasts pictures of Chechen civilians killed in the Russian war on terrorism. Numerous pro-Chechnya websites can be found on the Internet.

The Chechen terrorists are financed by the Chechen mafia as well as with Saudi money (for building mosques) and Arab relief fronts. There are some 150 Chechen mafia groups operating in or near Moscow, and they seem to prefer London, rather than Switzerland, as their money laundering center. They are constantly engaged in gang warfare with other Russian gangs, most notably the Solntsevskaya, and of course, in making whatever profit they can from criminal activity.

Chechen terrorism is largely successful because the Chechen mafia obtain and pass on intelligence obtained from bribing Russian military personnel. Both Chechen and Russian mafia groups have been involved in the nuclear black market, smuggling depleted plutonium, cesium, and other radioactive material that makes "dirty" bombs. An in-depth analysis of Chechen terrorism is called for.

6.6. Religious Terrorism in North Africa

Sudan is the largest country in Africa (roughly the size of Europe), and located south of Egypt. It has been a war zone since it's independence from Britain in 1954. Years of dictatorships and military coups have been the norm, with the situation escalating in the 1990s to genocide. Northern Sudan (the safer region) consists of 8 million Arabic-speaking Muslims, and an indigenous black Nuba population which the current government has been trying to exterminate.

Southern Sudan consists of 6 million black Africans who are Christians or animists (animism is a primitive religion that every object, even a rock, has a soul). The current government's goal is to become Africa's first all-Islamic nation, so Islamic Law and Jihad are used to persecute and execute any non-believers. Christians, in particular are regularly murdered, raped, maimed, or forced into slavery. The National Islamic Front regime which holds the capital city of Khartoum regards Christian missionary activity as Western invasion.

Osama bin Laden hid for many years in Sudan. Next to Iran, Sudan is one of the world's largest sponsors of terrorism, but it is trying to change that, and began cooperating with America's war on terror in 2002, but American intelligence and diplomatic officials are quite suspicious of Sudan's sincerity in this regard.

The United States has spent about $30 million in covert aid to the rebel forces in Sudan while at the same time sending $100 million in humanitarian aid. U.S. officials deny that the covert aid was military, describing it as 'non-lethal' - radios, uniforms, boots, tents, etc. The rebel groups are split and factionalised, the strongest one being the Sudan People's Liberation Army (SPLA). Other include the Sudan People's Liberation Movement (SPLM), and its armed wing, the SPLM/A (A for Army), the Sudanese Allied Forces (SAF), and the United Democratic Salvation Front (UDSF). In the opinion of most military experts, none of these rebel groups ever has a chance of winning against the stronger, government NIF/GoS forces.

Many religious cults tend to form in Africa, and much of it involves distorted forms of Christian fundamentalism which mix witchcraft with what might be called Pentecostalism. This is prevalent in Ghana, Malawi, Zambia, Zimbabwe, and Nigeria, but we'll focus on Uganda, a country located directly below Sudan. Like many Africans, Ugandans believe in witch-doctors, who not only attempt to heal the sick (usually by cutting off a body part), but provide financial and marital advice.

Christian missionaries in the region usually report having a hard time explaining things like witches and devils. Africans, however, are intensely interested in anything to do with salvation and putting troubles behind you to start a new life. At least one terrorist cult group, the LRA, has exploited these desires. The

LRA, in existance since 1989, has an agreement with the National Islamic Front/Government of Sudan (NIF/GoS) that they would support the NIF/GoS in their jihad against the Southern Sudanese, if the NIF/GoS would support the LRA.

6.7. Religious Terrorism in Middle East

At last count, there were 57 separate nations with Islam as the official religion or a substantial part of the population consisting of Muslims. These nations belong to a group called the Organisation of the Islamic Conference (OIC) which has gone on record saying there's no such thing as separation of church and state. There is even no such thing as a secular religion, like the official Church of England religion in Great Britain. There appears to be three schools of Muslim thought on the subject.

The majority group believes that it is the sacred mission of Islam to rule the world by use of the sword if necessary. Another group accepts cohabitation with other religions as long as Islam is the world's pre-eminent religion. A third group, the moderates, advocates co-existence primarily because of the economic benefits it brings. Bearing the scars of life and an inability to develop constitutional democracies, Middle Eastern countries take particular umbrage at the existence of Israel, the history of which follows.

The area known as Palestine is an ancient land which has always been populated by Arab Muslims, Arab Christians, and Arab Jews. In 1917, the British promised to help create a Jewish "national home" in Palestine. Arab protests began in 1920. In 1919 there were 568,000 Muslims, 74,000 Christians, and 58,000 Jews in Palestine. Fifteen thousand Jews a year immigrated during Hitler's rise to power, and some 100,000 death camp survivors came later. Today, there are 1,091,000 Muslims, 614,000 Jews, and 146,000 Christians in Palestine. Wars have been fought in 1948–49, 1956, 1967 (The Six Day War), 1973–74 (The Yom Kippur War), and 1982 between Israel and the Arab states.

The current conflict centers on two Israeli-controlled territories. The West Bank has the largest percentage of Arab Muslims, and the conflict there revolves around the status of Jerusalem (the center of three great religions). The Gaza Strip is another Muslim area where the intifadah (grassroots uprising) began, and refugee camp conditions are worse than in the West Bank. The religious backdrop to the situation is heavily mixed with anti-U.S. sentiment, where the U.S. is seen as supporting Israel only because of American oil interests. Further, the U.S. is seen as being responsible for militarising the region (the Middle East is the most militarised region in the world) and propping up corrupt Arab governments. In addition, American culture is seen as hopelessly racist, or at least stereotypical, in the way it portrays Arabs - as the bad guys in movies, cartoons, war films, and popular conception, up to and including the latest way Americans easily roll the words "Islamic terrorism" off their tongues.

It's hard to walk the line between cultural sensitivity and stereotype. Suffice it to say that opinions vary, but some believe Islam doesn't mean peace, but submission - to the will of Allah to "fight and slay the unbelievers wherever you find them, and seize them, beleaguer them, and lie in wait for them in every stratagem of war". If these viewpoints are true, then there really is such a thing as Islamic terrorism. There are, indeed, organisations dedicated to Islamic domination of the world, just as the great "breakout" of Islam during the 7th Century that resulted in the Arab "golden age." At the forefront of this idea are Muslim clerics most likely kept quiet by their governments, and in some ways is an adequate description of Osami bin Laden's goals for al-Qaeda.

In the Philippines and Malaysia, there's the Abu Sayyaf group. In Algeria there's the Armed Islamic group. In Egypt there's Al-Gam'a al-Islamiyya and Al-Jihad. Other Islamic groups simply hate Israel and want to destroy it. Hamas, Hezbollah, the Popular Front for the Liberation of Palestine, and the Palestinian Liberation Front are such groups.

Other Middle Eastern groups are more closely linked to Muslim fundamentalism than the Palestine issue, and fundamentalism in this context bridges both Sunnis and Shiites, and can be seen as anti-Americanism - an outright hatred of American values and culture couched in the language of religion. A few leaders of these groups have openly called for the deaths of Americans on a global scale. The foremost character in this regard is Osama bin Laden and his group, al-Qaeda, which are perhaps marginal players compared to the global Islamist threat or perhaps the strongest, most dangerous of such a threat.

Al Qaeda ideology, to which Osama Bin Laden and others like him represent, is an admixture of various Koranic misinterpretations and a hatred of the U.S. and/or all westernised things. When speaking of al-Qaeda, one should strive to be clear if they are speaking of: (a) *traditional* al-Qaeda, the group which attacked the US on 9/11; (b) *ideological* or doctrinal al-Qaeda, the leaderless followers who simply believe in the same ends; or (c) the *new* al-Qaeda, which is part of the insurgency in Iraq targeting other Muslims.

6.8. Rise of Religious Fundamentalism

One of the most important religious social transformations of the last century has been the gradual rise of fundamentalism, the embrace of anti-modern religious orthodoxies. Jurgensmeyer notes that religious fundamentalism across various religious cultures is on the rise globally for three common reasons: first, radical conservative religious movements reject the liberal values of secular institutions and blame society's decline on the loss of religious inspiration; second, these radical religious movements refuse to accept boundaries of secular society which keeps religion a private observance and not the public sphere; and third, these conservative movements are seeking to restore religion as central to social life.

Fundamentalisms generally require unquestioning acceptance of transcendent religious precepts, a strict adherence to compulsory rituals and a subjugation of the self to higher powers. Fundamentalism may be defined as a conservative religious reaction to secular society that typically includes the following characteristics: Exclusive truth claims are typically based on a sacred text. It often has Manichean truth claims in which non-believers are constructed as immoral and an apocalyptic view of the world. Fundamentalism seeks to restore a glorious past from which people had strayed.

Fundamentalism makes exclusive truth claims grounded in canonical religious, spiritual texts and seeks to recreate an idealised religious community while paradoxically embracing modern means: mass media, bureaucratic institutions, and destructive technologies in militancy. Christian, Jewish, Hindu, and Islamic fundamentalisms more or less follow this pattern.

Thus, fundamentalisms resist the usually hedonistic, secular, materialistic values of modernity. At the same time, fundamentalists are modernists in that they use elements of tradition in combination with modern methods-advanced technology, institutional forms, and instrumental rationality-to transform the political order.

Radical religious movements often position themselves to act in the public sphere as moral agents. From the viewpoint of religious radicals, it is not so much that religion has become political as much as politics has become religious. The reasons for this deep antagonism are not merely political. Secular modernity and its valorisation of Reason has made an assault on religious values and worldviews that erode the impact and power of religious institutions leading to a general crisis in religious belief. As secular society is suffering a crisis of morality and meaning, there is a space for religious critiques of secular modernity and transcendental alternatives. The West, celebrating the secular materialism of modernity, spread through a political economic imperialism and mass mediated consumerism has created spaces for radical religious movements, both in the developed and developing countries.

Islamic fundamentalisms arose in various Islamic states. For example, Wahabbism was embraced in Saudi Arabia, as the Ottoman Empire declined in the later 18th, early 19th Century. As Western power grew and the division of the Islamic world proceeded, Western interests encouraged the suppression of progressive movements in the Middle East such as socialism or even nationalism. For example, the US has strongly supported the (oil rich) House of Saud, where Islam has turned increasingly conservative and militant in resistance. Islamic fundamentalism is a response many factors, central among which are the domination by the West, the relative poverty and underdevelopment of the Muslim world, and the lack of political outlets to express discontents.

In the 20th Century, Westernisation did not yield its promised results. Modernity failed Islamic states, for a variety of reasons mentioned above, especially the conservatism of its religion, the underdevelopment inherent in colonialism and foreign sponsoring of local elites, the lack of education of the populace, and, the conservatism of religious leaders. Islamic states generally secured the wealth and power of the elites and sustained oppressive secular governments rather than seek expansions of democracy and human rights. With the failure of modernity to bring its promised benefits, conservative Islamic brotherhoods and movements, originally organised to address social justice issues attempted to reinvigorate, reform and re-establish Islam as the basis for revitalised Islamic states.

As westernising strategies in Islamic states failed and/or were suppressed in the 20th Century, conservative religious responses grew more pronounced, generating various Islamisms, Islamic fundamentalist movements. Note that in many developing nations, secular thought and autonomous institutions, especially democratically elected legislative bodies and executive are not very well formed or advanced. Religious ways of life and social-political institutions hold more public power, especially in Islamic countries. Hence, there is a strong link between religious belief and resistance to Western hegemony among radical religious movements in the Islamic world.

The rigid claims and orthodoxy of fundamentalism generally prevents a group from self-examination and critical reflection. This is not likely to change as long as the educational processes in the developing world remain tied to traditional religious institutions. Studying the Quran and/or Islamic studies does not much prepare the student for science, industry, commerce or critical thought. Conservative Islamic movements have pursued three main ends in Islamic society: reformism, revivalism, and radical defence. The main interest of these movements is to re-establish the moral and political virtues of traditional Islamic society.

Islamism is modelled on the attempt to recapture Muhammad's early role of rebel in Mecca in criticising moral corruption and need for lifestyle and political economic reforms grounded in religious mores. For revivalists, just as Muhammad challenged false gods and immoral ways instead of a righteous life, Islamism is seen as a path to justice and equality against the Western ways of corruption and worship of its false gods. Islamist ideological analysis offers these reasons for the decline of Islam:

i) Islamic society declined due to the departure from the practice of religious values and dictates;
ii) This decay made possible the Western intrusion; and,
iii) The solution is to revitalise and return to Islam by a) reintroducing the Shariah, Islamic law, while purging most Western cultural influences, but not science and technology and b) re-politicising Islam, along lines of Muhammad's role as administrator and law giver in Medina.

The rise of Islamic fundamentalism was the result of many factors beginning with general factors that have also fostered the growth of Christian fundamentalism, Orthodox Judaism and even Hindu fundamentalism. Further, various Islamic institutions have provided cheap alternatives to public education, in which young boys learn strict conservative forms of Islam, as for example the madrassas of Pakistan funded by Saudi Arabia. Islamism has often been directly reproduced through strictly enforced civic codes in which "moral police" vigorously patrol the borders of virtue as in Saudi Arabia, Kuwait, Iran and the former Taliban controlled Afghanistan.

There have been wide variations in the extent to which Muslim societies have embraced Islamisms, and within particular societies, there have been wide disparities in the appeal of Islamisms. For example, Afghanistan, under the Taliban, was an extreme, even by fundamentalist standards. But so too was (is) Afghanistan one of the poorest, least educated societies in the world. In contrast, Pakistan was (is) not a fundamentalist country. After General Zia took power, he tried to impose fundamentalism from the top down. It had few adherents, not more than about five percent of the people, primarily among tribal groups-looked down upon in Pakistani society.

The Saudis financed madrassas that were accepted by subsequent governments in order to divert scarce funds to nuclear weapons programmes, in response to India. Islamic fundamentalism was accepted by elements within Pakistani Security (the ISI) who used these schools to provide "volunteers" to fight against India in Kashmir as well as train US-financed mujahadeen that would fight a proxy war against Russia. In Algeria, a prolonged conflict between urban, Western modernists and rural fundamentalists has cost perhaps 200,000 lives.

Although fundamentalism has been widely embraced in the Muslim world, and it often promotes hatred of infidels, the vast majority of fundamentalists do not become terrorists, and not all terrorists in Islamic societies are "holy warriors". Nevertheless, the world wide rise of fundamentalism, with its Manichean division of the world into those who are good and those who are evil, with it assertions of patriarchy and promises of redemption, creates an atmosphere in which terrorism can thrive.

REFERENCES

Barnett, R., *Asymmetrical Warfare*, Washington DC: Brasseys, 2003.

Benjamin, D. & S. Simon, *The Age of Sacred Terror*, NY: Random House, 2002.

Choueiri, Youssef, *Islamic Fundamentalism*, Boston: Twayne Publishers, 1990.

Cooper, B., *New Political Religions, or An Analysis of Modern Terrorism*, Columbia: University of Missouri Press, 2004.

Ellis, M., *Unholy Alliance: Religion and Atrocities in Our Time*, Minneapolis: Fortress Press, 1997.

Esposito, J., *The Islamic Threat: Myth or Reality?*, NY: Oxford Univ. Press, 1999.

Hoffman, B., *Inside Terrorism*, NY: Columbia Univ. Press, 1999.

Juergensmeyer, M., *Terror in the Mind of God: The Global Rise of Religious Violence*, Berkeley: Univ. of California Press, 2001.

Lewy, G., *Religion and Revolution*, NY: Oxford Univ. Press, 1974.

Perlmutter, D., *Investigating Religious Terrorism and Ritualistic Crimes*, Boca Raton, FL: CRC Press, 2004.

Shay, S., *The Endless Jihad*, Herzliya, Israel: ICT, 2001.

Stern, J., *Terror in the Name of God: Why Religious Militants Kill*, NY: Harper Collins, 2003.

Tibi, Bassam, *The Challenge of Fundamentalism: Political Islam and the New World Disorder*, Berkeley: University of California Press, 1998.

7
Dynamics of Ethnic Terrorism

Ethnic violence also known as ethnic terrorism or ethnically-motivated terrorism refers to violence that is predominantly framed rhetorically by causes and issues related to ethnic hatred, though ethnic violence is more commonly related to political violence, and often the terms are interchangeable in a local context where reference to ethnicity is considered minimal or improper.

"Racist terrorism" is a form of ethnic violence which is typically dominated by overt forms of racism and xenophobic reactionism. This form typically involves attacks on minorities, and hold an association with right-wing extremism.

Racial supremacist groups such as Neo-Nazis often dominate the perception of an ethnic terrorist, though other violent actors associated with ethnic supremacism qualify.

"Ethnic violence" may and does also refer to violence committed by ethnic people, and not just against ethnic people.

7.1. Ethno-nationalistic Terrorism

Nationalist terrorism is mostly "traditional" terrorism (also called revolutionary or ideological terrorism), but it is also a large category of terrorism with many subtypes. For the most part, it is practiced by individuals belonging to an identifiable organisation with a well-defined command-and-control structure, clear political, social or economic objectives, and a comprehensible ideology or self-interest.

The usual targets of nationalist terrorism are usually selective and usually discriminate — ambassadors, bankers, dignitaries — symbols often blamed for an economic, political, or social injustice. They usually issue communiqués taking credit for, and explaining in great detail, their actions. Only rarely do such groups operate outside their home territory unless it is in their interest to do so or they claim to be representing the oppressed of some Third World (an outdated and archaic concept), or additionally, they belong to some diaspora.

Disapora is a term from the field of migration studies referring to the study of dispersed ethnic populations and carrying connotations of forced resettlement, expulsion, slavery, racism, war and conflict. To provide some further definitions, an ethnic group is a human population whose members identify with each other, usually on the basis of a presumed common genealogy or ancestry.

Ethnic groups are typically united by common cultural, behavioural, linguistic, or religious practices, and an important political science distinction is that an ethnic group is distinguished from a nation-state by the former's lack of sovereignty. Nationality (which is part of the root conception behind nationalism) refers to a person's legal relationship to a legal system, or set of laws which they perceive as applicable to them, although under international law, it is each nation's right to declare whom they believe their nationals are.

A person who is not a national of any state is referred to as a stateless person, many of whom are also refugees, asylum seekers, and/or sometimes present themselves as having dual citizenship (a term not allowed in some nations). Legally, nationality can only be acquired by *jus soli* (birthright), *jus sanguinis* (blood), or naturalisation (a process that is part of immigration law). Nationalism is an ideology which holds that some notion of nationality or some variant of what is often talked about in the field of "identity politics" should serve as the only legitimate basis for a nation-state. It must be remembered that in the field of terrorism studies, it is quite dangerous to talk about terrorism on the basis of nationality alone, but there are interesting things to discuss nonetheless.

Nationalism is the driving force behind a love of country so strong that one is willing to die trying to change or overthrow a government seen as corrupt and/or oppressive. It's an Enlightenment notion associated with the thought of Locke, Voltaire, Rousseau, and Montesquieu that the best form of democratic government is based on the natural desire of people to govern themselves as a distinct nation-state. It has been the underlying justification for the American Revolution, the French Revolution, the Mexican Revolution, and the Cuban Revolution.

The patriotic feeling of loyalty to one's national ties can take different forms depending upon the economic and cultural context. Most people are familiar with jingoistic nationalism where a common external enemy unites people in a war mentality. Others, especially Westerners, might be familiar with self-interest nationalism in which a presumed economic superiority permits the export of a civilisation in the name of prosperity. Militaristic nationalism tends to involve fascist or socialist movements that glorify the institutions, icons, and achievements of a state. And finally, there is ethnic nationalism which is rooted in ethnic identity as the basis for a cause. This last form has become a dominant model of terrorism in the 21st Century, and is called ethno-nationalist terrorism, or more simply, ethnoterrorism.

Ethnic identity has some unique sociological characteristics. First of all, it is egalitarian - *the identity of the masses*. Joan of Arc, for example, explained why she continually used familiar names for the French nobility by saying "After all, we're all French." Secondly, it allows a certain amount of freedom while at the same time reinforcing group solidarity. A person who says they are French-American-Canadian, for example, has a couple of second-order identities, but they are still French. Thirdly, there are no entry or exit points for ethnic identity. Nobody needs certificates or credentials to prove their ethnicity, and most people can come and go (exit the group and reenter) with relative ease. The most negative aspects of ethnicity involve stereotyping and de-individualisation. It's easier to gas the Jew, lynch the Black, or shoot the White Man than it is to understand such groups as individuals. Ethnicity also tends to find its way into public policy, no matter how fair the politicians try to be.

Nationalism, or more precisely, the concept of nation-state, was used by the great European powers to create and administer their colonies. It's easier to govern when the "people" think they're all part of a nation-state with borders. Unfortunately, it turns out in this post-colonial era that there were a diverse number of different ethnic groups within those borders. That's why scholars such as Horowitz say *ethnic conflict is nationalist conflict.* Control of *the* state, *a* state, *any* state becomes the goal of ethnic conflict. That's why nationalist terrorist groups are referred to as subnational organisations, para-states, states within a state, liberationists, separatists, or unifiers. One should never underestimate the power of such groups. They are not political parties fighting for their slice of a pie, nor are they simply elites with a grudge going back to some historical accident (they fantasise about some imagined loss instead, or in the case of the IRA, an exaggerated actual loss).

As Connor points out, such terrorists are emotional personalities with an "us-them syndrome" who are capable of the worst atrocities, up to and including genocide, because ethnonationalism is a passion or drive that goes straight to the core of an identity need to "find one's self." Ethnonationalist terrorism is less rational and comprehensible than plain, old nationalist terrorism.

One of the experts on ethno-nationalist terrorism is Daniel Byman argues that it has some built-in advantages that make it the most dangerous kind of terrorism. The following are the advantages:

— It polarises ethnic conflict and accentuates a primal fear of race war
— Well-timed and well-placed symbolic attacks reinforce the ethno-nationalist issue
— It easily provokes government over-reaction who see it as an insurgency or domestic problem
— It frequently produces government concessions which are seen as a sign of success
— It often raises money (donations) and public support quickly
— Long-standing logistical support and hiding places are easy to come by
— There is a ready-made audience or constituency (you're either in or out)
— There are no innocent bystanders (anyone not identifying with the right ethnic group is the enemy)

— Terrorised victims often cope by joining the terrorist movement
— Passivity (doing nothing) ensures escalation of the violence to genocide
— You can't trust their cease-fires, peace treaties, or statements of curtailing operations

Countering ethnoterrorism is quite difficult. Ethno-nationalists almost always hold the high ground on morality, being seen as "good patriots", so any moral outrage by a reactionary government is futile as it only reinforces group cohesion. Byman suggests that what might work is empowering the ethnic community, winning over moderates to the political system, and encouraging self-policing. This is all wishful thinking, as such measures can result in insurgency problems, fractionalisation, and escalation.

Despite the fact that most ethnoterrorism is confined to one country or theatres of operation, there have been many groups who developed an international presence. More often than not, these are Left-Wing groups, or splintered factions of Left-Wing groups, that take up the calling of oppressed people everywhere. In such cases, support is usually obtained from a sponsoring nation, but it would be a mistake to call it state-sponsored terrorism since they mostly rely upon popular support and the strength of a solid message.

It's also interesting to note that the leaders of many international terrorism groups were women. This is different from say, religious terrorism where women are more commonly used as cannon fodder, or terrorism in general, which is a male-dominated profession. How and why women achieve terrorist leadership roles are matters of speculation. Laqueur argues that they are more fanatical and have a greater capacity for suffering, but the field of criminology largely rejects this notion.

7.1.1. Pogrom

Pogrom is a form of riot directed against a particular group, whether ethnic, religious or other, and characterised by destruction of their homes, businesses and religious centres. Usually pogroms are accompanied by physical violence against the targeted people and even murder or massacre. The term has historically been used to denote extensive violence, either spontaneous or premeditated, against Jews, but has been applied to similar incidents against other, mostly minority, groups.

The term "pogrom" became commonly used in English after a large-scale wave of anti-Jewish riots swept through southwestern Imperial Russia in 1881-1884. The trigger for these pogroms was the assassination of Tsar Alexander II, for which some blamed "the Jews." The extent to which the Russian press was responsible for encouraging perceptions of the assassination as a Jewish act has been disputed.

Local economic conditions are thought to have contributed significantly to the rioting, especially with regard to the participation of the business competitors of local Jews and the participation of railroad workers, and it has been argued that this was actually more important than rumors of Jewish responsibility for the death of the Tsar. These rumors, however, were clearly of some importance, if only as a trigger, and they had a small kernel of truth: one of the close associates of the assassins, Gesya Gelfman, was indeed Jewish. The fact that the other assassins were all Christians had little impact on the spread of such Anti-Semitic rumors.

During these pogroms, which started in Elizavetgrad in April of 1881, thousands of Jewish homes were destroyed, and many families were reduced to poverty; and large numbers of men, women, and children were injured in 166 towns in the southwest provinces of the Empire (modern Ukraine). The new Tsar Alexander III initially blamed revolutionaries and the Jews themselves for the riots and issued a series of harsh restrictions on Jews. The pogroms continued for more than three years, and were thought to have benefited from at least the tacit support of the authorities, though there were also attempts on the part of the Russian government to end the rioting.

Although the pogroms claimed the lives of relatively few Jews (2 Jews were killed by the mobs, while 19 attackers were killed by tsarist authorities, the damage, disruption and disturbance were dramatic. The pogroms and the official reaction to them led many Russian Jews to reassess their perceptions of their status within the Russian Empire, and so to significant Jewish emigration, mostly to the United States. Changed perceptions among Russian Jews also indirectly gave a significant boost to the early Zionist movement.

7.1.2. Combat 18

Combat 18 (or C18) is the "armed wing" of the British neo-Nazi organisation Blood & Honour. The "18" in their name is commonly used by neo-Nazi groups, and is derived from the initials of Adolf Hitler; A and H are the first and eighth letters of the Latin alphabet.

The group was formed in the early 1990s in response to attacks by Anti-Fascist Action on meetings of the British National Party (BNP) and other far right groups. C18 soon attracted national attention for its members' violent attacks on immigrants and its left-wing opponents. In 1992, it started publishing *Redwatch* magazine, which contained photographs, names and addresses of political opponents. The later, more well-known website of the same name was set up by Simon Sheppard, who had been expelled from the BNP for a matter unrelated to the website.

Between 1998 and 2000, dozens of Combat 18 members in the UK were arrested on various charges during dawn raids by the police. These raids were part of several operations conducted by Scotland Yard in co-operation with MI5. Those arrested included Steve Sargent (brother of Charlie Sargent), David Myatt, Andrew Frain, Jason Marriner, and two serving British soldiers; Darren Theron (Parachute Regiment) and Carl Wilson (1st Battalion, The Queen's Lancashire Regiment). One of those whose house was raided was Adrian Marsden, who later became a councilor for the British National Party. Several of those arrested were later jailed, including Frain (seven years) and Marriner (six years). The number of arrests led some to believe Combat 18 was a government operation to entrap neo-Nazis.

A group calling itself the Racial Volunteer Force split from C18 in 2002, although they have retained close links to their parent organisation. Some journalists believed that the White Wolves were also a C18 splinter group. They alleged that the group had been set up by Del O'Connor, the former second-in-command of C18 and member of Skrewdriver Security.

7.1.3. Black Panther Party

The Black Panther Party was an African American organisation founded to promote civil rights and self-defense. It was active within the United States in the late 1960s into the 1970s. Founded in Oakland, California, by Huey P. Newton and Bobby Seale in October 1966, the organisation initially espoused a doctrine calling for armed resistance to societal oppression in the interest of African American justice, though its objectives and philosophy changed radically throughout the party's existence. While the organisation's leaders passionately espoused socialist doctrine, the party's black nationalist reputation attracted an ideologically diverse membership base. Ideological consensus within the party was difficult to achieve, and some members openly disagreed with the views of the leaders.

The group was founded on the principles of its Ten-Point Program, a document that called for "Land, Bread, Housing, Education, Clothing, Justice And Peace," as well as exemption from military service that would utilise African Americans to "fight and kill other people of color in the world who, like Black people, are being victimised by the White racist government of America."

While firmly grounded in black nationalism and begun as an organisation that accepted African American membership exclusively, the party reconsidered itself as it grew to national prominence and became an iconic representative of the counterculture of the 1960s. The Black Panthers ultimately condemned black nationalism as "black racism" and became more focused on socialism without racial exclusivity. They instituted a variety of community programs to alleviate poverty and illness among the communities it deemed most needful of aid. While the party retained its all-black membership, it recognised that different communities needed to organise around their own set of issues and encouraged alliances with these organisations.

The group's political goals are often overshadowed by their confrontational and even militaristic tactics, and by their suspicious regard of law enforcement agents; whom the Black Panthers perceived as a linchpin of oppression that could only be overcome by a willingness to take up armed self-defense. The Black Panther Party collapsed in the early 1970s, after party membership had started to decline during Huey Newton's 1968 manslaughter trial. There have been a variety of allegations about the lengths to which law enforcement officials went in their attempts to discredit and destroy the organisation; including allegations of assassination.

7.1.4. Ku Klux Klan

Ku Klux Klan (KKK) is the name of several past and present organisations in the United States that have advocated white supremacy, anti-Semitism, anti-Catholicism, racism, homophobia, anti-Communism and nativism. These organisations have often used terrorism, violence, and acts of intimidation, such as cross burning and lynching, to oppress African Americans and other social or ethnic groups.

The Klan's first incarnation was in 1866. Founded by veterans of the Confederate Army, its main purpose was to resist Reconstruction, and it focused as much on intimidating "carpetbaggers" and "scalawags" as on putting down the freed slaves. The KKK quickly adopted violent methods. A rapid reaction set in, with the Klan's leadership disowning violence and Southern elites seeing the Klan as an excuse for federal troops to continue their activities in the South. The organisation was in decline from 1868 to 1870 and was destroyed in the early 1870s by President Ulysses S. Grant's vigorous action under the Civil Rights Act of 1871 (also known as the Ku Klux Klan Act).

The name "Ku Klux Klan" has since been used by many different unrelated groups, including many who opposed the Civil Rights Act and desegregation in the 1950s and 1960s, with members of these groups eventually being convicted of murder and manslaughter in the deaths of civil rights workers and children. he modern KKK has been repudiated by all mainstream media, political and religious leaders.

REFERENCES

Binder, Leonard, *Ethnic Conflict and International Politics in the Middle East*, University Press of Florida. 1999.

Byman, Daniel, "The logic of ethnic terrorism", *Studies in Conflict and Terrorism*, 1998.

Carr, Caleb, "Terrorism as warfare: the lessons of military history", *World Policy Journal*, 1996.

Fox, Jonathan, "Do religious institutions support violence or the status quo?", *Studies in Conflict and Terrorism*, 1999.

Medhurst, Paul, *Global Terrorism*, United Nations Institute for Training and Research, New York: NY, 2000.

Smith, Jonathan B., *Colonialism - A Catalyst for Ethnic Terrorism*, March 6, 2005.

Volkan Vamik D., *Bloodlines: From Ethnic Pride to Ethnic Terrorism*, January 1999.

8
Democracy and Terrorism

Terrorism poses unique challenges to in the liberal democratic state. If liberal democracies take police state-like action in response to terrorism, then arguably the terrorists have achieved their ends. If societies must condone such policies, then those societies of the cooperating states must reach a minimal level of consensus of how to view justice, human rights, rule of law, civil liberties, etc; the operating level of these traits in a society describes a society's political culture.

The challenge of terrorism to liberal democracies must be analysed in a strategic context; it is not just an ancillary concern to security professionals. This is not an easy task, for as Ted Sorenson once remarked: "The touchstone of our nation's security concept – the containment of Soviet military and ideological power is gone. The primary threat cited over forty years in justification for most of our military budget, bases, and overseas assistance is gone. The principal prism through which we viewed most of our world-wide diplomatic activities and alliances has gone."

Many scholars argue that globalisation is the dominating force, while others claim that localisation or fragmentation dominates. The term, "globalisation" is a frequently used term that is cast in a variety of contexts, and, consequently, it has come to mean many different things to many different people. It has taken on the best of all possible meanings for some, and for others it is the epitome of all evil and inequity. Globalisation is a dynamic process that has potential for both good and bad, democratic and non-democratic, and security enhancing and security detracting.

James Rosenau differentiates between globalism as a world system that embraces universal values and globalisation as a process that describes forces in every sphere of human and environmental activity that transcends borders. He further distinguishes between globalisation and localisation: "In short, globalisation is boundary-broadening and localisation is boundary-heightening." He describes the combination of these forces as "fragmegration." Moreover, he argues that eventually the forces of globalisation will dominate.

According to Donald Hanle, "Terrorism is called terrorism because it violates the normative values of the target entity regarding the employment of lethal force." Philip B. Heymann illustrates the subjectivity of this term by reviewing several countries' definitions: According to the Office for the Protection of the Constitution, Germany's internal security agency, terrorism is the, "enduringly conducted struggle for political goals, which are intended to be achieved by means of assaults on the life and property of other persons, especially by means of severe crimes [such as murder, kidnapping, arson]." Britain's "Prevention of Terrorism Act" of 1974 defines terrorism as "the use of violence for political ends, and includes any use of violence for the purpose of putting the public or any section of the public in fear." The U.S. State Department views terrorism as any violent act conducted for political purposes by substate actors or "secret state agents" against normally noncombatants with the goal of influencing an audience.

U.S. laws defines a terrorist act as criminal violence that "appears to be intended (i) to intimidate or coerce a civilian population; (ii) to influence the policy of a government by intimidation or coercion; or (iii) to affect the conduct of a government by assassination or kidnapping." And according to a group of European Interior Ministers coordinating their efforts concerning the challenges of terrorism, they state: "Terrorism is..the use, or the threatened use, by a cohesive group of persons of violence (short of warfare) to affect political aims."

Paul Wilkinson views terrorism as a means to a political end:

> ..the systematic and premeditated use of violence to create a climate of fear for political purposes. Second, it is violence directed at a wider audience—a wider target—than the immediate victim of the violence. Third, as a consequence of this wider targeting, it inevitably involves random and

symbolic targets that include civilians. Fourth, it involves extra-normal means in quite a literal sense, which is to say, a deliberate violation of the norms of society regarding conflicts and disputes and political behaviour to create the impact of fear and the exploitation of that fear for the terrorists' ends.

For Peter Chalk, terrorism's aim is to upset the societal *status quo*. Its destructive acts are designed to attain "..the long-term objective of gradually removing the structural supports which ultimately give society its strength." Cindy Combs describes terrorism as a "synthesis of war and theatre, a dramatisation of the most proscribed kind of violence—that which is perpetrated on innocent victims—played before an audience in the hope of creating a mood of fear, for political purposes."

Bajhlit Singh sums up terrorism as a "threat or use of symbolic violent acts aimed at influencing political behaviour." The terrorist acts are conducted outside normal political bounds, involving symbolic violence usually perpetrated against innocent victims in order to weaken the bonds between the legitimate government and society.

The significant trends are the accessibility of information, accessibility of weapons of mass destruction, and democratisation. First, the accessibility of information has reduced the power of the nation-state, increased the availability of non-state sponsors of terrorism, introduced cyber-tools to terrorist tactics, and enhanced networking for terrorist strategies. Information accessibility disrupts hierarchies because it facilitates communication and coordination, functions that tend to flatten hierarchical structures. John Arquilla and David Ronfeldt describe such information networks and the challenge they pose to nation-states as netwar. Networks favour autonomy, flexibility, and adaptability, and they challenge traditional jurisdictional lines of responsibility.

Moreover, terrorists can quickly diminish users' perceptions of the integrity of the Internet. Attacks on the Internet may reduce states' ability to protect Internet commerce. While the terrorist use of the Internet for communication and propaganda is not revolutionary, its "global immediacy" is. Lorenzo Valeri and Michael Knights categorise the convergence of terrorism and the

Internet as Offensive Information Warfare, which they define as a: "..set of activities carried out by individuals and/or groups with specific political and strategic objectives, aimed at the integrity, availability and confidentiality of the data collected, stored and transferred inside information systems connected to the Internet." Clearly, states that rely heavily on information are extremely vulnerable to this terrorist method of attack. Moreover, the non-state, network organisation, and transnational nature of these terrorists complicate their identification and subsequent apprehension. It is evident that states cannot combat terrorism alone; international cooperation is paramount.

Second, the availability of weapons of mass destruction to terrorists is another trend that states must consider. Ashton Carter, John Deutch, and Philip Zelikow argue that "The danger of weapons of mass destruction being used against America and its allies is greater now than at any time since the Cuban Missile crisis of 1962." They propose a reorganisation of U.S. domestic agencies to deal with "catastrophic terrorism," and, moreover, they propose to universally criminalise the development of prohibited WMD. The universal nature of this law would allow "..the power of national criminal law to be used against people, rather than the power of international law against governments."

Robert Bunker introduces the idea of weapons of mass disruption, which not only target things, but also societal and political bonds. He establishes two criteria of such weapons: a threshold of effect based on a weapon's expansive properties that enable it to effect a massive area and an ability to affect "bonds and relationships." For example, he discusses biological weapons as weapons of mass disruption because "..their employment would also degrade and alter the bonds-relationship within a society, as would nuclear weapons.

Examples of such degradation include the loss of confidence in governmental competency and heightened perceptions of insecurity (literally terror) by citizens who would now view themselves in imminent danger." Accessibility of these weapons that have the potential for enormous destruction and disruption compels international coordination among states as a means to reduce accessibility to such weaponry.

Security professionals must address the global trend of democratisation and the unique challenge liberal democracies face with combating terrorism. States that are transitioning to democratic regimes are vulnerable to internal conflict that terrorists can exploit. Essentially, these transitioning states are replicating the early stages of state-making. Different power centers are competing for supremacy, which can easily erupt into conflict. According to Larry Diamond, "..elections are only one dimension of democracy. The quality of democracy also depends on its levels of freedom, pluralism, justice and accountability." He continues to explain liberal democracy as having the following conditions:

Freedom of belief, expression, organisation, demonstration, and other civil liberties, including protection from political terror and unjustified imprisonment; a rule of law under which all citizens are treated equally and due process is secure; political independence and neutrality of the judiciary and other institutions of "horizontal accountability" that check the abuse of power, such as electoral administration, audits, and a central bank; an open and pluralistic civil society, including not only associational life but the mass media as well; and civilian control of the military.

Democratic political culture fosters these traits of civil liberties, rule of law, civil society, and civilian control of the military, all of which are necessary to a liberal democracy. Francis Fukuyama claims that it is not the mere existence of democratic institutions that will secure the fate of transitioning democracies; rather, it will be in the critical realms of civil society and culture that will determine successful transitions. In fact, a number of studies indicate that even with the rise of electoral democracies, freedoms world-wide have decreased. The connection between democracy and liberty is not linear, and culture seems to be a critical intervening variable.

Samuel Huntington calls for policies that emphasise the liberalisation of electoral democracies. Mature democracies face a similar challenge when dealing with terrorism, and political culture stands out again. While the definitions of terrorism may differ, there seems to be a consensus concerning the imperative of society's support in its state's counter and anti-terrorist policies.

This consensus is important on several levels. First mature, liberal democracies cannot undermine their own values by imposing police-state like policies as a means of addressing terrorism. Grant Wardlaw warns that "The danger lies in the possibility of doing the terrorists' job for them by taking unnecessary steps in an attempt to counter the perceived threat and thereby fundamentally altering the nature of democracy."

8.1. Political Culture and Legitimacy

Inherent in the concept of political culture is the idea of a political community that describes a society's loyalties towards the political system. These concepts—political culture, legitimacy, and political community—are intricately interwoven, but because of their amorphous nature, they do not always receive the critical analysis necessary to understand political behaviour. These foundational concepts and then fold them back together to better understand how liberal democracies can best ward off threats that target their inner souls. This inner soul is the state's legitimacy. According to Max Weber, "If the state is to exist, the dominated must obey the authority claimed by the powers that be. Ralf Dahrendorf explains legitimacy and effectiveness as two keys to a state's stability. He argues that for governments to work ...two things have to be present: effectiveness and legitimacy. Effectiveness is a technical concept. It simply means that governments have to be able to do things which they claim they can do...they have to work. Legitimacy, on the other hand, is a moral concept. It means that what governments do has to be right....A government is legitimate if what it does is right both in the sense of complying with certain fundamental principles, and in that of being in line with prevailing cultural values.

Moreover, these two concepts are asymmetrically related. Governments, such as totalitarian regimes, may be effective without being legitimate. However, "Over time, ineffectiveness will probably erode legitimacy." Dahrendorf is most concerned about the erosion of legitimacy because for democracies "...there is a great danger that the response to a crisis of legitimacy will be authoritarianism and illiberty."

Augustus Norton agrees that the most important element for state survival is legitimacy, meaning "that authority which rests on the shared cultural identity of ruler and ruled." States base legitimacy on a "political formula" which justifies a leader's rule.

As Gaetano Mosca notes, political formulas are not 'mere quakeries aptly invented to trick the masses into obedience....The truth is that they answer a real need in man's social nature; and this need, so universally felt, of governing and knowing that one is governed not on the basis of mere material or intellectual force, but on the basis of moral principle, has...a practical and a real importance.

When legitimacy dissolves, the regime is vulnerable to change. Timothy J. Lomperis argues that "..a state can rule without legitimacy, but not well." Ted Robert Gurr and Muriel McClelland stress the importance of societal attitudes for legitimacy. They define legitimacy as "the extent that a polity is regarded by its members as worthy of support. This is not the same as citizens' compliance with laws and directives, but refers to a basic attitude that disposes them to comply in most circumstances...".

Along with this idea of an attitude towards the political system is the idea of a political community or identity. David Easton refers to the political community as a "domain of support" for the political system. Michael C. Hudson links the idea of community with legitimacy: "If the population within given political boundaries is so deeply divided within itself on ethnic or class lines...then it is extremely difficult to develop a legitimate order." Furthermore, this "legitimate order requires a distinct sense of corporate self-hood: the people within a territory must feel a sense of political community...".

These ideas of a political community and attitude towards the political system describe the concept of political culture. In fact Robert Dahl's work on political opposition groups helped reveal political culture based on a society's attitudinal orientations towards problem solving, the political system, cooperation and individuality, and people. Interestingly, even among democracies, political cultures differ. For example, citizens of Italy and France have been described as having alienated or apathetic attitudes towards their political systems; West German citizens exhibited detached attitudes; and citizens of the United States and Great Britain tended to have an allegiant orientation towards their political systems.

A civic culture, that is a democratic political culture, describes a culture in which people feel that they make a difference politically; they tolerate others; they trust their fellow citizen and political elites; and they have allegiance towards the political system. A liberal, democratic culture is the essence of democracy; it provides legitimacy for the democratic regime, making it the terrorist's bull's-eye.

8.2. Democracy in the Muslim World

Democracy building remains an uphill battle in most Muslim countries, asserted Kubba. Progress in liberalising society, modernising institutions, and developing infrastructure is slow and limited. In Kubba's view, the key to understanding the democracy predicament in Muslim countries does not lie in the texts or in the traditions of Islam but in the context of society, politics, and culture. In short, the basic problem is not about religion but about modernity. Noting that many Muslim states are stuck in a dysfunctional "deadlock" of corruption and repression, Kubba warned that apathy and despair breed radicalism.

According to recent study, "In the minds of nearly one billion Muslims who practice some form of democracy around the globe, there is no dispute between Islam and democracy." Pointing to the role that Muslims play in civil society in countries from the United States to Pakistan, study indicated that the international community is not confronted by a "clash of civilisations" or a clash of Islam versus democracy, but rather a "clash of myths." These myths are advanced by Islamists and Western ideologues alike. The greatest threats to human rights in the Muslim world, are not religious or theological but political.

To counter these myths, study stressed the importance of further examining three issues:

— The Koranic principle of Shura, a consultative decision-making process encouraged by the Koran, and its commonalities and differences with basic precepts of western democratic theory;

— The false dichotomy whereby the rule of law in a democratic state ("law of man") is portrayed as being inherently in conflict with the Sharia or Islamic law ("law of god"); and

— Democratic institutions and practices from ancient and modern Muslim history, such as the Loya Jirga in Afghanistan or the Constitution of Medina, that may provide useful lessons on how democratic principles can be woven effectively into a modern Islamic society.

8.3. Terrorism and the Rule of Law

On 11 September 2001 history of the sudden and unexpected kind was made. We all know what happened. It is one of those days in our lives when we will always remember where we were when we heard the news.

Of course, explosive attacks on civil society are not new, even in recent history. The Atlanta Olympics and Oklahoma City come to mind. There were Nairobi and Tanzania in 1998. There have been decades of attacks in Northern Ireland and England, in Israel and Palestine. And then we had Bali on 12 October 2002; Kenya again; Riyadh; Chechnya; Casablanca – and the list (unfortunately) continues to grow. Terrorism was well known before 11 September 2001 – and it has continued.

Conduct of this kind is criminal in nature. Often the perpetrators die; but there is no shortage of appropriate offences or of legal avenues for the prosecution of the survivors. The normal response of the lawful authorities is to investigate, identify suspects, prosecute and punish. Those events were also criminal – trans-national crime of a shocking kind. Some offenders remained alive; but the criminal justice response does not seem to have been given priority by those in power in the USA and in many states around the world.

Instead of following the criminal justice path, the war paradigm was invoked – the war on terrorism– and it has continued. It is, however, difficult to control and direct. As will be seen, it has enabled the rule of law to be bypassed in a number of respects. By definition, such a war may have no end and the measures introduced along the way may be with us forever. Although war was declared on an abstract noun, real places and real people were attacked, including sovereign states. On the military front Afghanistan was overcome and a new government installed; Iraq was later invaded and occupied.

Democracy, human rights, the rule of law: three expressions that sit together like air, earth and water. They are elemental for all right-thinking people. They are inter-dependant. As Lord Woolf, Lord Chief Justice of England and Wales, has said: "Human rights come with democracy, whether the government wants them or not".

Democracy is a given. Human rights come with it and in the words of the Vienna Declaration of 1993 they are universal, indivisible, interdependent and interrelated and should be promoted in a fair and equitable manner.

Democracy and human rights cannot be enjoyed without the rule of law. The Preamble to the Universal Declaration of Human Rights (1948) states that:

> "it is essential, if man is not to be compelled to have recourse, as a last resort, to rebellion against tyranny and oppression, that human rights should be protected by the rule of law."

So what is the rule of law? How does it operate? Why is it important? How may it protect human rights?

It does not mean:

— rule by law: that is, so long as there is a law on the subject the rule of law is operating;
— the law of the ruler;
— "law and order";
— the law of rules; or even
— the rule of the lawyer.

A clue to its meaning would be given by the addition of one word to the phrase: "the just rule of law". Justice requires the importation of principles that arise under other labels, such as peace, freedom, democracy and fairness. Such principles are echoed in the rule of law.

There are two principal features of the rule of law.

— The people (including the government) should be ruled by the law and obey it.
— The law should be such that the people will be able and willing to be ruled (or guided) by it.

From those features commentators have deduced 12 more particular requirements to be met before it can be said that the rule of law is truly in operation.

1. There must be laws prohibiting and protecting against private violence and coercion, general lawlessness and anarchy.
2. The government must be bound (as far as possible) by the same laws that bind the individual.
3. The law must possess characteristics of certainty, generality and equality. Certainty requires that the law be prospective, open, clear and relatively stable. Laws must be of general application to all subjects. They must apply equally to all.
4. The law must be and remain reasonably in accordance with informed public opinion and general social values and there must be some mechanism (formal or informal) for ensuring that.
5. There must be institutions and procedures that are capable of speedily enforcing the law.
6. There must be effective procedures and institutions to ensure that government action is also in accordance with the law.
7. There must be an independent judiciary, so that it may be relied upon to apply the law.
8. A system of legal representation is required, preferably by an organised and independent legal profession.
9. The principles of "natural justice" (or procedural fairness) must be observed in all hearings.
10. The courts must be accessible, without long delays and high costs.
11. Enforcement of the law must be impartial and honest.
12. There must be an enlightened public opinion – a public spirit or attitude favouring the application of these propositions.

If all these features exist in large part, the climate will exist for the protection and enforcement of human rights – those rights that are enjoyed by humans simply because they are human beings. Those rights are to be found in the great international instruments accepted by the community of nations. That climate will be one of acceptance, observance and incorporation into domestic law of those international standards and their enforcement in everyday life. Those 12 features also provide the internal mechanisms for that enforcement.

An enlightened citizenry might well demand of its leaders measured and lawful responses to common threats. Emergencies pass – urgent, short term measures must be dismantled and longer term responses must be found that are unobjectionable in principle. The world has responded in that way to many great challenges. There is a long history of legal responses to large scale or particularly serious international criminality, extending back at least to the 15th Century in Germany. In the early 1900s Americans were tried for offences in the nature of war crimes committed in the Philippines. In 1921 twelve German soldiers were tried for crimes committed in Leipzig. And so it went until the largest breakthroughs after the Second World War with the Nuremberg trials and the Tokyo trials.

In modern times we have had the International Tribunals for the former Yugoslavia and for Rwanda (where hundreds of thousands were killed). We have had the very successful Lockerbie trial, a collaborative effort between a number of states. And now we have the International Criminal Court – arguably the single most important development in international criminal justice in a hundred years.

There are also proceedings for crimes against humanity in tribunals in East Timor. A special, hybrid court has been set up in Sierra Leone with collaboration between the government and the UN – an imaginative model. Trials may be held in Cambodia of former Khmer Rouge.

During World War II the US Attorney General, Francis Biddle, said: "The Constitution has not greatly bothered any wartime President". Is this the case now?

Francis Biddle's statement is to be contrasted with that of Justice Breyer of the US Supreme Court, speaking to the Association of the Bar of the City of New York on 14 April this year, when he said: "The Constitution always matters, perhaps particularly so in times of emergency." He said that by searching for alternative methods that avoid "constitutional mistakes" lawyers, judges and security officials help the government avoid extreme positions (at both ends of the spectrum): that the Constitution does not matter or that security emergencies do not matter.

In 1962, however, Earl Warren, then Chief Justice of the US, wrote in the New York University Law Review that courts are unreliable in time of war or emergency and that "other agencies of government must bear the primary responsibility for determining whether specific actions they are taking are consonant with our Constitution." In a democracy, he wrote, "it is still the legislature and the elected executive who have the primary responsibility for fashioning and executing policy consistent with the Constitution... the day-to-day job of upholding the Constitution really lies elsewhere. It rests, realistically, on the shoulders of every citizen". Those statements are entirely in accord with our understanding of the nature of the rule of law; but they devalue the role of the courts in maintaining it.

In his declaration of war on terrorism President Bush spoke of "bringing the perpetrators to justice". However, it appears to be a special kind of justice. One cannot help wondering what the response would have been if the perpetrators of 11 September 2001 had all come from within western states, rather than from the shelter of the Taliban in Afghanistan and from other countries of inferior power, particularly in the Middle East.

Another consequence of adopting the war paradigm is the effect on the web of relations between states and the international mechanisms that bring them together, such as the UN.

There has indeed been much activity internationally. On 12 September 2001, the very day after the New York and Washington attacks, the UN Security Council adopted Resolution 1368. Among other things, it "Calls on all States to work together urgently to bring to justice the perpetrators, organisers and sponsors of these terrorist attacks and stresses that those responsible for aiding, supporting or harbouring the perpetrators, organisers and sponsors of these acts will be held accountable".

On 28 September 2001 Resolution 1373 was adopted. It mandated that all states shall prevent and suppress the financing of terrorist acts by various prescribed means, deny support to terrorists and take other quite specific and detailed measures to suppress and combat terrorism. The Resolution placed a heavy legal and administrative burden on all states, an obligation that the vast majority of smaller and less developed states (and some wealthy developed states) are still struggling to discharge.

These measures were followed in due course by Resolution 1456 of 20 January 2003 which reinforced the earlier resolutions. It contains two paragraphs of particular relevance to the place of laws and legal systems in the response to terrorism:

> "States must bring to justice those who finance, plan, support or commit terrorist acts or provide safe havens, in accordance with international law, in particular on the basis of the principle to extradite or prosecute...

States must ensure that any measure taken to combat terrorism complies with all their obligations under international law, and should adopt such measures in accordance with international law, in particular international human rights, refugee, and humanitarian law".

The Council of Europe (now of 45 nations) in its Common Position of 27 December 2001 defined a "terrorist act". It is but one of the attempts made around the world to define terrorism. It is capable of embracing state-sponsored terrorism, even that committed in the course of a "war on terrorism". Perhaps for fear of that happening, and for other unspecified fears held for US servicemen abroad, the USA has pursued misplaced and unfortunate opposition to the International Criminal Court. It is coercing states (at the latest US count, 44 who are prepared to admit to it and seven who are not) to exclude the Court's jurisdiction over Americans in those places. These are called "Article 98 agreements".

On 24 January 2002 the Assembly of the Council of Europe adopted Resolution 1271. It states the need to "take stock" of the means to combat terrorism and paragraph 5 states, significantly, that "The combat against terrorism must be carried out in compliance with national and international law and respecting human rights". It calls on all member states to take various specific steps to assist in the prevention and suppression of terrorism.

The 12th point made above in relation to the rule of law was reinforced by Justice Potter Stewart of the US Supreme Court, when in 1971 the Court ruled on an application by the Nixon administration to prevent the New York Times from publishing Pentagon papers about the history and origins of the Vietnam War (what the Vietnamese call the "American War"). He addressed the role of the press on national security issues, noting that on those matters the usual legislative and judicial checks on executive power scarcely operate – Congress and the courts defer to the President. In an echo of Earl Warren nine years before, he said: "The only effective restraint upon executive policy and power in the areas of national defence and international affairs may lie in an enlightened citizenry". However, in the absence of an enlightened citizenry, an informed and enlightened public opinion, the rule of law may be corrupted.

8.3.1. Ignoring the Rule of Law

When the rule of law is cast aside anywhere, we all have reason for concern. Legislation has been passed in many countries that seriously interferes with the previously accepted rights of the citizenry; but action has also been taken that does not seem to require legislation.

In accordance with the Third Geneva Convention of 1949, the expression "enemy combatant" encompasses lawful and unlawful combatants, each of which is subject to capture and detention for the duration of a conflict. They are to be treated differently, however. Lawful combatants become prisoners of war and subject to the internationally recognised protections (such as keeping personal effects, corresponding with people outside detention, practising religion, having living conditions equivalent to the armed forces of the detaining power). Unlawful combatants, however, do not have these protections and, in accordance with *Ex parte Quirin*, may be *"subject to trial and punishment by military tribunals for acts which render their belligerency unlawful"*. It would seem to be towards unlawful combatants that the present designation "enemy combatant" is directed.

The *Quirin* case, however, does not stand for the proposition that any detainees may be held incommunicado and denied access to counsel. In that case the defendants, unlawful enemy combatants, had counsel, were put on trial within weeks of capture and, patently, were able to appeal to the US Supreme Court.

REFERENCES

Baljit Singh, "An Overview," in *Terrorism: An Interdisciplinary Perspective*, ed. Yonah Alexander and Seymour Maxwell Finger, New York: John Jay Press, 1977.

Chris Dishman, "Review Article: Trends in Modern Terrorism," *Studies in Conflict and Terrorism*, vol 22, 4, 1999.

Cindy Combs, *Terrorism in the 21st Century*, Upper Saddle River, New Jersey: Prentice Hall, 1997.

David A. Charters, "Conclusion," in *The Deadly Sin of Terrorism: Its Effect on Democracy and Civil Liberty in Six Countries*, ed. David A. Charters, Westport, Conn: Greenwood Press, 1994.

Francis Fukuyama, "The Primacy of Culture," *Journal of Democracy*, vol 6, no. 1, 1995.

Michael Brown, "Introduction," ed. *The International Dimensions of Internal Conflict*, Cambridge: The MIT Press, 1996.

Paul Wilkinson, "Freedom and Terrorism," in *Terrorism: Roots, Impact, Responses*, ed. Lance Howard, New York: Praeger, 1992.

Peter Chalk, *West European Terrorism and Counter-Terrorism: The Evolving Dynamic*, New York: St. Martin's Press, 1996.

Philip B. Heymann, *Terrorism and America: A Commonsense Strategy for a Democratic Society*, Cambridge, MA: The MIT Press, 1998.

Robert Cooper, "Integration and Disintegration," *Journal of Democracy*, 10.1, 1999.

Russell Bova, "Democracy and Liberty: The Cultural Connection," *Journal of Democracy*, vol 8, no 1, 1997.

Samuel P. Huntington, "After Twenty Years: The Future of the Third Wave," *Journal of Democracy*, vol. 8, no. 4, October 1997.

9
Psychology of Terrorists

Violence is "caused" by a complex interaction of biological, social/contextual, cognitive, and emotional factors that occur over time. Some causes will be more prominent than others for certain individuals and for certain types of violence and aggression. Most violence can be usefully viewed as intentional. It is chosen as a strategy of action. It is purposeful (goal-directed) and intended to achieve some valued outcome for the actor. It is not the product of innate, instinctual drives, nor is it the inevitable consequence of predetermining psychological and social forces. Obviously, many factors influence that decision and the competing options available, but humans typically are not passive vessels for involuntary displays of behaviour. Certainly, there are exceptions. One can conceive of circumstances where an individual might have some brain dysfunction that causes general disinhibition and/or emotional instability that may result in aggression or violence. This would be inconsistent, though, with the kind of organisation and planning necessary to carry out a terrorist attack.

9.1. Theoretical Approach

In reviewing explanatory theories and empirical models, it is perhaps not surprising to learn that the discipline of psychology has yet to develop or discover (much less agree upon) any that substantially explain violent behaviour, particularly across its many contexts, motivations and actors. The problem is not that researchers, scholars and practitioners have not tried to locate such an explanation, but the "holy grail" has proved to be elusive. In fact, it is probably fair to say that psychological theoretical development in explaining violence has been given less attention, and has made less progress than in many behavioural realms of substantially lesser social importance or consequence.

The following are some of the main psychological theories that have been applied to understanding violence:

9.1.1. Instinct Theory

Psychoanalytic: "The most widely recognised theory that addresses the roots of all forms of violence is the psychoanalytic model. Despite its influence on writers in the political science, sociology, history, and criminology literature, this model has weak logical, theoretical, and empirical foundations". Freud viewed aggression more generally as an innate and instinctual human trait, which most should outgrow in the normal course of human development.

A later development in Freud's theory was that humans had the energy of life force (eros) and death force (thanatos) that sought internal balance. Violence was seen as the "displacement" of thanatos from self and onto others. A number of more narrow violence-related theories have drawn on psychoanalytic concepts and ideas, but none are widely regarded as psychoanalytic theories of violence.

Ethology: Ethology has been alternately defined as the scientific study of animal behaviour, especially as it occurs in a natural environment and as the study of human ethos, and its formation. Ethologist, Konrad Lorenz advanced the notion that aggression arises from a very basic biological need—a "fighting instinct" that has had adaptive value as humans have evolved. He argued the drive from aggression is innate and that, in humans, only its mode of expression is learned through exposure to, and interaction with the environment. The theory of an instinctual drive for aggression suggests that it builds up over time, is fuelled by emotional or psychophysiological arousal, and is subsequently discharged by a process of catharsis, which ostensibly decreases drive. Empirical research, including physiologic studies, however, do not support this "hydraulic" (building until discharge, then receding) theory of aggressive energy. Moreover, anthropologists and other social scientists have found significant differences both in the nature and level of aggression in different cultures, and experimental research has demonstrated that aggression can be environmentally manipulated; both findings that argue against a universal human instinct.

9.1.2. Drive Theory (Frustration-Aggression)

The link between frustration (being prevented from attaining a goal or engaging in behaviour) and aggression has been discussed in psychology for more than half a century. Some even view it as a "master explanation" for understanding the cause of human violence. The basic premise of the frustration-aggression (FA) hypothesis is twofold:

i) Aggression is always produced by frustration, and

ii) Frustration always produces aggression.

When subjected to empirical scrutiny, however, research has shown that frustration does not inevitably lead to aggression. Sometimes, for example, it results in problem solving or dependent behaviours. And aggression is known to occur even in the absence of frustration. Thus it is not reasonable to view frustration alone as a necessary and sufficient causal factor. In an important reformulation of the FA hypothesis, Berkowitz posited that it was only "aversive" frustration that would lead to aggression.

The newly proposed progression was that frustration would lead to anger, and that anger—in the presence of aggressive cues—would lead to aggression. While subsequent research findings have, at times, been inconsistent or contradictory, "it is reasonable to conclude that aversive stimuli do facilitate, but probably not instigate, aggressive behaviour". In a now classic work, Ted Gurr was among the first to apply a systematic FA analysis to the problem of political violence, framing the frustration as one of "relative deprivation".

9.1.3. Social Learning Theory

Fundamental learning theory suggests that behavioural patterns are acquired by links (contingencies) established between the behaviour and its consequences. When behaviour is followed by desired results (reward), that behaviour is "reinforced" (made more likely). Conversely, when behaviour is followed by undesirable or aversive consequence, that behaviour is "punished" (made less likely). Social learning theory is a simple extension of this basic idea, suggesting that behaviour (e.g., aggression) is learned not only through one's direct experience, but also through observation of how such contingencies occur in one's environment. Some have referred to this as vicarious learning. In this model, aggression is viewed as learned behaviour. Accordingly, it is argued that through observation we learn consequences for the behaviour, how to do it, to whom it should be directed, what provocation justifies it, and when it is appropriate. "If aggression is a learned behaviour, then terrorism, a specific type of aggressive behaviour, can also be learned".

9.1.4. Cognitive Theory

The core elements in a "cognitive theory" of aggression derive from an area of study called "social cognition." The basic notion is that people interact with their environment based on how they perceive and interpret it. That is, people form an internal (cognitive) map of their external (social) environment, and these perceptions—rather than an objective external reality—determine their behaviour. Moreover, there are internal and external factors that can affect one's perceptions of provocation or intent. Two common cognitive/processing deficits found among people who are highly aggressive are: (1) an inability to generate non-aggressive solutions to conflicts (and lack of confidence in their ability to use them successfully) and (2) a perceptual hypersensitivity to hostile/aggressive cues in the environment, particularly interpersonal cues.

Crenshaw suggests that the principles of social cognition apply both to terrorists and to their organisations. She notes "the actions of terrorists are based on a subjective interpretation of the world rather than objective reality. Perceptions of the political and social environment are filtered through beliefs and attitudes that reflect experiences and memories".

9.2. Biological Approaches

Consideration of biological factors affecting aggression does not constitute a theory, in any formal sense. Nevertheless they are an important element in a comprehensive biopsychosocial understanding of behaviour. Oots and Wiegele argue that "social scientists who seek to understand terrorism should take account of the possibility that biological or physiological variables may play a role in bringing an individual to the point of performing an act of terrorism". Yet, it is rare that any biological studies are conducted on terrorists. One notable exception is an early finding by psychiatrist David Hubbard that a substantial portion of the terrorists he examined clinically suffered from some form of inner-ear problems or "vestibular dysfunction."

Neurochemical factors: Serotonin (5-HT), of all neurotransmitters in the mammalian brain, has received the most research attention and has shown the most consistent association with aggressive behaviour. Lower levels of serotonin have been linked to higher levels of aggression in normal, clinical, and offender samples. The association between 5-HT deficits and aggression seem to be specific to (or at least principally affect) impulsive, rather than premeditated aggressive behaviour, which also appears to be mediated by perceived threat or provocation. Low levels of 5-HT may heighten one's sensitivity or reactivity to cues of hostility or provocation. "In the absence of provocative stimuli, decreased 5HT functioning may have little effect on the level of aggressive behaviour exhibited by humans. Because Serotonin is primarily an inhibitory neurotransmitter, it is possible that deficits in 5-HT reduce inhibition of aggressive ideas/ impulses that would otherwise be suppressed—there is not real evidence that it creates them.

Hormonal factors: The effects of androgens / gonadotropic hormones on human behaviour—particularly aggressive behaviour—are weaker and more complex than one might expect. There is not good empirical evidence to support "testosterone poisoning" as a cause of disproportionate violence in males. Testosterone has—at best—a limited role. A meta-analysis of the relationship between testosterone and scores on the Buss-Durkee Hostility Inventory showed a "low but positive relationship between T levels and the overall inventory score of 230 males tested over five studies".

Psychophysiological Factors: Lower than average levels of arousal (e.g., low resting heart rate) and low reactivity are consistently found in studies of people who engage in aggressive and antisocial behaviour.

Neuropsychological Factors: Cognitive abilities relating to selfawareness and self-control are referred to as "executive functions." The frontal lobe of the brain, and the prefrontal cortex in particular, has been identified as the primary neuroanatomic site of these functions. "Evidence of the relation between executive deficits and aggression has been found among incarcerated subjects, among normal subjects in laboratory situations, and among nonselected populations. Effect sizes are small to moderate, but consistent and robust. Theoretical and empirical evidence suggests that dysfunction or impairment in the prefrontal cortex may be responsible for the psychophysiologic deficits found in people who engage in antisocial and aggressive behaviour. Specifically, brain imaging, neurological, and animal studies suggest that prefrontal dysfunction may account for low levels of arousal, low (stress) reactivity, and fearlessness.

9.3. Raw Empirical Approaches

These theoretically-based approaches, psychological researchers also have attempted to apply statistical models to explain violence and to identify its predictors. This line of inquiry has yielded some positive findings on risk factors for violent behaviour. The use of risk factors in the behavioural sciences is a concept borrowed from the field of Public Health, specifically the discipline of epidemiology. Technically, a risk factor is defined as an aspect of personal behaviour or lifestyle, an environmental exposure, or an inborn or inherited characteristic which on the basis of epidemiological evidence is known to be associated with health-related condition(s) considered important to prevent. Applied to this study, it is any factor, that when present, makes violence more likely than when it is absent.

Notice that this definition does not imply anything about causation. It is possible to identify risk factors, without a clear understanding of the causal mechanisms by which they operate. In fact, this is why we have a well-developed base of empirical knowledge on risk factors for violence and so little explanation of its cause. Static risk factors are those that are historical (e.g., early onset of violence) or dispositional (e.g., gender) in nature, and that are unlikely to change over time. Dynamic factors are typically individual, social or situational factors that often do change and, therefore might be more amenable to modification through intervention.

While it may be tempting to apply these risk factors to determine risk for terrorism, they are unlikely to be useful predictors. Although terrorism is a type of violence, risk factors tend to operate differently at different ages, in different groups, and for different—specific—types of violent behaviour. For example, the factors that predict violent behaviour in the urban gang member with a drug addiction often differ from those that predict violence among predatory child molesters or perpetrators of domestic violence.

Most of the risk factor research in the social sciences has focused on predicting "general violence risk." General violence risk here represents the likelihood that an individual might engage in any aggressive act toward anyone over a specified period of time. That is not the question posed in terrorist threat assessments. Most people who have a collection of general violence risk factors will never engage in terrorism. Conversely, many known terrorists—including some field leaders of the 9/11 attacks—did not have a large number of key general violence risk factors, although they were actively preparing to engage in acts of terrorism. That the correlates of general violence and terrorism are different has at least two important implications: (1) it is likely that the causal (explanatory) mechanisms also are different; (2) one cannot reasonably use the risk factors from one to predict the other.

9.4. First Generation of Psychological Research on Terrorism

The "first generation" of psychological research on terrorism is not officially designated or bounded by any time period, but for purposes of this discussion, will roughly encompass a term from the late 1960s to the mid-1980s. The term "research" is used loosely, as virtually none of the professional literature was based on any empirical studies. Rather, the writings that were produced were based largely on clinical speculations and theoretical formulations, most of which were rooted in a psychoanalytic tradition.

Terrorism was pathologised as manifestation of psychological and behavioural deviance. Accordingly, within a psychoanalytic framework, the "psychopathology of terrorism" was believed to be driven by unconscious motives and impulses, which had their origins in childhood.

9.4.1. Psychoanalytic Theory

Freud wrote: "one has, I think, to reckon with the fact that there are present in all men destructive, and therefore anti-social and anti-cultural, trends and that in a great number of people these are strong enough to determine their behaviour in human society". Early writings on psychological dimensions of terrorist behaviour were dominated by psychoanalytic formulations, reflecting, in part, the prevailing theoretical orientation in clinical practice at the time. The two themes consistently at the center of these formulations were (1) that motives for terrorism are largely unconscious and arise from hostility toward one's parents and (2) that terrorism is the product of early abuse and maltreatment.

One of the earliest examples of the former was Feuer's "conflict of generations" theory, "which is based on a Freudian interpretation of terrorism as a psychological reaction of sons against fathers, a generational phenomenon rooted in the Oedipus complex and, thus, in maleness". The idea that terrorism is rooted in childhood abuse (often unconscious sequelae) is a relatively common theme, and is still held by some contemporary analysts. Psychohistorian Lloyd De Mause observes that "The roots of terrorism lie not in this or that American foreign policy error, but in the extremely abusive families of the terrorists."

9.4.2. Narcissism

Many first generation attempts to understand and explain terrorism within a psychodynamic framework, focused on the trait of narcissism as a defining and driving factor. The premise was that terrorist behaviour was rooted in a personality defect that produced a damaged sense of self. The essence of pathological narcissism is an overvaluing of self and a devaluing of others. It is not difficult to see how one might observe these traits among terrorists. In fact, political scientist Richard Pearlstein concluded: "the psychoanalytic concept of narcissism is the most complete and thus most intellectually satisfying theory regarding the personal logic of political terrorism."

Crayton for example, posed the "psychology of narcissism" as a framework for understanding (not excusing) terrorist behaviour, using Kohut's concepts to guide his argument. According to Clayton, the two key narcissistic dynamics are a grandiose sense of self and "idealised parental imago". With regard to the effect of groups, he argues that narcissistically vulnerable persons are drawn to charismatic leaders and that some groups are held together by a shared grandiose sense of self. As others have posited, he suggested that narcissistic rage is what prompts an aggressive response to perceived injustice. Indeed "narcissistic rage" has been posed by more than one observer as the primary psychological precipitant of terrorist aggression.

In developmental context the way in which this evolves is that as children the nascent terrorists are deeply traumatised, suffering chronic physical abuse and emotional humiliation. This creates a profound sense of fear and personal vulnerability that becomes central to their self concept. To eliminate this fear and create a more tolerable self-image, such individuals feel the need to "kill off" their view of themselves as victims. They buttress their own self-esteem by devaluing others. The result of this devaluation of others—what some have termed "malignant narcissism"—muffles their internal voice of reason and morality. Furthermore, whatever sense of "esteem" has developed in that process is extraordinarily fragile. This makes the individual particularly vulnerable to any slights, insults or ideas that threaten to shatter the façade of self-worth.

Such insults are known as "narcissistic injuries" and are the triggers of narcissistic rage. The influence of psychoanalytic formulations generally, and emphasis on narcissism specifically, has abated considerably in contemporary research. While some cling to—or attempt to reify—old ideas, these first generation notions did not generate much empirical support. Most current experts in the field have moved on to other approaches in search of more accurate and more useful insights for understanding terrorists.

9.4.3. Early Typologies

Some of the first generation conceptualisations and writings began to presage Laqueur's notion that there is not one terrorism, but many terrorisms. Typologies began to emerge to categorise and classify terrorist groups, acts, and actors. Focusing on the diversity in motivations, psychiatrist Frederick Hacker proposed one of the first psychological typologies. His 1976 book, *Crusaders,*

Criminals and Crazies, was perhaps the first major popular press release on the psychology of terrorism. Although Hacker's formulations did have a psychoanalytic bent, they were also much broader than those of his contemporary writers. His book introduced the now popular and colloquial terrorist typology of Crusaders (idealistically inspired and acting in service of a higher cause), Criminals (who simply use terrorism for personal gain) and Crazies (often motivated by false beliefs and perceptions arising from their mental illness). Hacker notes immediately (and correctly) "of course, the pure type is rarely encountered." Nevertheless, this effort introduced the notion that there were differences among terrorists and that the phenomenon and the actors were not monolithic.

In the early 1980s, built on the earlier models that sought to explain terrorism a form of psychopathology or personality defect, arguing that two different forms of dysfunction produced two different patterns of terrorist behaviour. The first type was the Anarchicideologue. These individuals were hypothesised to come from severely dysfunctional families where they likely had suffered severe abuse or maltreatment, leading them to have hostile feelings toward their parents. Their extremist ideology was a displacement of their rebellion and hostility onto the "state" authority. That is, they acted out hostility by rebelling against the "state" of their parents. In contrast, the second type, the Nationalist-secessionist was not hostile, but loyal to his parents, and his extremism was motivated to retaliate or avenge the wrongs done to his parents by the state. In essence, they rebelled against external society out of loyalty to their parents.

9.5. Contemporary Psychological Research

There are many factors at the macro and micro level that affect political violence generally, and terrorism specifically. Indeed, "there is substantial agreement that the psychology of terrorism cannot be considered apart from political, historical, familial, group dynamic, organic, and even purely accidental, coincidental factors."

Psychologists John Horgan and Max Taylor have structured the issues in a most perspicuous way for terrorism researchers by drawing on contributions from theoretical and developmental criminology "to consider involvement in terrorism as a process comprised of discrete phases to 'becoming' a terrorist, 'being' a terrorist (or what might be construed as both a) remaining involved and b) engaging in terrorist offences) and disengaging from terrorism".

9.5.1. Motives and Vulnerabilities

Among the key psychological factors in understanding whether, how and which individuals in a given environment will enter the process of becoming a terrorist are motive and vulnerability. By definition, motive is an emotion, desire, physiological need, or similar impulse that acts as an incitement to action, and vulnerability refers to susceptibility or liability to succumb, as to persuasion or temptation.

One's motivation for engaging in terrorism is often presumed to be the "cause" or ideology of the group. However, as Martha Crenshaw notes, "the popular image of the terrorist as an individual motivated exclusively by deep and intransigent political commitment obscures a more complex reality." That reality is that motives to join a terrorist organisation and to engage in terrorism vary considerably across different types of groups, and also within groups—and they may change over time.

Martha Crenshaw for example, suggests that there are at least four categories of motivation among terrorists: (1) the opportunity for action, (2) the need to belong, (3) the desire for social status, and (4) the acquisition of material reward. Horgan has framed the issue of vulnerability in the perhaps most lucid and useful way as "factors that point to some people having a greater openness to increased engagement than others." There are three motivational themes—injustice, identity, and belonging—appear to be prominent and consistent. These themes also relate to one's potential openness or vulnerability.

Injustice: Perceived injustice has long been recognised a central factor in understanding violence generally and terrorism specifically, dating back to some of the earliest writings. In the mid-1970s, Hacker concluded that "remediable injustice is the basic motivation for terrorism". A desire for revenge or vengeance is a common response to redress or remediate a wrong of injustice inflicted on another. It is not difficult to imagine that "one of the strongest motivations behind terrorism is vengeance, particularly the desire to avenge not oneself but others. Vengeance can be specific or diffuse, but it is an obsessive drive that is a powerful motive for violence toward others, especially people thought to be responsible for injustices".

Identity: One's psychological identity is a developed, stable sense of self and resolved security in one's basic values, attitudes, and beliefs. Developmentally, its formation typically occurs in a crisis of adolescence or young adulthood, and is tumultuous and emotionally challenging. However, "the successful development of personal identity is essential to the integrity and continuity of the personality". An individual's search for identity may draw him or her to extremist or terrorist organisations in a variety of ways. One may fall into what psychologist Jim Marcia calls "identity foreclosure" where a role and set of ideas and values (an identity) are adopted without personal, critical examination. The absolutist, "black and white" nature of most extremist ideologies is often attractive to those who feel overwhelmed by the complexity and stress of navigating a complicated world.

A similar mechanism is one in which a desperate quest for personal meaning pushes an individual to adopt a role to advance a cause, with little or no thoughtful analysis or consideration of its merit. Taylor and Louis describe a classic set of circumstances for recruitment into a terrorist organisation: "These young people find themselves at a time in their life when they are looking to the future with the hope of engaging in meaningful behaviour that will be satisfying and get them ahead. Their objective circumstances including opportunities for advancement are virtually nonexistent; they find some direction for their religious collective identity but the desperately disadvantaged state of their community leaves them feeling marginalised and lost without a clearly defined collective identity".

Belonging: In radical extremist groups, many prospective terrorists find not only a sense of meaning, but also a sense of belonging, connectedness and affiliation. Luckabaugh and colleagues argue that among potential terrorists "the real cause or psychological motivation for joining is the great need for belonging." For these alienated individuals from the margins of society, joining a terrorist group represented the first real sense of belonging after a lifetime of rejection, and the terrorist group was to become the family they never had. This strong sense of belonging has critical importance as a motivating factor for joining, a compelling reason for staying, and a forceful influence for acting.

9.6. Psychopathology and Preventing Terrorism

Psychology, as a discipline, has a long history of (perhaps even a bias toward) looking first to explain deviant behaviours as a function of psychopathology (i.e., mental disease, disorder, or dysfunction) or maladjusted personality syndromes. In reality, psychopathology has proven to be, at best, only a modest risk factor for general violence, and all but irrelevant to understanding terrorism.

9.6.1. Major Mental Illness

It is rather difficult to study the prevalence of psychopathology and maladaptive personality traits in terrorist populations. Most studies that have examined this question using actual psychological measures have included only terrorists that have been captured and/or referred for a mental health examination. Obviously, those viewed as needing a mental health assessment may be different from the general terrorist population.

9.6.2. Psychopathy/Antisocial Personality

Terrorism is regarded by most as a form of antisocial behaviour. Indeed to the victims and observers many of the acts could be seen as heinous and the actors as callous, "cold blooded killers." Given the general tendency to view extreme deviance as a sign of abnormality or psychopathology, some have posited that terrorists might best be understood as a collective of psychopaths. Certainly such concepts were invoked to characterise at least some of the hijackers in the 9/11 attacks on America.

It's not difficult to see how the idea of "terrorist as psychopath" holds some intuitive appeal. Pearce, for example, regarded the terrorist as "an aggressive psychopath, who has espoused some particular cause because extremist causes can provide an external focal point for all the things that have gone wrong in his life." To understand the limitations and inaccuracies in such a generalisation, however, requires some examination of the essential elements of psychopathy and the way in which those traits interact with the demands of participation in a terrorist organisation.

First to clarify an issue of terminology, the designation of "antisocial personality disorder" (ASPD) is a clinically recognised diagnosis characterised by a lifelong history (including before age 18) of engaging in a range of delinquent and antisocial behaviours, which might include lying, stealing, aggression, and criminal activity. Psychopathy, though widely recognised as a clinical syndrome, is not formally listed as a diagnosis in the American Psychiatric Association's Diagnostic and Statistical Manual of Mental Disorders. Similar to ASPD, the construct of psychopathy includes a longstanding pattern of antisocial behaviour and impulsive lifestyle, but in contrast it also has essential elements deficient emotional experience (e.g., lack of guilt, empathy, and remorse) and interpersonal exploitativeness (e.g., callous, use of others, parasitic lifestyle). Only about 25% of those with ASPD also have those core personality deficits that comprise a psychopathic syndrome.

9.6.3. Psychological/Personality Abnormality

Andrew Silke observed that after researchers failed to find any strong links between terrorism and major psychopathology, "a trend has emerged which asserts that terrorists possess many of the traits of pathological personalities but do not possess the actual clinical disorders. This development has effectively tainted terrorists with a pathology aura, without offering any way to easily test or refute the accusations."

Despite more than two decades of research and theoretical speculation attempting to identify what makes terrorists "different," "perhaps the best documented generalisation is negative: terrorists do not show any striking psychopathology". In fact, argues that "the outstanding common characteristic of terrorists is their normality"

9.6.4. Suicide Attacks

While suicide attacks have been a part of conflict throughout the history of the world, most contemporary researchers mark the

1983 suicide attack on the U.S. embassy in Beirut, as the beginning of a modern era of suicide terrorism. Since that time, "there have been at least 188 separate suicide terrorist attacks worldwide, in Lebanon, Israel, Sri Lanka, India, Pakistan, Afghanistan, Yemen, Turkey, Russia, and the United States. The rate has increased from 31 in the 1980s, to 104 in the 1990s, to 53 in 2000-2001 alone".

The rate of suicide terrorism was rising, even while the overall number of terrorist incidents was on the decline. U.S. Senator John Warner echoed the sentiments of many who observed this trend when he said: "Those who would commit suicide in their assaults on the free world are not rational and are not deterred by rational concepts." Available data, however, suggest a different conclusion.

Existing research reveals a marked absence of major psychopathology among "would-be" suicide attackers; that the motivation and dynamics for choosing to engage in a suicide attack differ from those in the clinical phenomenon of suicide; and that there is a rational "strategic logic" to the use of suicide attack campaigns in asymmetric conflict.

In some ways, the absence of suicidal risk factors among suicide attackers is not surprising. They are different phenomena. Suicide attackers view their act as one of martyrdom, whether for their faith, their people, or their cause. In the case of jihadists, for example, "the primary aim of suicide terrorists is not suicide, because to the terrorist group, suicide is simply a means to an end with motivation that stems from rage and a sense of self-righteousness. They see themselves as having a higher purpose and are convinced of an eternal reward through their action".

Suicide terrorism also is not exclusively a tactic of the religious extremist. Sprinzak points out that "the Black Tigers {Liberation Tigers of Tamil Eelam -LTTE} constitute the most significance proof that suicide terrorism is not merely a religious phenomenon and that under certain extreme political and psychological circumstances secular volunteers are fully capable of martyrdom." In fact, that group alone is responsible for nearly half of the suicide attacks worldwide that have occurred in the past decade. Certainly there are logistical and tactical advantages: the operations are relatively inexpensive, the attackers are unlikely to be captured and compromise the security of the group; and the psychological effects on the target population can be devastating. Moreover, this tactic has shown disproportionate lethality. Even excluding the 9/11 attacks on America, in the span of two decades between 1980 and 2001, suicide attacks accounted for only 3% of all terrorist incidents, but they were responsible for 48% of the terrorism-related deaths.

9.7. Understanding Terrorist Personality Traits

Personality traits consistently have failed to explain most types of human behaviours, including violent behaviours. Certainly they have been shown repeatedly to contribute less to an explanation than situational and contextual factors. Crenshaw, for example, has argued that "shared ideological commitment and group solidarity are much more important determinants of terrorist behaviour than individual characteristics." Bandura seems to agree, as reflected in his more general conclusion that "It requires conducive social conditions rather than monstrous people to produce heinous deeds."

The most effective method for explaining behaviour, however, is by combining personal and situational factors. Past analyses of acts of targeted violence reveal that the "person"-related factors are only one part of the equation, and often not the most critical. Risk for engaging in terrorism is the product of factors related not only to the individual, but also to the situation, setting, and potential target. Contextual factors such as the support or rejection of friends and family to the extremist ideology or justifications for violence, the degree of security or target hardening that exists, the recency or severity of experiences that might exacerbate hostility toward the target all could affect the nature and degree of risk posed by a person of investigative concern.

Although the possible existence of a "terrorist personality" holds some intuitive appeal, it most certainly is devoid of empirical support. Further complicating this effort is the fact that terrorists can assume many different roles—only a few will actually fire the weapon or detonate the bomb. The "personality" of a financier, may be different from that of an administrator or strategist or an assassin. Taylor and Quayle's research explored whether some systematic differences might be discerned between those who engage in terrorism and those who do not; yet their search led them to the conclusion that "the active terrorist is not discernibly different in psychological terms from the non-terrorist; in psychological terms, there are no special qualities that characterise the terrorist."

Nearly a decade later, psychologist John Horgan again examined the cumulative research evidence on the search for a terrorist personality, and concluded that "in the context of a scientific study of behaviour (which implies at least a sense of rigour) such attempts to assert the presence of a terrorist personality, or profile, are pitiful." This appears to be a conclusion of consensus among most researchers who study terrorist behaviour. "With a number of exceptions, most observers agree that although latent personality traits can certainly contribute to the decision to turn to violence, there is no single set of psychic attributes that explains terrorist behaviour".

9.8. Understanding Individual's Life Experiences and Preventing Terrorism

9.8.1. Childhood and Adult Experiences

The role of life experiences in understanding a pathway to terrorism is based mainly on certain emotional and behavioural themes; in the contemporary literature three experiential themes appear to be robust: Injustice, Abuse, and Humiliation. They often are so closely connected that it is difficult to separate the effects and contributions of each. By definition, most abuse is unjust. Humiliation often results from extreme forms of abuse (often involving the anticipated judgments of others). Moreover, those experiences may have different effects when they present in different forms (e.g. parental abuse vs. prison abuse) or at different points in one's development (e.g., during childhood vs. during adulthood).

Field spent more than eight years studying terrorism and the "troubles" in Northern Ireland, where she found "the children there have suffered severe disruption in the development of moral judgment-a cognitive function-and are obsessed with death and destruction about which the feel helpless, and against which they feel isolated and hopeless." She apparently was not surprised by the findings: "common sense and experience can tell us that people who are badly treated, and/or unjustly punished, will seek revenge. It should be not be surprising, then, that young adolescents, who have themselves been terrorised, become terrorists, and that in a situation where they are afforded social supports by their compatriots reacting against the actions of an unjust government, the resort to terrorist tactics becomes a way of life".

Twenty years later, some in the psychiatric community continue to share this view. Akhtar concludes that "evidence does exist that most major players in a terrorist organisation are themselves, deeply traumatised individuals. As children, they suffered chronic physical abuse, and profound emotional humiliation. They grew up mistrusting others, loathing passivity, and dreading reoccurrence of a violation of their psychophysical boundaries." The nature and strength of the evidence to which she refers, however, is less clear. Many researchers and terrorist case histories have noted that periods of imprisonment and incarceration often facilitated experiences of injustice, abuse and humiliation. Post and colleagues offer a rich account of the impact of such experiences among the 35 incarcerated middle-eastern terrorists whom they interviewed. They found that "the prison experience was intense, especially for the Islamist terrorists. It further consolidated their identity in the group or organisational membership that provided the most valued element of personal identity. The impact of the prison experience showed more divergence between the secular and Islamist groups. Only a small percentage of either group stated that they were less connected to the group after their incarceration.

Many terrorists are involved in extremist groups before their incarceration and certainly we know that more people have personal histories of having been abused and humiliated than become terrorists. Nevertheless, some of these life experiences may be seen as markers of vulnerability, as possible sources of motivation, or as mechanisms for acquiring or hardening one's militant ideology.

9.8.2. Role of Ideology in Terrorist Behaviour

Ideology plays a crucial role in terrorist's target selection; it supplies terrorists with an initial motive for action and provides a prism through which they view events and the actions of other people. Ideology is often defined as a common and broadly agreed upon set of rules to which an individual subscribes, which help to regulate and determine behaviour. These "rules" are, of course, also linked to (perhaps even guided by) one's beliefs, values, principles, and goals.

The difference and relationship between an ideology and a worldview may depend on one's perspective—perhaps a worldview is broader or just less overt—nonetheless they serve a similar function of acting not only to provide guidelines for behaviour, but also as a lens through which we perceive and interpret information, cues, and events in our environment. Many religions either embrace or sustain an ideology. The doctrine or core beliefs are certainly a central element of a religious system, but those beliefs generally are at least implicitly tied to a set of "rules," which would comprise an ideology.

The substance of ideologies among individuals and groups probably extend through the entire range of human interest and values. There do, however, appear to be some commonalities in the process or structure of terrorist ideologies that may help inform an understanding of terrorist behaviour. Aaron Beck recently applied a cognitive model to terrorist ideologies and concluded that "the thinking of the terrorist evidently shows the same kind of cognitive distortions observed in others who engage in violent acts, either solely as individuals or as members of a group. These include overgeneralisation that is, the supposed sins of the enemy may spread to encompass the entire population. Also, they show dichotomous thinking that a people are either totally good or totally bad.

There are three general conditions seem necessary for an ideology to support terrorism.

First, the ideology must provide a set of beliefs that guide and justify a series of behavioural mandates. Bandura argues that "people do not ordinarily engage in reprehensible conduct until they have justified to themselves the morality of their actions." Terrorists, like most others, seek to avoid internal conflict or dissonance by acting in ways that are consistent with their own beliefs and that allow them to see themselves as basically good.

In essence, "terrorists must develop justifications for their terrorist actions".

Second, those beliefs must be inviolable and must be neither questionable nor questioned. "In his classic volume, *The True Believer*, Eric Hoffer pointed out the importance of belief for the human mind and the problems that arise when uncertainty in belief cannot be tolerated. Belief provides meaning and purpose-it reduces uncertainty and facilitates adaptation and adjustment. It offers "deep assurance" and "communion" with others. Of special significance in this syndrome is the inability to tolerate doubt and uncertainty". The beliefs on which the terrorist ideology is based cannot be doubted, criticised or skeptically examined. Indeed, among those who subscribe to the ideology, "to rely on the evidence of the senses and of reason is heresy and treason.

Third, the behaviours must be goal directed and seen as serving some meaningful cause or objective. People strive for meaning, and perhaps no cause has greater meaning than the polemic struggle between good and evil, in its various forms. Evidence of this dynamic figures prominently into most terrorist ideologies. Falk even suggests that "the terrorist mindset is dominated by its melodramatic preoccupation with the destruction of evil." Kernbergargues that such dichotomous, absolutist, "black and white" thinking, especially concerning matters of morality, is a common feature of fundamentalist ideologies in general. He has observed that such ideologies, "divide the world into ideal and evil realms; their own ideology belongs to the ideal realm. The ideas beliefs and behaviour of the realm of evil are immoral, dangerous, destructive, and threatening. Typically, such an ideology projects all aggression on to the evil social group, while justifying aggression against the infidel as a necessary defence and retribution if not a moral imperative".

9.9. Influence of Culture on Terrorist Ideologies

The role and influence of culture on terrorism generally and on terrorist ideologies specifically has been virtually neglected by most social science researchers. Brannan and colleagues have stated the problem quite clearly: "There is one fundamental issue relevant to such understanding that is rarely mentioned in terrorism studies and yet the virtual absence of which is an unambiguous sign of the flawed methodology currently in vogue. This is the issue of culture".

At the most general, anthropological level, culture is often defined as "socially patterned human thought and behaviour." Even early on in the study of terrorism, there was some recognition of the fact that one's social environment could impact the development of beliefs and values, but this would not provide a complete and satisfactory explanation for the phenomenon. Eric Shaw, in crafting his developmental pathway model, recognised the potentially significant role of early socialisation experiences as part of a complex of influences that might predispose an individual to move along a path to terrorism.

Ideologies generally are based on a set of shared beliefs that explain and justify a set of agreed upon behavioural rules. For terrorists, ideology helps to provide "the moral and political vision that inspires their violence, shapes the way in which they see the world, and defines how they judge the actions of people and institutions". To state simply that ideology controls actions (which may generally be true), however, does not explain why or how that control occurs. This is a relevant consideration because it is the strength of behavioural control—not just the appeal of the rhetoric—that determines whether violent mandates will be followed. Taylor has provided perhaps the clearest behavioural explanation: "the way ideology controls behaviour is by providing a set of contingencies that link immediate behaviour (e.g., violence) to distant outcomes (e.g., new state, afterlife reward)." Because the connection is distant, however, to exert any effect, the contingency must be absolutely certain (hence the need for unquestioning acceptance). In addition, the outcomes or rewards need to be powerful motivators or reinforcers. That is, they need to be fervently desired.

The alternative—albeit related—framework for analysis of control is to consider ideologically-driven action as a form of rule-following behaviour. A rule can be conceptualised as "a verbal description of relationships between behaviours and consequences, especially aversive events and reinforcement". At this juncture, it is relevant to examine whether and the extent to which religion—particularly compared to secular based ideologies—affects the nature and degree of ideological control over behaviour. Religious extremists are called to participate in the religion and to follow the rules. Three factors appear to exert primary influence in maintaining religious participation:

1. Hearing that one's existing practice will produce spiritual as well as materialistic reinforcers.
2. No longer hearing that one's current practices are producing negative sanctions.
3. Hearing that our enemies are in supernatural trouble.

Ideologies—especially religious ones—may also contain mandates or imperatives that impel its adherents to action. Two types of mandates are particularly noteworthy: the moral mandate and the divine mandate. Moral mandates share the same characteristics of other strong attitudes-that is, extremity, importance and certainty-but have an added motivational and action component, because they are imbued with moral conviction. The divine mandate is one of the unique—and potentially most concerning—features of the extremist driven by religious ideology.

REFERENCES

Akhtar, S., "The Psychodynamic Dimension of Terrorism", *Psychiatric Annals*, Jun; 29(6):350-355, 1999.

Crenshaw, M., "The psychology of political terrorism", In M.G. Hermann (Ed.) *Political psychology: contemporary problems and issues* (pp.379-413). London: Josey-Bass, 1986.

deMause, L., "The childhood origins of terrorism", *Journal of Psychohistory*, 2002.

Johnson, P. W. and Feldman, T. B., "Personality types and terrorism: Self-psychology perspectives", *Forensic Reports*, 1992.

Oots, Kent & Thomas Wiegele, "Terrorist and Victim: Psychiatric and Physiological Approaches," *Terrorism: An International Journal*, 1985.

Rex A. Hudson, *The Sociology and Psychology of Terrorism: Who Becomes a Terrorist and Why?*, Washington, DC: Library of Congress, Federal Research Division, 1999.

Silke, A., "The psychology of suicidal terrorism", Silke, A., Ed. *Terrorist, victims, and society: Psychological perspectives on terrorism and its consequence*, London: John Wiley, 2003.

10
Globalisation, Terrorism and Democracy

The September 11 terrorist attacks and the subsequent wars in Afghanistan and Iraq put on display contradictions and ambiguities embedded in globalisation that demand critical and dialectic perspectives to clarify and illuminate these events and globalisation itself.

In a globalised network society, the transmutations of technology and capital work together to create an increasingly globalised and interconnected world. A technological revolution involving the creation of a computerised network of communication, transportation, and exchange is the presupposition of a globalised economy, along with the extension of a world capitalist market system that is absorbing ever more areas of the world and spheres of production, exchange, and consumption into its orbit. The technological revolution presupposes global computerised networks and the movement of goods, information, and peoples across national boundaries. Hence, the Internet and global computer networks make possible globalisation by producing a technological infrastructure for the global economy.

Computerised networks, satellite communication systems, and the software and hardware that link together and facilitate the global economy depend on breakthroughs in microphysics. Technoscience has generated transistors, increasingly powerful and sophisticated computer chips, integrated circuits, high-tech communication systems, and a technological revolution that provides an infrastructure for the global economy and society.

From this perspective, globalisation cannot be understood without comprehending the scientific and technological revolutions and global restructuring of capital that are the motor and matrix of globalisation. Many theorists of globalisation, however, either fail to observe the fundamental importance of scientific and technological revolution and the new technologies that help spawn globalisation, or interpret the process in a technological determinist framework that occludes the economic dimensions of the imperatives and institutions of capitalism. Such one-sided optics fail to grasp the co-evolution of science, technology, and capitalism, and the complex and highly ambiguous system of globalisation that combines capitalism and democracy, technological mutations, and a turbulent mixture of costs and benefits, gains and losses.

In order to theorise the global network economy, one therefore needs to avoid the extremes of technological and economic determinism. Technological determinists frequently use the discourse of post-industrial, or post-modern, society to describe current developments. This discourse often produces an ideal-type distinction between a previous mode of industrial production characterised by heavy industry, mass production and consumption, bureaucratic organisation, and social conformity, contrasted to the new post-industrial society characterised by "flexible production," or "post-fordism," in which new technologies serve as the demiurge to a new post-modernity.

For post-modern theorists such as Baudrillard, technologies of information and social reproduction (e.g. simulation) have permeated every aspect of society and created a novel social environment of media, consumption, computers, and socially constructed identities. In the movement toward post-modernity, Baudrillard claims that humanity has left reality and modern conceptions behind, as well as the world of modernity. This post-modern adventure is marked by an implosion of technology and the human, which is generating an emergent post-human species and post-modern world.

There are positive and negative models of technological determinism. A positive discourse envisages innovative technologies as producing a "new economy," interpreted affirmatively as fabricating a renewed "wealth of nations." On this affirmative view, globalisation provides opportunities for small business and individual entrepreneurs, empowering excluded persons and social groups. Technophiles claim that new technologies also make possible increased democratisation, communication, education, culture, entertainment, and other social benefits, thus generating a utopia of social progress.

Few legitimating theories of the information and technological revolution, however, contextualise the structuring, implementation, marketing, and use of new technologies in the context of the vicissitudes of contemporary capitalism. The ideologues of the information society act as if technology were an autonomous force and either neglect to theorise the complex interaction of capital and technology, or use the advancements of technology to legitimate market capitalism.

A negative version of technological determinism, by contrast, portrays the new world system as constituted by a monolithic or homogenising technological system of domination. The German philosopher and Nazi supporter Martin Heidegger talked of the "complete Europeanisation of the earth and man", claiming that Western science and technology were creating a new organisation or framework, which he called Gestell, and that was encompassing ever more realms of experience. French theorist Jacques Ellul depicted a totalitarian expansion of technology, or what he called la technique, imposing its logic on ever more domains of life and human practices.

A large number of theorists conceive globalisation simply as a process of the imposition of the logic of capital and neo-liberalism on various parts of the world rather than seeing the restructuring process and the enormous changes and transformations that scientific and technological revolution are producing in the networked economy and society. Capital logic theorists, for instance, portray globalisation primarily as the imposition of the logic of capital on the world economy, polity, and culture, often engaging in economic determinism, rather than seeing the complex new configurations of economy, technology, polity, and culture, and attendant forces of domination and resistance. In the same vein, some critical theorists depict globalisation as the triumph of a globalised hegemony of market capitalism, where capital creates a homogeneous world culture of commercialisation, commodification, administration, surveillance, and domination.

From these economistic perspectives, globalisation is merely a continuation of previous social tendencies; i.e. the logic of capital and domination by corporate and commercial interests of the world economy and culture. Defenders of capitalism, by contrast, present globalisation as the triumph of free markets, democracy, and individual freedom. Hence, there are both positive and negative versions of economic and technological determinism. Most theories of globalisation, therefore, are reductive, undialectical, and one-sided, either failing to see the interaction between technological features of globalisation and the global restructuring of capitalism, or the complex relations between capitalism and democracy.

Dominant discourses of globalisation are thus one-sidedly for or against globalisation, failing to articulate the contradictions and the conflicting costs and benefits, upsides and downsides, of the process. Hence, many current theories of globalisation do not capture the novelty and ambiguity of the present moment that involves both innovative forms of technology and economy-and emergent conflicts and problems generated by the contradictions of globalisation. In particular, an economic determinism and reductionism that merely depicts globalisation as the continuation of market capitalism fails to comprehend the new forms and modes of capitalism itself that are based on novel developments in science, technology, culture, and everyday life.

Some poststructuralist theories that stress the complexity of globalisation exaggerate the disjunctions and autonomous flows of capital, technology, culture, people, and goods, thus a critical theory of globalisation grounds globalisation in a theory of capitalist restructuring and technological revolution. To paraphrase Max Horkheimer, whoever wants to talk about capitalism, must talk about globalisation, and it is impossible to theorise globalisation without talking about the restructuring of capitalism. The term "technocapitalism" is useful to describe the synthesis of capital and technology in the present organisation of society.

Unlike theories of post-modernity (i.e. Baudrillard), or the knowledge and information society, which often argue that technology is the new organising principle of society, the concept of technocapitalism points to both the increasingly important role of technology and the enduring primacy of capitalist relations of production. In an era of unrestrained capitalism, it would be difficult to deny that contemporary societies are still organised around production and capital accumulation, and that capitalist imperatives continue to dominate production, distribution, and consumption, as well as other cultural, social and political domains. Workers remain exploited by capitalists and capital persists as the hegemonic force-more so than ever after the collapse of communism.

The term technocapitalism points to a new configuration of capitalist society in which technical and scientific knowledge, computerisation and automation of labour, and information technology and multimedia play a role in the process of production analogous to the function of human labour power, mechanisation of the labour process, and machines in an earlier era of capitalism. This process is generating novel modes of societal organisation, forms of culture and everyday life, conflicts, and modes of struggle.

The emergence of novel and original forms of technology, politics, culture, and economy marks a situation parallel to that confronted by the Frankfurt school in the 1930s. These German theorists who left Nazi Germany were forced to theorise the new. In their now classical texts, the Frankfurt school analysed the emergent forms of social and economic organisation, technology, and culture; the rise of giant corporations and cartels and the capitalist state in "organised capitalism," in both its fascist or "democratic" state capitalist forms; and the culture industries and mass culture which served as powerful modes of social control, manipulative forms of ideology and domination, and novel configurations of culture and everyday life.

Today, critical theorists confront the challenge of theorising the emergent forms of technocapitalism and novelties of the present era constructed by syntheses of technology and capital in the emergence of a new stage of global capitalism. The notion of technocapitalism attempts to avoid technological or economic determinism by guiding theorists to perceive the interaction of capital and technology in the present moment.

Capital is generating innovative forms of technology just as its restructuring is producing novel configurations of a networked global economy, culture, and polity. In terms of political economy, the emergent post-industrial form of technocapitalism is characterised by a decline of the state and increased power of the market, accompanied by the growing power of globalised transnational corporations and governmental bodies and declining power of the nation-state and its institutions-which remain, however, extremely important players in the global economy, as the responses to the terror attacks of September 11 document.

Globalisation also is constituted by a complex interconnection between capitalism and democracy, which involves positive and negative features, that both empowers and disempowers individuals and groups, undermining and yet creating potential for revitalised types of democracy. Yet most theories of globalisation are either primarily negative, presenting it as a disaster for the human species, or as positive, bringing a wealth of products, ideas, and economic opportunities to a global arena.

A critical theory is sharply critical of globalisation's oppressive effects, skeptical of legitimating ideological discourse, but also recognises the centrality of the phenomenon in the present age. It affirms and promotes globalisation's progressive features, while criticising negative ones and noting contradictions and ambiguities.

The processes of globalisation are highly turbulent and have generated new conflicts throughout the world. Benjamin Barber describes the strife between McWorld and Jihad, contrasting the homogenising, commercialised, Americanised tendencies of the global economy and culture with traditional cultures which are often resistant to globalisation. Thomas Friedman makes a more benign distinction between what he calls the "Lexus" and the "Olive Tree." The former is a symbol of modernisation, of affluence and luxury, and of Westernised consumption, contrasted with the Olive Tree that is a symbol of roots, tradition, place, and stable community.

Barber, however, is too negative toward McWorld and Jihad, failing to adequately describe the democratic and progressive forces within both. Although Barber recognises a dialectic of McWorld and Jihad, he opposes both to democracy, failing to perceive how both generate their own democratic forces and tendencies, as well as opposing and undermining democratisation. Within the Western democracies, for instance, there is not just top-down homogenisation and corporate domination, but also globalisation-from-below and oppositional social movements that desire alternatives to capitalist globalisation. Thus, it is not only traditionalist, non-Western forces of Jihad that oppose McWorld. Likewise, Jihad has its democratising forces as well as the reactionary Islamic fundamentalists who are now the most demonised elements of the contemporary era. Jihad, like McWorld, has its contradictions and its potential for democratisation, as well as elements of domination and destruction.

Friedman, by contrast, is too uncritical of globalisation, caught up in his own Lexus high-consumption life-style, failing to perceive the depth of the oppressive features of globalisation and breadth and extent of resistance and opposition to it. In particular, he fails to articulate contradictions between capitalism and democracy and the ways that globalisation and its economic logic undermines democracy as well as circulates it. Likewise, he does not grasp the virulence of the pre-modern and Jihadist tendencies that he blithely identifies with the Olive tree and the reasons why globalisation and the West are so strongly resisted in many parts of the world.

Hence, it is important to present globalisation as a strange amalgam of both homogenising forces of sameness and uniformity, and heterogeneity, difference, and hybridity, as well as a contradictory mixture of democratising and anti-democratising tendencies. On one hand, globalisation unfolds a process of standardisation in which a globalised mass culture circulates the globe creating sameness and homogeneity everywhere. But globalised culture makes possible unique appropriations and developments all over the world, thus proliferating hybridity, difference, and heterogeneity. Every local context involves its own appropriation and reworking of global products and signifiers, thus proliferating difference, otherness, diversity, and variety.

As Friedman shows, capitalist corporations and global forces might very well promote democratisation in many arenas of the world, and globalisation-from-below might promote special interests or reactionary goals, as well as destructive projects like Al Qaeda terrorism. While on one level, globalisation significantly increases the supremacy of big corporations and big government, it can also give power to groups and individuals that were previously left out of the democratic dialogue and terrain of political struggle. Such potentially positive effects of globalisation include increased access to education for individuals excluded from entry to culture and knowledge and the possibility of oppositional individuals and groups to participate in global culture and politics through gaining access to global communication and media networks and to circulate local struggles and oppositional ideas through these media. The role of new technologies in social movements, political struggle, and everyday life forces social movements to reconsider their political strategies and goals and democratic theory to appraise how new technologies do and do not promote democratisation.

In general, globalisation involves both a disorganisation and reorganisation of capitalism, a tremendous restructuring process, which creates openings for progressive social change and intervention. In a more fluid and open economic and political system, oppositional forces can gain concessions, win victories, and effect progressive changes. During the 1970s, new social movements, new non-governmental organisations (NGOs), and new forms of struggle and solidarity emerged that have been expanding to the present day.

10.1. Globalisation, September 11 and Terror War

Momentous historical events, like the September 11 terrorist attacks and the subsequent Terror War, test social theories and provide a challenge to give a convincing account of the event and its consequences. Certain dominant social theories were put in question during the momentous and world-shaking events of September 11, and offer an analysis of the historical background necessary to understand and contextualise the terror attacks. The term "Terror War" to describe the Bush administration's "war against terrorism" and its use of unilateral military force and terror as the privileged vehicles of constructing a U.S. hegemony in the current world (dis)order. The Bush administration has expanded its combat against Islamic terrorism into a policy of

Terror War where they have declared the right of the U.S. to strike any enemy state or organisation presumed to harbour or support terrorism, or to eliminate "weapons of mass destruction" that could be used against the U.S. The right-wing of the Bush administration seeks to promote Terror War as the defining struggle of the era, coded as an apocalyptic battle between good and evil and has already mounted major military campaigns against Afghanistan and Iraq, with highly ambiguous and unsettling results.

Social theories generalise from past experience and provide accounts of historical events or periods that attempt to map, illuminate, and perhaps criticise dominant social relations, institutions, forms, trends, and events of a given epoch. In turn, they can be judged by the extent to which they account for, interpret, and critically assess contemporary conditions, or predict future events or developments. One major theory of the past two decades, Francis Fukuyama's *The End of History*, was strongly put into question by the events of September 11 and their aftermath. For Fukuyama, the collapse of Soviet communism and triumph of Western capitalism and democracy in the early 1990s constituted "the end of history." This signified for him "the end point of mankind's ideological evolution and the universalisation of Western liberal democracy as the final form of human government." Although there may be conflicts in places like the Third World, overall for Fukuyama liberal democracy and market capitalism have prevailed and future politics will devolve around resolving routine economic and technical problems, and the future will accordingly be rather mundane and boring.

Samuel Huntington polemicises against Fukuyama's "one world: euphoria and harmony" model in his *The Clash of Civilisations and the Remaking of World Order*. For Huntington, the future holds a series of clashes between "the West and the Rest." Huntington rejects a number of models of contemporary history, including a "realist" model that nation-states are primary players on the world scene who will continue to form alliances and coalitions that will play themselves out in various conflicts. He also rejects a "chaos" model that detects no discernible order or structure. Instead, Huntington asserts that the contemporary world is articulated into competing civilisations that are based on irreconcilably different cultures and religions. For Huntington, culture provides unifying and integrating principles of order and cohesion, and from dominant cultural formations emerge civilisations that are likely to come into conflict with each other, including Islam, China, Russia, and the West.

On Huntington's model, religion is "perhaps the central force that motivates and mobilises people" and is thus the core of civilisation. Although Huntington's model seems to have some purchase in the currently emerging global encounter with terrorism, and is becoming a new dominant conservative ideology, it tends to overly homogenise both Islam and the West, as well as the other civilisations he depicts. As Tariq Ali argues, Huntington exaggerates the role of religion, while downplaying the importance of economics and politics. Moreover, Huntington's model lends itself to pernicious misuse, and has been deployed to call for and legitimate military retribution against implacable adversarial civilisations by conservative intellectuals like Jeane Kirkpatrick, Henry Kissinger, and members of the Bush administration, as well as, in effect, to give credence to Al Qaeda and Jihadist attacks against the "corrupt" and "infidel" West.

Globalisation includes a homogenising neo-liberal market logic and commodification, cultural interaction, and hybridisation, as well as conflict between corporations, nations, blocs, and cultures. Benjamin Barber's book *McWorld vs. Jihad* captures both the sameness and conflictual elements of globalisation. Barber divides the world into a modernising, stanardising, Westernising, and secular forces of globalisation, controlled by multinational corporations, opposed to pre-modern, fundamentalist, and tribalising forces at war with the West and modernity. The provocative "Jihad" in the title seems to grasp precisely the animus against the West in Islamic extremism. But "Jihad" scholars argue that the term has a complex history in Islam and often privilege the more spiritual senses as a struggle for religion and spiritualisation, or a struggle within oneself for spiritual mastery. From this view, bin Laden's militarisation of Jihad is itself a distortion of Islam that is contested by its mainstream.

Leading dualistic theories that posit a fundamental bifurcation between the West and Islam are thus analytically suspicious in that they homogenise complex civilisations and cover over differences, hybridisations, contradictions, and conflicts within these cultures. Positing inexorable clashes between bifurcated blocs a la Huntington and Barber fails to illuminate specific discord within the opposing spheres and the complex relations between them. These analyses do not grasp the complexity in the current geopolitical situation, which involves highly multifaceted and intricate interests, coalitions, and conflicts that shift and evolve in response to changing situations within an overdetermined and constantly evolving historical context.

As Tariq Ali points out, dualistic models of clashes of civilisation also occlude the historical forces that clashed in the September 11 attacks and the subsequent Terror War. Consequently, the events of September 11 and their aftermath suggest that critical social theory needs models that account for complexity and the historical roots and vicissitudes of contemporary problems like terrorism rather than bifurcated dualistic theories. Critical social theory also needs to articulate how events like September 11 produce novel historical configurations while articulating both changes and continuities in the present situation.

The causes of the September 11 events and their aftermath are highly multifaceted and involve, for starters, the failure of U.S. intelligence and the destructive consequences of U.S. interventionist foreign policy since World War II and the failure to address the Israeli-Palestinian crisis; U.S. policies since the late 1970s that supported Islamic Jihadist forces against the Soviet Union in the last days of the Cold War; and the failure to take terrorist threats seriously and provide an adequate response. In other words, there is no one cause or faction responsible for the 9/11 terror attacks, but a wide range of responsibility to be ascribed and a complex historical background concerning relations between the U.S. and radical Islamic forces in the Cold War and then conflicts starting with the 1990-1991 "crisis in the Gulf" and subsequent Gulf War.

In the aftermath of September 11, there was a wealth of commentary arguing that "everything has changed," that the post-September 11 world is a different one, less innocent, more serious, and significantly altered, with momentous modifications in the economy, polity, culture and everyday life. In the context of U.S. politics, September 11 was so far-reaching and catastrophic that it flipped the political world upside down, put new issues on the agenda, and changed the political, cultural, and economic climate almost completely overnight. To begin, there was a dramatic reversal of the fortunes of George W. Bush and the Bush administration. Before September 11, Bush's popularity was rapidly declining. After several months of the most breathtaking hardright turn perhaps ever seen in U.S. politics, Bush seemed to lose control of the agenda with the defection of Vermont Republican Senator Jim Jeffords to the Democratic Party in May 2001. Jeffords' defection gave the Democrats a razor-thin control of Congress and the ability to block Bush's programs and to advance their own. Bush seemed disengaged after this setback, spending more and more time at his Texas ranch. He was widely perceived as incompetent and unqualified, and his public support was seriously eroding.

With the terror attacks of September 11, however, the bitter partisanship of the previous months disappeared and Bush was the beneficiary of a extraordinary outburst of patriotism. Support for the Bush administration was strongly fuelled by the media that provided 24/7 coverage of the heroism of the fireman, police, and rescue workers at the World Trade Center. The response of ordinary citizens to the tragedy showed American courage, skill, and dedication at its best, as rescue workers heroically struggled to save lives and deal with the immense problems of removing the Trade Center ruins. New York City and the country pulled together in a remarkable display of community, heroism, and resolve, focused on in the ongoing media coverage of the tragedy. There was an explosion of flags and patriotism and widespread desire for military retaliation, fanned by the media.

The U.S. media's demonising coverage of bin Laden and his Al Qaeda network of terrorists and constant demand for strong military retaliation precluded developing broader coalitions and more global and less militarist approaches to the problem of terrorism. Bush articulated the escalating patriotism, vilification of the terrorists, and the demand for stern military retaliation, and a frightened nation supported his policies, often without seeing their broader implications and threat to democracy and world peace. There was a brief and ironical ideological flip-flop of Bush administration policy, in which it temporarily put aside the unilateralism that had distinguished its first months in office in favour of a multilateral approach. As the Bush administration scrambled to assemble a global coalition against terrorism with partners such as Pakistan, China, and Russia, that it had previously ignored or in the case of China even provoked, illusions circulated that the U.S. would pursue a more multilateral global politics.

Crucially, the September 11 events dramatised that globalisation is a defining reality of our time and that the much-celebrated flow of people, ideas, technology, media, and goods could have a down side as well as an upside, and expensive costs as well as benefits. The 9/11 terror attacks also call attention to the complex and unpredictable nature of a globally-connected networked society and the paradoxes, surprises, and unintended consequences that flow from the multidimensional processes of globalisation.

Moreover, the terror attacks of 9/11 put in question much conventional wisdom and forced U.S. citizens and others to reflect upon the continued viability of key values, practices, and institutions of a democratic society. In particular, the events of September 11 force the rethinking of globalisation, technology, democracy, and national and global security. 9/11 and its aftermath demonstrate the significance of globalisation and the ways that global, national, and local scenes and events intersect in the contemporary world. The terror spectacle also pointed to the fundamental contradictions and ambiguities of globalisation, undermining one-sided pro or anti-globalisation positions.

9/11 was obviously a global event that dramatised an interconnected and conflicted networked society where there is a constant worldwide flow of people, products, technologies, ideas and the like. September 11 could only be a mega-event in a global media world, a society of the spectacle, where the whole world is watching and participates in what Marshall McLuhan called a global village. The 9/11 terror spectacle was obviously constructed as a media event to circulate terror and to demonstrate to the world the vulnerability of the epicenter of global capitalism and American power.

Thus, September 11 dramatised the interconnected networked globe and the important role of the media in which individuals everywhere can simultaneously watch events of global significance unfold and participate in the dramas of globalisation. Already, Bill Clinton had said before September 11 that terrorism is the downside, the dark side, of globalisation, and after 9/11 Colin Powell interpreted the terrorist attacks in similar fashion.

Worldwide terrorism is threatening in part because globalisation relentlessly divides the world into have and have-nots, promotes conflicts and competition, and fuels long simmering hatreds and grievances-as well as bringing people together, creating new relations and interactions, and new hybridities. This is the objective ambiguity of globalisation that both brings people together and brings them into conflict, that creates social interaction and inclusion, as well as hostilities and exclusions, and that potentially tears regions and the world apart while attempting to pull things together.

Moreover, as different groups gain access to technologies of destruction and devise plans to make conventional technologies, like the airplane, instruments of destruction then dangers of unexpected terror events, any place and any time proliferate and become part of the frightening mediascape of the contemporary moment. Globalisation is thus messier and more dangerous than previous theories had indicated. Moreover, global terrorism and megaspectacle terror events are possible because of the lethality and power of new technology, and its availability to groups and individuals that previously had restricted access.

Hence, 9/11 exhibited a technological terror that converts benign instruments like airlines and buildings into instruments of mass destruction. Within a short time after the 9/11 terror attacks, in early October, 2001, the mail system was polluted by anthrax. Since infected letters were sent to politicians and corporate media, there was maximum public attention on the dangers on a lethal anthrax attack, making postal work, mail delivery, and the opening of mail a traumatic event, infused with fear. This is exactly the goal of terrorism and media hysteria over anthrax attacks went far in promoting war fever and hysterical fear that led the public to unquestionably support whatever military retaliation, or domestic politics, the Bush administration choose to exert.

10.2. ATTACKS ON DEMOCRACY

Democracy is in part a dialogue that requires dissent and debate as well as consensus. Those who believe in democracy should oppose all attempts to curtail democratic rights and liberties and a free and open public sphere. Democracy also involves the cultivation of oppositional public spheres and as in the 1960s on a global scale there should be a resurrection of the local, national, and global movements for social transformation that emerged as a reaction to war and injustice in the earlier era. This is not to call for a return to the 1960s, but for the rebirth of local/global movements for peace and justice that build on the lessons of the past as they engage the realities of the present.

There is little doubt that the Bin Laden and Al Qaeda terrorists are highly fanatical and religious in their ideology and actions, of a sort hard to comprehend by Western categories. In their drive for an apocalyptic Jihad, they believe that their goals will be furthered by creating chaos, especially war between radical Islam and the West. Obviously, dialogue is not possible with such groups, but equally as certain an overreactive military response that causes a large number of innocent civilian deaths in a Muslim country could trigger precisely such an apocalyptic explosion of violence as was dreamed of by the fanatic terrorists. It would seem that such a retaliatory response was desired by the Bin Laden group which carried out the terrorist attacks on the U.S. Thus, to continue to attack Arab and Islamic countries could be to fall into the Bin Laden gang's trap and play their game-with highly dangerous consequences.

Terrorists should be criminalised and international and national institutions should go after terrorist networks and those who support them with the appropriate legal, financial, judicial, and political instruments. Before and during Bush administration military intervention in Afghanistan, an intelligent campaign was underway that had arrested many participants and supporters of the bin Laden and other terror networks, that had alerted publics throughout the world to the dangers of terrorism, and that had created the conditions of possibility for a global campaign against terror.

References

Axford, Barrie, *The Global System*, Cambridge, U.K.: Polity Press, 1995.

Barber, Benjamin R., *Jihad vs. McWorld*, New York: Ballatine Books, 1995.

Burbach, Roger, *Globalization and Postmodern Politics, From Zapatistas to HighTech Robber Barons*. London: Pluto Press, 2001.

Castells, Manuel, *The Rise of the Network Society*, Oxford: Blackwell, 1996.

Held, David, *Democracy and the Global Order*, Cambridge and Palo Alto: Polity Press and Stanford University Press, 1995.

Huntington, Samuel, *The Clash of Civilizations and the Remaking of World Order*, New York: Touchstone Books, 1996.

King, Anthony D. ed., *Culture, Globalization and the World-System: Contemporary Conditions for the Representation of Identity*, Binghamton: SUNY Art, 1991.

Steger, Manfred, "Globalism", *The New Market Ideology*, Lanham, MD: Rowman and Littlefield, 2002.

Stiglitz, Joseph E., *Globalization and Its Discontents*, New York: Norton, 2002.

Waters, Malcolm, *Globalization*, London: Routledge, 1995.

Bibliography

AbuKhalil, As'ad, *Bin Laden, Islam, and America's New 'War on Terrorism'*, Open Media Pamphlet Series, New York: Seven Stories Press, 2002.

Akhtar, S., "The Psychodynamic Dimension of Terrorism", *Psychiatric Annals*, Jun; 29(6):350-355, 1999.

Axford, Barrie, *The Global System*, Cambridge, U.K.: Polity Press, 1995.

Baljit Singh, "An Overview," in *Terrorism: An Interdisciplinary Perspective*, ed. Yonah Alexander and Seymour Maxwell Finger, New York: John Jay Press, 1977.

Barber, Benjamin R., *Jihad vs. McWorld*, New York: Ballatine Books, 1995.

Barnett, R., *Asymmetrical Warfare*, Washington DC: Brasseys, 2003.

Benjamin, D. & S. Simon, *The Age of Sacred Terror*, NY: Random House, 2002.

Binder, Leonard, *Ethnic Conflict and International Politics in the Middle East*, University Press of Florida. 1999.

Bruce Hoffman, *Inside Terrorism*, 1999.

Burbach, Roger, *Globalization and Postmodern Politics*, From Zapatistas to HighTech Robber Barons. London: Pluto Press, 2001.

Byman, Daniel, "The logic of ethnic terrorism", *Studies in Conflict and Terrorism*, 1998.

Carr, Caleb, "Terrorism as warfare: the lessons of military history", *World Policy Journal*, 1996.

Castells, Manuel, *The Rise of the Network Society*, Oxford: Blackwell, 1996.

Choueiri, Youssef, *Islamic Fundamentalism*, Boston: Twayne Publishers, 1990.

Chris Dishman, "Review Article: Trends in Modern Terrorism," *Studies in Conflict and Terrorism*, vol 22, 4, 1999.

Cindy Combs, *Terrorism in the 21st Century*, Upper Saddle River, New Jersey: Prentice Hall, 1997.

Cooper, B., *New Political Religions, or An Analysis of Modern Terrorism*, Columbia: University of Missouri Press, 2004.

Cosgrove, Michael, "Terrorist Strategy and Global Economic Implications", *Journal of Business and Economics Research*, Vol. 1 (6), 2003.

Crenshaw, M., "The psychology of political terrorism", In M.G. Hermann (Ed.) *Political psychology: contemporary problems and issues* (pp.379-413). London: Josey-Bass, 1986.

Daniel Byman, *Deadly Connections: States That Sponsor Terrorism*, University Press, 2005.

David A. Charters, "Conclusion," in *The Deadly Sin of Terrorism: Its Effect on Democracy and Civil Liberty in Six Countries*, ed. David A. Charters, Westport, Conn: Greenwood Press, 1994.

deMause, L., "The childhood origins of terrorism", *Journal of Psychohistory*, 2002.

Eaton, David J., ed. *Weapons of Mass Destruction: Foreign and Domestic Options for Containment: Proceedings of a Conference May 6, 1998*, Austin, TX: Lyndon B. Johnson School of Public Affairs, The University of Texas at Austin, 1999.

Ellis, M., *Unholy Alliance: Religion and Atrocities in Our Time*, Minneapolis: Fortress Press, 1997.

Esposito, J., *The Islamic Threat: Myth or Reality?*, NY: Oxford Univ. Press, 1999.

Falkenrath, Richard, "Problems of preparedness: US readiness for a domestic terrorist attack", *International Security*, 25 (4): 147-186, 2001.

Fox, Jonathan, "Do religious institutions support violence or the status quo?", *Studies in Conflict and Terrorism*, 1999.

Francis Fukuyama, "The Primacy of Culture," *Journal of Democracy*, vol 6, no. 1, 1995.

Freedman, Lawrence et al., *Terrorism and International Order*, Routledge and Kegan Paul for the Royal Institute of International Affairs, 1986.

Grant Wardlaw, *Political Terrorism: Theory, Tactics, and Counter-Measures*, 2nd ed., rev. and extended, 1989.

Gurr, Nadine, Benjamin Cole, *The New Face of Terrorism: Threats from Weapons of Mass Destruction*, 2002.

Held, David, *Democracy and the Global Order*, Cambridge and Palo Alto: Polity Press and Stanford University Press, 1995.

Hoffman, B., *Inside Terrorism*, NY: Columbia Univ. Press, 1999.

Huntington, Samuel, *The Clash of Civilizations and the Remaking of World Order*, New York: Touchstone Books, 1996.

Johnson, P. W. and Feldman, T. B., "Personality types and terrorism: Self-psychology perspectives", *Forensic Reports*, 1992.

Juergensmeyer, M., *Terror in the Mind of God: The Global Rise of Religious Violence*, Berkeley: Univ. of California Press, 2001.

King, Anthony D. ed., *Culture, Globalization and the World-System: Contemporary Conditions for the Representation of Identity*, Binghamton: SUNY Art, 1991.

Laqueur, Walter, "Postmodern Terrorism", *Foreign Affairs*, Vol.75 (5), 1996.

Laqueur, Walter, The Age of Terrorism, Weidenfeld and Nicolson, 1987.

Lenzy Kelley, *Combat Terrorism: Foreign and Domestic; Steps and Procedures to Protect Yourself, Your Family, and Your Employees Against the Next Wave*, Paperback - February 2001.

Lerner, Brenda Wilmoth & K. Lee Lerner, eds., *Terrorism: Essential primary sources*, Thomson Gale, 2006.

Lewy, G., *Religion and Revolution*, NY: Oxford Univ. Press, 1974.

Mark Juergensmeyer, *Terror in the Mind of God: The Global Rise of Religion's Violence*, 2000.

Martha Crenshaw (ed.), *Terrorism in Context*, 1995.

Medhurst, Paul, *Global Terrorism*, United Nations Institute for Training and Research, New York: NY, 2000.

Michael Brown, "Introduction," ed. *The International Dimensions of Internal Conflict*, Cambridge: The MIT Press, 1996.

Mullins, Wayman C., *A Sourcebook on Domestic and International Terrorism: An Analysis of Issues, Organizations, Tactics, and Responses*, 2nd ed. Springfield, IL: Charles C. Thomas, 1997.

Nadine Gurr, Benjamin Cole, *The New Face of Terrorism: Threats from Weapons of Mass Destruction*, Paperback - November 2000.

Oots, Kent & Thomas Wiegele, "Terrorist and Victim: Psychiatric and Physiological Approaches," *Terrorism: An International Journal*, 1985.

Paul Wilkinson, "Freedom and Terrorism," in *Terrorism: Roots, Impact, Responses*, ed. Lance Howard, New York: Praeger, 1992.

Paul Wilkinson, *Terrorism and the Liberal State*, 2nd ed., rev., extended, and updated, 1986.

Perlmutter, D., *Investigating Religious Terrorism and Ritualistic Crimes*, Boca Raton, FL: CRC Press, 2004.

Peter Chalk, *West European Terrorism and Counter-Terrorism: The Evolving Dynamic*, New York: St. Martin's Press, 1996.

Philip B. Heymann, *Terrorism and America: A Commonsense Strategy for a Democratic Society*, Cambridge, MA: The MIT Press, 1998.

Raymond L. Garthoff, *Reflections on the Cuban Missile Crisis*, Brookings Institution, 1987.

Rex A. Hudson, *The Sociology and Psychology of Terrorism: Who Becomes a Terrorist and Why?*, Washington, DC: Library of Congress, Federal Research Division, 1999.

Richard A. Falkenrath, Robert D. Newman, and Bradley A. Thayer, *America's Achilles' Heel: Nuclear, Biological, and Chemical Terrorism and Covert Attack*, 1998.

Robert Cooper, "Integration and Disintegration," *Journal of Democracy*, 10.1, 1999.

Robert O. Slater and Michael Stohl, "States, Terrorism and State Terrorism," *Current Perspectives on International Terrorism*, Macmillan, 1988.

Rosalyn Higgins and Maurice Flory, eds., *Terrorism and International Law*, London, Florence, KY Routledge, 1997.

Russell Bova, "Democracy and Liberty: The Cultural Connection," *Journal of Democracy*, vol 8, no 1, 1997.

Silke, A., "The psychology of suicidal terrorism", Silke, A., Ed. *Terrorist, victims, and society: Psychological perspectives on terrorism and its consequence*, London: John Wiley, 2003.

Smith, Jonathan B., *Colonialism - A Catalyst for Ethnic Terrorism*, March 6, 2005.

Stern, J., *Terror in the Name of God: Why Religious Militants Kill*, NY: Harper Collins, 2003.

Stiglitz, Joseph E., *Globalization and Its Discontents*, New York: Norton, 2002.

Tibi, Bassam, *The Challenge of Fundamentalism: Political Islam and the New World Disorder*, Berkeley: University of California Press, 1998.

Vohryzek-Bolden, Miki, Gayle Olson-Raymer, and Jeffrey O. Whamond, *Domestic Terrorism and Incident Management: Issues and Tactics*, Springfield, IL: Charles C. Thomas, 2001.

Volkan Vamik D., *Bloodlines: From Ethnic Pride to Ethnic Terrorism*, January 1999.

Walter Laqueur, *The New Terrorism: Fanaticism and the Arms of Mass Destruction*, 1999.

Waters, Malcolm, *Globalization*, London: Routledge, 1995.

Wave," *Journal of Democracy*, vol. 8, no. 4, October 1997.

Wilkinson, Paul, *Terrorism and the Liberal State (2nd edition)*, Macmillan, 1986.

Index

Abu Nidal Organisation (ANO), 70
African National Congress (ANC), 19
Alpha 66, 88
Al-Qaeda terrorist network, 129
Al-Qaida, 3
Anarchism, 7
Anti-Cuban terrorism, 39
Anti-globalisation positions, 199
Antisocial Personality Disorder (ASPD), 178
Anti-Terrorism Act, 98
Arab Liberation Front (ALF), 73
Army of God (AOG), 89

Bin Laden, Osama, 12, 131
Black Liberation Army, 89
Black Panther Party, 146
Black Sea Tigers, 121
Border Management Programme (BMP), 63
British National Party (BNP), 145

Central Intelligence Agency (CIA), 31
Chechen terrorism, 130
Christian fundamentalism, 137
Civil disorder, 24
Civil War Draft Riots, 89
Civilian population, 150
Cognitive Theory, 168
Combat 18, 145

Computerised networks, 187
Confucianism, 128
Counter radicalisation, 56
Counter terrorism, 56
Counter-terrorist activity, 60
Cross-border terrorism, 101

Defensive terrorism, 27
Department for Education and Skills (DfES), 58
Dictatorial governments, 1
Disgruntled population, 17
Drive Theory, 167

Earth Liberation Front (ELF), 89
Economic determinism, 190
Erode legitimacy, 154
Ethno-nationalistic Terrorism, 139
Ethology, 166
European Convention on Human Rights (ECHR), 61
Explanatory theories, 165

Farabundo Marti National Liberation Front (FMLN), 71
Federal Bureau of Investigation (FBI), 18
Federally Administered Tribal Area (FATA), 111
Foreign and Commonwealth Office (FCO), 57
Foreign Terrorist Organisations (FTOs), 48

French revolution, 1
Fundamentalism, 83

Globalisation, 149
Globalisation, process of, 11
Globalised network society, 187
Government Communications Headquarters (GCHQ), 59
Guerrilla forces, 18

Harkat-ul-Mujahideen, 93
Huntington, Samuel, 153
Indigenous Kashmiri organisations, 96
Indiscriminate violence, 7
Instinct theory, 166
International Court of Justice, 32
International law, 34
International terrorism, 35
Inter-Services Intelligence agency (ISI), 50
Irish terrorism, 126
Islamic extremism, 196
Islamic Movement of Uzbekistan (IMU), 130
Islamic radicalism, 6
Islamist sectarianism, 109
Israeli Defence Forces (IDF), 45

Jaish-e-Mohammed (JEM), 48, 49
Japanese Red Army (JRA), 70, 75
Jihadi organisations, 95

Ku Klux Klan (KKK), 88, 147
Kurdistan Worker's Party (PKK), 116

Laqueur, Walter, 13
Lashkar-e-Taiba (LET), 48
Liberation Tigers of Tamil Eelam (LTTE), 116, 179
Limited Political Terrorism, 27

MacMichael, David, 35
McLuhan, Marshall, 199

Mujahidin-e-Khaiq (MEK), 73
Muslim fundamentalism, 133
Muttahida Majlis-e-Amal (MMA), 51

Narcissism, 172
Narodnaya Volya, 1
Nationalism, 7, 140
Non-Governmental Organisations (NGOs), 11, 194
Non-political terrorism, 26
Non-religious terrorist groups, 96
Non-violent civil disobedience, 2
North West Frontier Province (NWFP), 51

Organisation of the Islamic Conference (OIC), 132
Organisations, proscription of, 60

Palestine Islamic Jihad (PIJ), 70
Palestine Liberation Organisation (PLO), 21
Palestinian Islamic Jihad (PIJ), 116
Palestinian National Council (PNC), 43
Persian Gulf War, 19
Pluralistic civil society, 153
Pogrom, 143
Popular Struggle Front (PSF), 76
Pre-state Zionist movement, 42
Preventing Extremism Together' (PET), 58
Psychological theoretical development, 165
Psychological typologies, 173

Quasi-terrorism, 27

Racist terrorism, 139
Radical religious movements, 135
Radicalism, proliferation of, 12
Religious mass-casualty terrorism, 9
Revolutionary terrorism, 22

Right-wing Christian terrorists, 9
Rosenau, James, 149
Royal Ulster Constabulary (RUC), 127

Satellite communication systems, 187
Secret Intelligence Service (SIS), 59
Severe Acute Respiratory Syndrome (SARS), 14
Sipah-e-Sahaba Pakistan (SSP), 48
Social learning theory, 167
Socialist movements, 141
Stolper-Samuelson Theorem, 77
Sudan People's Liberation Army (SPLA), 131
Sudan People's Liberation Movement (SPLM), 131
Sudanese Allied Forces (SAF), 131
Suicide terrorism, 115

Taylor, Max, 174
Technocapitalism, 191
Technological determinism, 189
Technological revolution, 190

Unconventional warfare, form of, 17
United Democratic Salvation Front (UDSF), 131
Universal Declaration of Human Rights, 158

Weapons of Mass Destruction (WMD), 13
Western democratic theory, 156
Westernisation, 135
Wilkinson, Paul, 6
World-wide diplomatic activities, 149
Worship terrorism, 123